Nine Romantic Stories To Remember

Leisure Entertainment Service Co., Inc.
(LESCO Distribution Group)
And
Dorchester Media LLC.

For Paul J. Gross,
a man who turned good ideas
into great things. Sorely missed
and deeply loved by family and
friends

Leisure Entertainment Service Co., Inc. (LESCO Distribution Group)
65 Richard Road Ivyland, PA 18974   www.leisureent.com

Published by special arrangement with Dorchester Media, LLC.

Printed in the United States of America.

A Special LESCO Edition

FIRST TIME IN PAPERBACK

Dorchester Media is
a consumer magazine publisher.

Our Women's Romance Group of
eight titles includes the world's
largest and best selling women's
romance magazine, *True Story*.
True Story has a great history
(1919) and heritage and continues to
touch the heart, mind and soul of
readers by sharing everyday
experiences of romantic life.

In addition to *True Story*, sister
publications include *True Confessions*,
True Romance, and *True Love*.
Special collector magazines from
the substantial archive include
True Story Remember When.

For more information on all of
Dorchester Media publications, write
to Publisher, Dorchester Media,
333 Seventh Avenue, 11th Floor,
New York, N.Y. 10001.

We hope you enjoy the book.

Table Of Contents

This book consists of true stories. Names, characters,
places and incidents were changed. Any resemblance
to actual events, locales, or persons, living or dead, is
entirely coincidental.

An *Original* Publication of Dorchester Media, LLC.

ISBN:
First LESCO Edition Printing: February 2006
1-60016-011-5
Printed in the U.S.A.

Leisure Entertainment Service Co., Inc.
(LESCO Distribution Group)
65 Richard Road Ivyland, PA 18974
www.leisureent.com

NINE ROMANTIC STORIES TO REMEMBER

THE BEST OF MY THREE LOVERS

I listened to the howling wind and watched the snow fall around me and waited for death. I had neither the strength nor the will to go on. I had no reason to live. I had destroyed my life years ago when I married Lawrence Williams. Now, I had come to this wilderness searching for the one man who held my heart in his hands. Well, I had found him.

"Oh, Tim!" I sobbed to the wailing wind. "Why didn't I realize years ago that I loved you?"

It was too late for regrets. My baby was dead. My other son was with Lawrence, and I would never see him again. I could never go back and change my life. I couldn't live with the pain another moment. I closed my eyes and dreamed of what my life might have been with a man named Tim O'Brien. . . .

I had met him when I was seventeen. I remembered his teasing grin, and those piercing eyes that were so full of life, looking at me from the kitchen of the little café where we both worked. He cooked and I waited tables all night on weekends. He had dropped out of school and was living with his sister. I was still in high school, saving every dime for college. I had big dreams. I wanted to be a writer or an artist . . . whatever would bring me success and a ticket out of the poverty I'd been born into.

Tim enjoyed life as it was. He seemed to have no ambitions. He never cared that much about money. Good friends and good times were the best things in life to him . . . and, of course, his music. Tim played the guitar with a natural flair. He took it everywhere with him and made up songs.

I used to ask him why he never wrote the lyrics down that he sang. "That was just the way I felt at the moment," he'd say. "Besides, there's more songs than that one in my head."

He didn't understand my drive to be somebody. "You already are somebody," he'd tell me. "I never met anyone like you. Why are you so set on changing what you are?"

I had been singing a little tune to myself as I worked the first night he asked me out. "Hey, Susan," he'd called out to me, "come here and try that again."

Business was slow that night. It was a couple of hours after midnight, plus there had been a big storm earlier and all the drunks that we usually had were tucked in their beds. I was embarrassed at first. All the other girls who worked in the café had been trying to get Tim's attention. He was very cute and new in town. Most of them were prettier than I was. He grabbed his guitar and strummed a few chords, sitting on a chopping block in the back.

"Tim," I said. "I'm supposed to be working."

"Do you see anybody in here that needs to be

waited on?" he asked, looking around the restaurant. There was only one cop at the coffee bar, and he was in Sally's station.

"Well, what if the boss came in?" I asked.

"Okay, you win," Tim said. "I'll take you out to Point's Peak for breakfast. What do you say?"

We watched the sun come up over the towering mountains. Tim played and sang to the sunrise, and I joined him on some of the songs I knew.

"Your voice is really unusual," he said. "It's really a pure sound."

I laughed self-consciously.

"Your face has a purity, too," he went on. "I think you're special. Let's make a habit of this. I'd like to get to know you."

Tim was eighteen then. We'd dated for three months when he asked me to wear his ring. I never knew what he saw in me, but it didn't matter. I loved having him by my side. I loved the feel of his kisses and the slow fire he built in me. But I never thought of him as the man I wanted forever. I had too many dreams to fulfill.

My parents had divorced about four months before I met Tim. My older brother, after his tour of duty in the Army, had moved to Augusta, Georgia. Now my mother wanted to move there, too. The jobs in the little California town we lived in didn't pay much, and I guess she had a lot of bad memories to run away from. It was getting close to Christmas, and she wanted us to be together, so one weekend she announced that she had rented a van and wanted to pack up and leave.

Tim was in Placerville, where his mother lived at the time. I called him, telling him I was moving and promising to write.

"When are you pulling out?" he asked.

"I guess as soon as we get everything packed," I said. "Monday, I'll have to get my stuff at school. Tim, I'm going to miss you so much. . . ."

The next morning, after I had packed and cleaned all night, there he was at the door. I threw my arms around him and cried into his big sheepskin coat. "How did you ever get here so fast?" I asked him, crying and laughing at the same time.

"I flew over. I couldn't let you go without telling you that I love you, Susan," he said. "I always will. I'm a one-girl man. I want to marry you someday. Don't think about that now. You'll still be free to do whatever you want. I'd go with you if I could, but my mother's not well. I love you with all my heart. I just wanted you to know."

We drove Tim back to the airport and left from there for Augusta. I cried for awhile as we drove, but then I began to think about my new life and what was ahead for me in Augusta.

Mom went to work seven days a week. She told me she wanted me to concentrate on school and not work at all. It was the middle of my junior year, and I worked as hard as I could. I got an award for best feature writer on the school paper, made the honor roll every quarter, won awards for art projects, and was totally, miserably lonely.

Instead of making new friends, I retreated from people. I was ashamed of the tiny house by the railroad tracks that Mom and my two other brothers and me were crammed into.

I didn't want anyone to know me. I'd walk to school early in the morning and study in the cafeteria. I'd stay in the library until it closed at night, and then walk home and write to Tim, telling him about my dreams of going to college and all the things I wanted to have. I wanted a big, beautiful house in the mountains, with blue rugs and white furniture and a huge fireplace. I didn't quite know how I was going to get those things, but somehow, someday, I would have them all.

Pretty soon, I got so absorbed in school and those dreams of mine that I stopped writing to Tim. He was part of the past . . . the past I wanted to forget forever. My high school counselor told me that I stood a good chance for a scholarship if I continued to do well in my senior year. I had no room in my heart for Tim anymore.

One night I'd just washed my hair and had it wrapped up in a towel when the doorbell rang. When I answered it, there stood Tim, a suitcase and his guitar in his hands and a question in his eyes. I just stared at his worried face, his old jeans, and that old sheepskin coat. I was speechless. He put down the suitcase and guitar and took me in his arms. His kiss was the sweetest thing I'd ever known. I clung to him. I felt a need that I'd never felt before.

Then he held me at arm's length. "Why haven't you written, Susan?" he asked.

"I-I don't know," I said weakly. "I've changed. I can't help it. I've missed you, but I don't know what I want anymore, except to go to college. I don't know who I am, even."

He gathered me to him again. At that moment, I wanted him more than I had ever wanted anything else in my life. I kissed him with all the longing I felt.

THE BEST OF MY THREE LOVERS

When he slipped his hand under my robe, I held him tight against me. No one else was home.

He was the one who broke away. "Let's go for a walk," he said. "I'll wait in here while you get dressed."

"Tim—" I tried to pull him to me again.

"Don't," he said. "I don't want it like this for us."

That was his rule. He wanted me for his wife. I wanted him for my lover.

His mom had recovered so he came to be with me. He stayed in Augusta that summer and worked. I got a summer job and we'd walk in the park after work. He spent every moment he could beside me.

Sometimes I would get angry with him because he would never make love to me. "It's a special thing, Susan," he'd say. "I can't marry you yet, so let's wait."

Then, because the need between us got too strong even for him, he decided to leave Augusta. "Please try to understand," he begged. "I love you, but I want to make a life for us. When I can take care of you, I'll come for you."

I got a letter from him a week later. He had joined the Army. He would see me on his first leave, he said.

I missed him. But when he wasn't near me, the aching need for him faded and I could question whether I really loved him . . . in a marrying way, I mean.

He kept writing faithfully all through my senior year. I wrote back to him . . . sometimes. After awhile I even wrote to him about the boys I'd started dating. Once I wrote to him and told him I loved him like a brother. He wrote back and told me that

14

he had plenty of sisters and didn't need another one!

At the end of my senior year I got a scholarship to a state university. I couldn't believe it. They were going to pay for everything! Tim came to visit on his first leave just like he promised. It was right before graduation. He told me how proud he was of me.

I was dating a college student from the university so I fixed Tim up with one of my girlfriends. She thought I was out of my mind and told me I was a fool to let him out of my sight.

Tim took me for a drive the night he left. After we parked out in the country, he took my face in his hands and looked deeply into my eyes. "You and I are meant to be," he said. "I don't think you know that yet, but someday you will. I'm never going to give up on you. Date all the guys you want, but when you realize I'm the one who's right for you, come to me. I'll be waiting.

"I wrote you a song," he went on. "Well, actually, I wrote you a lot of songs. But I wrote this one down." He reached for his guitar, leaned over it, then sang the song to me. It had a haunting melody. "She is my music," the words went. "She's the soft light of dawn and the rain on my face. She's everything that time won't erase. She is the beauty of the first breath of spring. She is my woman, my everything. . . ."

The words went straight to my heart ant I began crying. Tim stared at me and laughed softly. "You see?" he said. "Why do you keep running away from it? You can't run forever. Why don't you just—"

"I can't!" I sobbed. "Don't you understand? I have to make it. I don't want just to exist. I want to live!"

"And do what?" Tim demanded. "Did I ever say I'd hold you back from anything? Let me be the one beside you—"

"I have to do it on my own," I insisted. "Until then, I don't know how I really feel about you. Can you understand that?"

"No, but I guess I'll have to live with it," he said.

He left for North Carolina the next morning to take airborne training. I hated to see him go . . . but, at that same time, I was relieved.

I started at the state university that fall. I got a job on weekends at a tourist type restaurant. I waited tables, sang with the musicians, and danced and sang on stage with a troupe of cancan girls from the university. It really boosted my self-confidence. None of us were professionals, so we just had fun with the whole thing. I dated a lot of boys who worked there, too, but it was just for fun.

I had just finished singing one Saturday night when one of the other waitresses told me that someone wanted to see me at one of her tables. I expected a guy from the university to drop by that night, so I was surprised to see a total stranger sitting there. He was the most incredible man.

He was handsome. He had copper colored hair and green eyes. He had deep lines on the sides of his face, which were attractive when he smiled. He was immaculately groomed. He had on a pale-gray suit. I could tell it had cost him a fortune.

"Did you want to see me for something?" I asked him as soon as I got to the table.

"I'm Lawrence Williams," he said. "I wanted to tell you that you have a beautiful voice and that you're going out with me tonight." He grinned, a very boyish grin.

"I don't go out with customers, Mr. Williams," I told him. "It's against the rules here. But I wouldn't go out with you anyway. I don't know you. Now, I must get back to work."

He didn't look a bit discouraged. "Look," he said. "I got a big promotion today. I think you are a very attractive young lady . . . and I stress the word lady. I would really like it if you would help me celebrate. I'll wait for you in the bar when the restaurant closes. You're going with me."

"And you think I will . . . just like that? I demanded.

He nodded. "I promise you a night you'll never forget. I won't lay a hand on you. What else did you have planned for this evening? I could arrange to get you off early. Your boss is a personal friend of mine."

"No, thank you, Mr. Williams," I said.

I went back to work. Ten minutes later Mr. Lindy, my boss, met me in the kitchen and told me I could go ahead and leave with Lawrence Williams. "I didn't know you knew Lawrence," he said. "I've know him for three years. Fine man. Go ahead. If you'd asked me, Susan, I would have given you the night off. I know he's only in town for a couple of days." With that, he pushed me out of the kitchen.

I saw Lawrence grinning from ear to ear at his table. I marched over and demanded, "Who in the world do you think you are?"

"My name is Lawrence Williams," he said holding back a laugh. "I'm from Atlanta and I don't take no for an answer when I really want something. And I really want to get to know you. You sing like an angel. Please, I'm asking you as humbly as I know how. Will you go out with me tonight?'

I hesitated. There was something about him. He had a quality I hadn't encountered before, and I was curious.

"Why me?" I asked him.

"Why not you?" he countered. "Look, I'm not asking you to marry me. I want just to go out with you. Come on. We're wasting time. Where do you live?"

I've regretted going with him that night many times. I watched him put a twenty-dollar tip on the table. He took my elbow and led me to a gleaming luxury car. I felt self-conscious riding in it, like I would soil the upholstery or something.

I could have died with embarrassment as he walked into the living room of our house. He sat down on the worn easy chair like he was one of the family. "Don't be long," he said. "I made reservations for nine o'clock."

I changed into a black miniskirt and black high-heeled sandals. Taking a deep breath, I walked back into the living room.

"No, no. That's all wrong!" Lawrence said, "What else do you have?" He proceeded to go through my closet, and finally pulled out a long pale-yellow gown that I'd worn as a bridesmaid's dress. "This might do," he said. "Try it on, and let your hair down. It's your biggest asset."

I was beginning to get mad and Lawrence knew it. "Please don't be offended," he said. "I'm an executive with one of the biggest corporations in Atlanta. People expect certain things from me. We're going to a private club. You would've felt out of place."

THE BEST OF MY THREE LOVERS

"Look, maybe we should just call this whole thing off," I said, trying to fight down tears of humiliation.

He cupped my face in his hands. "Don't be so sensitive," he said. "I thought you were a little tougher than this. Come on, change and come with me. You won't regret it. Besides, where else am I going to find a date at this hour?"

He took me to a club that looked like something out of *Gone with the Wind*. Certainly no one in the room had on a miniskirt, and I was grateful to Lawrence.

"You never have to feel out of place with me, Susan," he told me. "I wasn't always so knowledgeable. My mom was so poor we went hungry lots of times. I just promised myself my life would be better. It's only been a couple of years since I've felt comfortable in a place like this. These are just people. They are no better than you or me."

"I'm not planning on being poor forever, either," I said.

"Tell me about your dreams," Lawrence begged.

I let go of all my bitterness and shame, and told him about all the things I wanted to achieve. We talked until the club closed. Then we walked around the gardens outside and talked some more. Lawrence listened intently, a funny smile on his face. All I found out about him was that he was twenty-seven and he was from Nebraska originally.

I wasn't ready for the night to end. Just thinking that someone like Lawrence could treat me like I was special was thrilling to me. He took me for breakfast when the sun began to rise and then drove me home. Lawrence was such the gentleman that he never even kissed me good-bye.

THE BEST OF MY THREE LOVERS

I was so glad it was Sunday. I fell into bed and set the alarm for two-thirty. I had to be to work at three.

There were two-dozen yellow roses at the front desk waiting for me. Lawrence had written, "I have reserved your table. See you at seven. I'll take you home tonight. Love, Lawrence."

"You shouldn't have," I told him when he arrived at seven. Everyone stared at us.

"You will find that I never do what I should do," he said. "I try hard to do what I shouldn't do. Come with me tonight and I'll prove it to you. I have a pool to myself. Let's go skinny-dipping."

"I can't, Lawrence," I said, grinning in spite of myself at his absurd suggestion.

"One of the most eligible bachelors in town is trying to sweep you off your feet and you're turning him down?" he teased.

"I have classes tomorrow," I answered.

"So skip your first one and I'll have you there for the second one. If I have to, I'll get you a bathing suit, if that's what's bothering you," he said. "This is my last night in town, so I'll pick you up at ten . . . okay?"

I nodded, hoping I wasn't making a big mistake.

I discovered that Lawrence lived in one of the high rises downtown. We rode an elevator up to the top floor, and when the door opened I couldn't believe my eyes. Plush white carpeting covered the floor and the walls were all glass. You could see for miles. Everything was white . . . and beautiful.

"What is this place?" I asked him.

"My penthouse," he said. "I've always wanted one. I got it this year. Like it?"

"It's like a dream," I answered.

"Dreams do come true if you go after them with all you've got," he told me. "Come on, I'll show you the pool."

I followed him through double French doors and gasped. There were huge plants everywhere. Smooth blue ceramic tiles surrounded a glittering pool. Soft light came from nowhere. It looked almost like a natural lake.

"You can use the bedroom to change," Lawrence said. "The suit I bought for you is in there."

He needn't have bothered with the suit. As soon as I felt his body next to mine in the warm, silky water, I lost all control. I clung to him, whispering his name, as he unfastened the bikini top. I felt his strong arms lifting me to him, his lips touching my skin, and I sobbed out my need against his shoulder.

"Just like I thought," he whispered hoarsely. "You're terrific . . . sensational! We're going to be great together!"

Suddenly I was ashamed . . . so ashamed I pulled away from him and ran from the pool, slipped on the wet tiles, and bruised my chin. I got up and kept running. What a fool I'd been! He was so sure of himself . . . and of me. Well, I wasn't about to lose my virginity by being one of his fast weekend conquests.

I ran to the shower and let the water soothe me. Then I wrapped a towel around me and went to get my clothes. How ridiculous the waitress uniform looked in this place! I laughed bitterly. Lawrence certainly had style. He had made me believe I was something special to him. How he must have laughed to himself as I had melted to his touch!

THE BEST OF MY THREE LOVERS

He came in the bedroom and watched as I buttoned my blouse. He had two brandy snifters in his hands. He held one out to me.

I turned away from him, trying to control the tears.

"What is it? Do you want me to say I love you and tell you a bunch of lies?" he asked. "I could pull that off. I have before. But I respect you more than that. I want you. You're a beautiful, desirable woman. What do the other guys tell you?"

"I've never—" I bit back the words. How foolish he would think I was. A nineteen-year-old virgin! I refused to give him the satisfaction of laughing at me again. "Could you just take me home, Lawrence?" I asked.

He turned me around to face him. "You're for real, aren't you?" he said. "You've never had a man before? Either that or you're a sensational actress!"

I laughed through my tears, and then I cried some more. "I-I just can't believe I was so easy. . . ." I sobbed.

"Here, take a drink," he said. "You'll feel better. Sex is a natural thing, but it isn't all it's cracked up to be. I would enjoy sleeping with you, but if you're looking for true love, I'm the wrong guy. On the other hand, if you're willing to settle for excitement, passion, and experience . . . well, I'm your man. I'm not giving up on you yet."

"I will love somebody someday," I told him. "And when I do, I'll love him forever. If I didn't believe that, I don't think life would be worth living."

"Good luck," Lawrence said softly, apparently not at all put out at having his romantic plans fall through. He took me home and told me he was leaving in the morning for Atlanta. "I have an early flight. I go right by the university on the way to the airport. I'll give you a ride."

As he kissed me good-bye the next morning, he looked at me and said, "Save yourself for me, will you? I'll be gone for a couple of months. Maybe you'll be educated in the ways of the world by then. I'm not much for writing. Maybe I'll give you a call. I'd like to see you again."

He left me in a state of confusion. I couldn't get him out of my mind. He was so totally different. He saw right through everything and had his own way of thinking. I respected him for that. I began to dream of the day when he'd fall in love with me and tell me he was wrong . . . that he would love me forever.

Tim came home on his way to the Gulf War. I was really glad to see him. He stood for all the little-girl dreams that were fading fast. I was very discouraged with college. It seemed as if there were so many roads to nowhere. I couldn't find the right one. He took me out to dinner, dressed in his uniform. He looked very handsome, and his eyes never left me. I couldn't help comparing him to Lawrence, but in many ways he came out the winner.

"Please don't keep me hanging on, Susan," he begged me as he parked the car in front of my house. "Tell me you love me. Tell me you'll be waiting for me when I get back. I'll have enough saved by then to build us a home in the mountains. I can make all your dreams come true. Just say the word."

"Tim, I'm so confused right now," I told him. "Everything is all wrong, then everything is right. I care about you so much . . . but I still don't know if I want to marry you. There's so much more I need to find out about myself. I'm sorry—"

"You make it so hard on yourself," he cut in. "Why don't you just give in to what you feel? I know you love me. If I didn't think so, I wouldn't be here. It's been three long years, waiting for you. I can't hold out forever. There's a girl that I met in North Carolina. She's crazy about me. But I want you . . . ."

"If you can be happy with her, Tim, don't let me stand in your way. I can't promise you anything, and it's not fair to you," I told him.

"Are you in love with someone else, Susan?" he asked.

"I don't know. I've been seeing someone," I admitted. "He's kind of special, but I don't think anything will come of it. He's not like you."

"What's that supposed to mean?" Tim said angrily. "Are you going to bed with him?"

His hands gripped the steering wheel tightly, and he looked straight ahead, as if he was afraid of the answer I would give him.

"Oh, Tim," I said, "I'm not sleeping with anyone. I never have. No one is special enough to me to do that."

He kissed me, over and over again. I felt the same slow tide of longing that I had always felt with him. A sweet, sharp yearning that was nothing like it had been with Lawrence. I was still in control of my actions, and I wanted him very much.

"Am I special enough? Will you stay with me tonight?" Tim asked me.

I looked at his dear, familiar face and nodded.

He took me to a nice motel and led me into the bedroom. We kissed and fumbled with each other's clothes. My anticipation of this moment was almost too much for me because I had wanted for so long to show him how much I appreciated his feelings for me. He made love to me in a very simple and tender way. It was awkward and a little clumsy, but I knew that he loved me.

Lying in his arms afterwards I savored that Tim was my first and realized that what had happened meant as much to me as it did to him. Even though there were no bells in my head, or great tides of emotion between us, it had been as it should be . . . gentle and flowing, satisfying and good.

Before he left, I gave him my senior class ring. "To keep you safe," I said, and wondered at my tears and the pain in my heart.

Lawrence called me the next weekend from Atlanta. "Go down to Miller's Department Store and charge a party dress to my account there," he said. "I want to see you tonight. I'm flying in at seven. I'll pick you up at seven-thirty sharp. Pick out something sexy, but subtle. Maybe something in white. I'll be glad to see you. I've missed you, and that's unusual for me."

"Lawrence, I just can't walk in that store and tell them to charge it," I protested. "I've never even been in there."

"Come on, I really want you to do this," he insisted. "Just mention my name."

There was just no saying no to this man. It was aggravating, but I liked it, too.

I went to the store and was appalled at the prices. Who in her right mind would pay three thousand hundred dollars for a dress? I searched but couldn't find anything much more reasonable. I chose a white toga-type gown that had a low back and flowing, simple lines. Since I had no shoes to go with the thing, I got some white sandals to match. I didn't dare look at the total bill as I signed where the very obliging clerk indicated.

Lawrence picked me up and drove to a quiet place on the outskirts of the city. He ordered for both of us. There were white roses at the table with a note that said: "To a lady who's become a special part of my life. Love, Lawrence." At my place, casually wrapped, was a pair of pearl earrings.

"I can't keep these, Lawrence," I exclaimed.

"You can't or you shouldn't?" he asked, taking my hand. "You know how I feel about that. Stop worrying so much about going by the rules. They don't matter half as much as everyone thinks they do. I want to tell you something. If everyone played by the rules, this would be a boring world. I want you to have the earrings. No strings or hidden meanings. So, that settles that."

I put on the earrings and smiled at Lawrence. Tonight was my night, I decided. I felt like throwing caution to the wind and just enjoying life. It was a warm and balmy night in early spring. It was a night for lovers.

We danced for hours. Dancing with Lawrence was like gliding in the wind. Soon, I was ready for anything. Lawrence took me out on the patio and kissed me.

"Having a good time?" he asked.

"The time of my life," I answered. "You make me feel like I'm all the things I've always wanted to be."

It was true. With Tim, I had to be more honest with myself. I always felt like I was just plain, poor

Susan Sandborn around him. He knew everything there was to know about me. With Lawrence, I felt brand new . . . like a rose just ready to bloom. Lawrence stood for all the "somedays" I had dreamed of, while Tim stood for all the reality that I didn't want to face.

It was easy to say yes to Lawrence that night. He took me to his penthouse and poured us a nightcap. With the brandy warming my blood, I said to him, "I've been educated. I'm not a virgin anymore."

He raised his eyebrows. "And when did this big event take place? Who did the honors?"

"A very dear friend," I said. "I've known him for years. He was leaving for The Gulf War."

"Ah, the lonely soldier," Lawrence said, starting to unbutton his shirt.

"It doesn't matter to you, does it?" I asked, excitement creeping through my body.

"Well, I am a little disappointed," he said lightly. "I liked that quality you had, but I'm not going to let that stop me. You're all mine tonight."

He knelt before me, close to where I was lying on the couch, and then he kissed me. I trembled with the same desperate need he had made me feel that night in the pool. He could sense my yearning and slowly undressed me. His touch was so different from Tim's. His hands knew just where to go and what to do and I melted beneath them. So many beautiful moments later, when he made love to me, it was like two worlds colliding and bursting into flame. I'd never known passion until that moment.

Toward dawn, he took me home. I felt I had to at least act like a good little daughter to Mother. I felt like a stranger to myself, bewildered by the emotions Lawrence had made me feel. It scared me to think that one man had so much power over me. I slept fitfully, knowing I might be in way over my head and that no one could throw me a lifeline if I needed one. No one at all.

Red roses arrived the next day, just as Lawrence called me on the phone.

I was relieved to hear from him. I didn't know what to expect after our night together. "I'm going to have to open a flower shop soon," I told him lightly.

"I'll buy you one," he said teasingly. "How did you sleep?"

"A little restless," I said.

"You're kidding! I didn't move a muscle all night," he told me. "You wore me out!"

"Lawrence—" I began. I wanted to tell him all what I had felt, but I was tongue-tied.

"Let's go out tonight," he cut in. "I want to show you off. I'll make reservations at the club. I'll pick you up something to wear on the way. I'll see you at seven-thirty."

He brought me a tangerine-colored dress made out of some shimmering fabric that floated around my knees. The color brought out all the highlights in my hair. "When will you stop doing this?" I asked him.

"When you have enough clothes to go out with me every night," he said. "Because that is what you'll be doing. I'm staying here for a while. I asked for an assignment down here so I could get to know you."

"How long will that be?" I asked him.

"As long as it takes," he answered.

THE BEST OF MY THREE LOVERS

I quit my job at the restaurant . . . on Lawrence's instructions. I went to school during the day and out with Lawrence every night. I felt like I was living in a fairy tale. I didn't think much about the future. I savored each moment I had. My schoolwork slid into the background. My first thought in the morning was Lawrence, as was my last thought at night.

I almost hoped that maybe the insane reckless way he made me feel when we made love would diminish, but it didn't. *Love me,* my mind would cry out to him. *Love me for however long you can. Just don't let me be another passing affair in your life.* He wouldn't ever say it, but sometimes I thought I could see it in his eyes.

I learned a lot about him. He scoffed at compassion. He hated weakness in others. He had no time for any problems I might have on my mind. He had no philosophy . . . he didn't wonder about the meaning of life. He had no respect for people who dreamed about things and did nothing to achieve their dreams. He was ruthless in his business dealings, and lying about a certain property or product that he handled didn't phase him a bit.

I knew all these things, but still I loved him hopelessly. I would have done anything for him that he asked. He knew this about me, and he prided himself on it. I saw the sense of power it gave him.

Of course, I was angry at myself for letting this happen. Sometimes I would think of the inevitable day when he would leave me, and I'd wonder how on earth I could be sane and still be involved with him. My friends didn't see me anymore, and my family was appalled at my behavior. I didn't care. Lawrence was everything to me. It wasn't just love.

He had become an obsession, and I couldn't stop seeing him. If he had asked me to go to the moon, I'd have found a way there.

One weekend he had to go to Atlanta, and I moped around the house, missing him. A letter from Tim arrived, and I read it guiltily.

"It sounds like you're having a good time in college," he said. "Just be careful and don't let some guy hurt you. I'll always treasure the time we had. I hope you will still be around when I get home. I love you more and more every moment. I'll see you in six months, God willing, and hold you in my arms. I'll never let you go. . . ."

Dear uncomplicated Tim, I thought. *What would he think of me now? How could I have done this to him?* I missed him. I wished that he was here so that I could pour out all my confused feelings to him and he could make me feel clean again.

I realized it was time I faced the fact that I was Lawrence's mistress. That's all I was. That's all I ever would be to him. I knew he'd never marry me. But I knew I'd be ready and willing the next time he called. I could feel the pain already of the day he'd leave me, and I really didn't know if I could cope with it.

I missed my period that month. I kept thinking: *Tomorrow I'll start. I'm not pregnant. I can't be pregnant. Lawrence would be furious!*

I told him when we were out at dinner one night. His face showed no reaction.

"Have you seen a doctor yet?" he asked.

"No," I said. "Not yet."

"How could you let this happen?" he demanded. "Or did you do it intentionally?" He was so cold.

THE BEST OF MY THREE LOVERS

"No, certainly not!" I said. "And you don't have to worry. I'm not asking anything from you. It's my problem. I'll handle it."

"How?" he asked. "How will you handle it if you are pregnant?"

"I'll have the baby," I said. "I would never have an abortion. No one could ever make me do that, not even you."

"And how do you intend to support him?"

"I'll go back to work at the restaurant," I said defiantly. "Mr. Lindy told me I'd always have a job there. I'll live at home until I can get my own place. Maybe I'll move to Sacramento or somewhere—"

Suddenly he took my hand. "I think have a better idea," he said. "Let's get married."

"No," I said quietly. "I don't want to marry you, Lawrence. You don't love me. I can't live with that."

"Maybe I do love you," he said, "Maybe I'm just too cynical—or stubborn—to admit it. At any rate, I'd like to give it a try. I don't want any son of mine wanting for anything in his life. And I think you'd make a wonderful mother. I'm not getting any younger. I planned to marry when I got the top job in my firm. I thought I'd pick out some gorgeous blonde to show off or some rich society debutante. But I like you. We're good together. I can't think of anyone else I'd rather have bear my children. Let's give it a try."

"This is all wrong," I said, shaking my head.

"You and your romantic notions!" he teased. "Do you want me to go down on my knees and declare my undying devotion to you? I could probably pull it off, but I wouldn't mean a word of it. So let's skip all that. You're marrying me, so that's settled. Let's order dinner and go celebrate somewhere."

"I don't want this," I said. "I have no control with you. I love you too much."

"That's sickening!" Lawrence said. "Don't go sappy on me, Susan. I can't handle it."

I bit my lip to stop the tears. I couldn't. They slid silently down my cheeks. I hid behind the menu, choking back the sobs. "I'll be back in a minute," I managed to say.

I found a phone booth in the lobby and called my brother. "Kenneth, could you please come and get me?" I asked. "I'll meet you at the bank building on Pine and Orchard. I don't feel well."

I walked out the front door and down the street. I was grateful that the downtown streets were empty at this hour. I hid between the pillars of the bank and watched for Kenneth's little red car. I felt so lucky to have a family that really cared about me. How could I have done this? At that moment, nothing was more precious to me than the sight of Kenneth's car pulling up beside me.

As we drove off, I told him everything. I'd just about finished by the time we got to his house. We went inside and he made us some coffee. Then we sat down.

"I think you're in love, little sister," Kenneth said. "I wish it was Tim . . . I trust him. But you've got it bad for Lawrence. The more you love somebody, the more they can make you hurt. The more you love somebody, the more you can hate them. It sounds crazy, but it's true. There's no doubt in my mind that you love this guy. You might as well give in and make an honest man of him."

"I'm afraid loving him the way I do will destroy

me," I said. "It swallows me up. It's a destructive thing. It leaves me wanting more than he can give me."

"I know what you mean," Kenneth agreed. "But think of the baby. He'd have it all, wouldn't he?"

The phone rang. It was Mom. Lawrence had called her, frantic with worry. Kenneth told her I was there and alright.

"At least that's something," I said. "He cares enough to worry. Don't tell him I'm here . . . just that I'm alright. I need some time to think."

I stayed with Kenneth and his wife that night. By morning, I had made my choice. I would go away and get a job . . . someplace where Lawrence would never find me. Maybe Kenneth or Mom could loan me enough money to leave. I'd find a way. I thought of all the dreams I left behind when I met Lawrence, especially the career I'd wanted. Those days seemed very far away. I'd learned something about myself. Love was all that mattered to me . . . the kind of love only Tim had offered me.

Lawrence was waiting in the living room at Mom's when Kenneth took me home. I saw his car in the driveway and cringed. "Might as well get it over with," Kenneth said.

Lawrence looked haggard and angry. Mom said he had waited there all night. She left for work almost right away. I gathered all my wits, took a deep breath, and faced him.

"I'm not going to marry you," I told him. "I think we would both be miserable. I'll take good care of the baby. You can help with his education if you want."

"How generous of you," he shouted. "He's my

child, too. I want this baby. I want you for my wife. If it means anything to you, I thought about it all night long. I'm sorry I hurt you last night. I guess I wanted to get back at you for being so blasted independent. I like it when you need me. It makes me feel like I'm worth something.

"I know I come on like I don't care most of the time, but what you don't understand is how afraid I am. I'm afraid I'm never going to be good enough for someone as decent as you. I'm afraid that people won't love me. I'll never tell another human being that as long as I live. Please give me a chance. I do care about you. I always have."

I looked at him as if I'd never seen him before. His hands were actually trembling. I wondered for a moment if he was just playing with my emotions.

"Lawrence, is this really what you want to do?" I asked. "What if there wasn't any baby? Would you still want to marry me?"

"To tell you the truth, I had been thinking about it," he told me. "The baby was a shock. If you had-n't been so matter of fact . . . if you'd acted like you might need me . . . I probably wouldn't have gotten so angry. I'm really getting excited about it. I like the idea. I'd like a son to spoil, to give the kind of child-hood I never had.

"If you want to know the real me, I'll tell you," he went on. "God knows who my father is. My mother was the town tramp. Everyone in that little town made sure I knew I was nothing but dirt. I hated my mother, the town, and everyone in it. I hated the whole human race.

"I left home when I was thirteen. I hopped a freight to Augusta and got arrested for stealing a car. I was sent to a group home for troubled youth, because no one would claim me. That was the best thing that could have happened to me. For the first time in my life, I felt like someone cared if I lived or died.

"Eventually I got a grant to go to school. I went to the university and got a degree in business, although I cheated my way through most of the classes. I dated every sorority girl I could, just to prove that I could make it with a woman. They were all too willing. When one of them told me she loved me, I laughed in her face. I've had nothing but contempt for women until I met you."

He paced the floor. "I should tell you I was married once. I thought I was in love with this girl. She wouldn't let me touch her until I married her. Four days later I came home from work and found her with my boss. I kicked her out and got an annulment. I swore I'd never let myself be fooled again.

"My next job was with the corporation I'm with now. I've worked like a dog to get where I am. I want to be a millionaire by the time I'm thirty.

"Susan, I've never been this honest with anyone. I really would like to have you by my side. Maybe it's too late for me to learn to love someone. On the other hand, maybe you could teach me how. I need you. You stand for all the love I never had. You stand for all the decency I never knew. I don't want to be alone anymore."

He was silent. He stood at the window and looked out. "You wouldn't lack for anything," he said finally. "Neither would our son. I want so much for him. I want to give him all I never had. You can do anything you want with your life. Just don't take my son. Just don't be unfaithful to me. That's all I'll ever ask from you."

I watched him, waiting there at the window for my answer. So much was clear to me now. I admired his determination. I longed to put my arms around him and take away some of the pain he must have felt during all those lonely years. But I knew all too well what his reaction would be to that. I decided to make a light remark to ease the tension in him.

"Well, we could have a girl, you know," I said. "Would you still want me and my baby then?"

He turned back to me and smiled . . . a winner's smile. "I'd try to make do," he said.

He bought me a diamond that was outrageous, it was so big. I told him I wanted to wait to get married until Tim returned so I could tell him face to face.

"No way," Lawrence said. "We're getting married now—before I have to adopt my own baby. Write him a letter. He'll get over it."

So I wrote Tim a letter. I didn't tell him about the baby, just about Lawrence. I sent him a wedding invitation, too, and told him he'd always be dear to my heart.

He wrote back right away. "Sorry I can't make it to the wedding," he said, "but the best of luck to you. If you ever need any thing, just call your old buddy. I might just still be around. I'll never stop loving you. Don't feel guilty. Be happy . . . that's all I ever wanted for you."

Lawrence and I flew to Greece for our honeymoon. I felt like I was in a dream. Lawrence was loving and attentive. The happiest time I remember was when we rented a beach house for a week. We were totally alone . . . totally uninhibited. I made love to him with all the feeling I had in me, trying to tell him with my body how much I loved him. I gave him all the pleasure I knew how to give. It seemed we made love from sun up to sun down, only stopping every now and then to eat and sleep. My uncontrollable need for him was growing with so much intensity that I had only hoped the same was happening in him.

When the honeymoon was over, we went back to Atlanta. Kyle was born on a sunny November morning. He worked a miracle with Lawrence. Lawrence held him, cooed to him, spoiled him. As Kyle grew, he looked more and more like Lawrence. He had the same coppery hair and green eyes. You would have thought he was the only baby in the world. I couldn't take good enough care of him to suit Lawrence.

"He's crying," Lawrence would say the minute Kyle woke up from a nap. "Aren't you going to pick him up?"

"Do you think he's warm enough in that?" he'd say. Or "Are you sure the doctor said he was alright?"

It was cute, at first. Then I began to resent it. But I understood his feelings.

Sometimes, as he watched me breast feeding our baby, I knew he almost loved me. But he never said it. I ached to hear those three little words . . . just once.

I really thought we might make it. Lawrence took us on all his business trips and spent all his free time with us. I stopped holding my breath and waiting for the world to crash in on me. But then one day when I took Kyle for a walk downtown, it did.

I saw Lawrence coming out of a hotel with a gorgeous brunette. He kissed her, right there on the street. It wasn't a friendly peck on the cheek, either.

I walked Kyle home in his stroller, fed him, and rocked him to sleep. Then I gave in to the torrent of anguish within me and cried hysterically.

Lawrence came home with a bouquet of yellow roses for me. "Get on your glad rags, woman," he said. "Call Mrs. Willcock to sit with Kyle. I got promoted to vice president today. We're going to dance all night!"

"Was the brunette a company bonus?" I asked him. "Or did you just pick her up and have your own private celebration? Well, you'll have to take her to celebrate your victory again tonight, I'm afraid. Kyle and I are leaving for Augusta at nine."

He stared in shock at my outburst and how ragged I must've looked with red swollen eyes. All I could do was plead, "Oh, Lawrence, why? How could you?"

"You want to go home? Fine," Lawrence sneered. "I'll drive you to the airport. But Kyle is staying with me. He's my son."

"He's mine, too! You can't take him away from me!" I protested. "I'm his mother."

"And how do you intend to support him?" Lawrence demanded. "With welfare checks and food stamps? Not on your life. No son of mine is going to live in a dump."

"There's alimony," I said. "I'm sure the courts will award me a generous amount."

"Get a divorce if you want," Lawrence said coldly. "But I'll fight you for Kyle with all I have. I'll win, no matter what I have to do."

"I'll have to take my chances," I told him. "The

courts usually side with the mother."

"I'll take him from you," Lawrence threatened. "You won't be able to stop me. I can go to the ends of the earth and live for the rest of my life with what I have in one bank in Atlanta. You had better think twice before you walk out the door. I'm dead serious."

"I can't stay here with you," I cried. "I hate you for what you've done to me. How many other women have there been? I loved you, Lawrence. I loved you."

I choked on my sobs and Lawrence tried to take me in his arms. "Don't touch me!" I warned him. "Don't you ever touch me again!"

"Susan, I'm so sorry," Lawrence said softly. "I don't want to hurt you. That's the last thing I'd ever want to do. That woman meant nothing to me, I swear it. Oh, honey, I don't want to lose you. I'd be so empty. None of this would mean anything without you!"

He sank down on the sofa and put his face in his hands. I was torn between slapping him for getting to me again and cradling him like a little child. The tears got to me finally. I went over to him and put his head against my bosom and rocked him. He held me so tightly it hurt.

"It's alright, Lawrence. I won't leave you," I said, comforting him. "But don't expect me to be a saint. I'm only human. I can only take so much. Don't do this to me again. Ever."

"Just give me some time," he said. "I know I've got problems . . . emotional scars. But you're healing me."

It was months before I felt anything when he

made love to me. I just didn't trust him enough to let my feelings go. He was devoted to Kyle and me. He called me twice a day from the office and often came home for lunch. He told me he loved me when I woke up each morning and as we went to sleep each night. Part of me was still angry with myself for not leaving. Yet part of me was happier than ever before. He tried so hard to earn my trust. I knew that what he felt for me was real.

One night he came home and said, "Would you like to go home for a visit?"

"Are you trying to get rid of me?" I teased him.

"No," he said, "I just thought you'd like to go. You haven't seen your family since Kyle was born."

"I would like that," I said. "Very much."

It was his way of telling me he trusted me not to take Kyle from him. I understood that, and it meant a lot to me.

It was wonderful to be home again. How I had missed my family! It seemed to me their lives were so uncomplicated and real. The simple things seemed to have so much more meaning in their lives. It was good to put on an old pair of jeans and play a game of softball in the park. I didn't even wear makeup while I was there. And for the first time in Kyle's life, he wore nothing but a diaper and got dirty from head to toe in a sandbox. He loved it.

It was such a relief not having to act just right like I did around all of the people we knew in Atlanta. I could just be myself and do whatever I wanted to do. I felt like a teenager again.

One hot afternoon Kenneth and I sat watching Kyle and Lillie, Kenneth's little girl, play. "You don't seem very happy," he said.

"I'm deliriously happy," I told him. "It's so good to be home where I really feel like I belong. I never appreciated you guys enough. I miss those talks we used to have."

"How is life in the fast lane?" he teased.

"Very complicated," I admitted. Then I told him about Lawrence and his affair.

He whistled softly. "It has been rough, hasn't it?"

"Oh, I guess I'm not the only woman to go through something like that," I said. "But I don't think I'd ever have had to face it with Tim. Have you heard anything from him?"

"Yeah," Kenneth said. "He called a while back. He's home now. I think he said he was working in Sacramento. He was planning on building a house soon. He seemed fine. He asked about you and if you were happy. He was surprised to hear about Kyle. I guess you didn't tell him, right?"

I turned the glass of tea around in my hands. "No. I didn't want him to figure out the obvious," I said. "When I married Lawrence, I wanted Tim to be free of me. I'd kept him stringing along for far too long."

"You regret it, don't you?" Kenneth asked.

"Sometimes," I admitted. "But I guess everyone does that once in a while. I miss him. He was the best friend I'd ever had."

"Why don't you write him a letter?' Kenneth suggested. "It couldn't hurt. You are old friends. He'd probably be happy to hear from you."

"Lawrence would never understand that," I said. "He would accuse me of having an affair or something. I'd better not. But I do wish I knew how he was doing."

"Is your relationship with Lawrence that fragile?"

Kenneth asked.

"I'm afraid so," I said. "It always has been. But I'm learning to live with it. Maybe someday it will be what it should be. It's already getting better."

Lawrence picked me up at the airport in Atlanta. "I have a surprise for you," he said.

He drove out on a country road and pulled up in front of a huge brick house. There was a garden of flowers in the front. Ivy covered the walls. I stepped inside and couldn't believe my eyes. Everything was lovely. All of our things had been moved in.

"I thought it was time we had a real home," Lawrence explained. "Kyle has a big playground in back. I'll put a pool in this month. Do you like it?"

I put my arms around him and said, "Lawrence, you couldn't have made me happier. It means a lot. You're really something, you know."

Kyle raced all around the yard, and we watched him discover each new treasure in his little world. "I love you, Susan," Lawrence said. For the very first time, I knew that he really meant it.

Two months later, I found out I was pregnant again. This time, it was as it should be. Lawrence was ecstatic. "Now we'll have our girl," he said. "Kyle will have a little sister."

Only it wasn't a girl. It was a little boy born two months prematurely. Lawrence was in Europe at the time. I called him after Seth was born, and the woman who answered the phone sounded very French and very sexy. She told me Lawrence was sleeping and asked if she could take a message.

"No, no," I said quickly. "It's not important. This is his secretary calling from Atlanta. I'm sorry to bother you. I'll call later."

THE BEST OF MY THREE LOVERS

After I hung up, all I could think was: *How could I have been so stupid! How could I let him do this to me again?* I cried out all the rage within me, and then I thought carefully of a plan. I thought of all my options. I'd have to call the housekeeper, who was staying with Kyle. Lawrence called me every morning. I'd have to tell her not to tell him about the baby. I'd say I didn't want to worry him. When I got out of the hospital, I'd take the children somewhere where Lawrence couldn't find us.

Suddenly I knew it would never work. Seth was so ill, he couldn't leave the hospital.

I walked down the hallway and looked in at my baby. He was so tiny. There were tubes everywhere running in and out of him. "Oh, Seth. What are you and I going to do?" I cried.

The doctors said his heart was not fully formed, and he couldn't breathe on his own. He was full of infections.

"Why?" I asked them. "Was it anything I did?"

"No, no," they assured me. "Premature babies are just more susceptible to infections. We're doing everything possible."

I spent the next twenty-four hours by Seth's side. Then a call came from Lawrence.

"Did you call last night, Susan?" he asked. I could hear both fear and anger in his voice.

"Yes, I did," I said. "I don't want to talk about it now. We have a son. He might not make it. That's all I care about right now. Are you coming home?"

"What's wrong with him?" Lawrence asked.

"He was born prematurely. His lungs don't work right yet. He has a malfunction in his heart. He's developed a bad infection. If he doesn't fight it off, we'll lose him."

"Why was he born prematurely?" Lawrence demanded. "Did you fall or something?" he asked accusingly.

So he was up to his old tricks. He felt guilty, so he was passing the blame on to me. I had no time or energy for his games.

"I'm going back to the nursery, Lawrence," I said quietly. "Come home when you can."

I hung up the phone and went back to our baby. The doctors were with him. He was bent backward and his arms were outstretched and shaking.

"What's wrong with him?" I asked, terrified.

"He's having a seizure," one of the doctors explained. "The infection has attacked his nerve centers. It doesn't look good, Mrs. Williams. Have you called your husband? Would you like a priest?"

I nodded numbly. My heart was breaking.

The priest came and baptized Seth. He asked me to pray with him, but I couldn't. I had lost God in my life. I didn't think He would listen to me.

The seizures continued all night. Seth hung on by a thin thread. The doctors said that every moment he lived was in his favor. He was fighting hard, they said.

I watched him helplessly, and then suddenly I found I could pray. "If it isn't your will that he lives, take him now. He is suffering so much. . . ."

God, I cried silently, *give me his pain. Have mercy on him. He's only an innocent child. Please, God, stop the pain.*

I looked up in the quiet room and there my mother stood. "Oh, Mom," I cried. "How did you know?"

"Lawrence called me. He thought you might need

me. Why didn't you call me?" she asked, holding me in her arms, stroking my hair.

"I just thought of the baby, Mom," I said. "In haven't thought of anything except him. Oh, Mom, I wish God would just take him. He's suffering so much."

"No, no," she said. "As long as he's willing to fight, you've got to fight right along with him."

She went to the isolette and lifted Seth up, talking softly to him. "Oh, my, what a strong fellow you are!" she crooned. "Yes, you're going to be fine. Just fine."

She rocked him gently and he fell asleep. I was amazed. Her touch was like a miracle. The dawn broke and we watched his gentle breathing. "Now, why don't you rest, Susan?" she asked me. "He's sleeping peacefully, and you must be exhausted."

I went back to my bed and fell asleep feeling that everything would be alright. I had already forgiven Lawrence. My mother had shown me the love that I had received all my life. Lawrence truly had been unloved, and I knew in my heart that even if he never changed, I was the only person he had to depend on.

When I woke up, he was there. "Why aren't you with him?" he demanded. "If he's so sick, why aren't you with him? Don't you care about our son?"

"Lawrence, I'm so glad to see you," I tried to say, holding my arms out to him. "I think he'll be alright. He fell asleep last night. He looked so much better."

"Then why did you tell me he was dying? Were you just trying to punish me?"

"Lawrence, he was very ill," I tried to explain. "The doctors asked me if I wanted a priest. Do you want to see him?"

"Of course I want to see him," he said. "Where is Kyle?"

"Mrs. Willcock is with him. She didn't mind staying—"

"Of course she didn't mind," Lawrence sneered. "I pay her enough—"

A nurse came into the room and interrupted us. "Mrs. Williams, you might want to come," she said. "It's Seth. He's in trouble. His heart—"

I stumbled down the hallway. The doctors stood over my baby, watching a monitor. I watched as they massaged his heart and put a tiny air bag over his mouth. They worked for what seemed like hours. Every once in a while, a little blip would show on the screen. Lawrence stood near the door, but Mama came to me and held my hands as we watched together. Then the little blips stopped happening. The doctor shook his head.

"Give him to me," I said. I reached across the wall of men in white and held my baby, willing him to live, willing him to breathe. But it was no use. "Oh, Seth, I loved you so." I sobbed.

Lawrence left the room. My mother stayed with me.

"Seth's gone, Susan," she said softly. "He'll never feel pain again. He'll never know how cruel life can be. God will accept him into His world. I know how much it hurts, but you wouldn't have wanted him to go on suffering, would you? Let's go now. Lawrence needs you, and Kyle needs you. You must be strong for them."

Lawrence was gone. He'd left a message at the nurses' station that he was home with Kyle. I cried on my mother's shoulder. I needed my husband, but he hadn't cared enough to stay with me.

After I was discharged from the hospital, Kyle became my whole world. It seemed as though his voice was the only thing I heard. I managed to get through the days. Lawrence spent all his free time with Kyle, too. I knew that whatever bond had held us together, Kyle was the only thing we could share now.

I also knew Lawrence would never give up his son. So I stayed with him, going through the motions. Mrs. Willcock stayed to help with Kyle's care. I took a lot of sleeping pills, and even when I was awake I'd slip in and out of reality. I started to fear for my sanity, but it seemed there wasn't anything I could do about it.

Lawrence started criticizing everything I did. I knew he was trying to drive me out, or put all the blame on me. I just tuned him out. He meant nothing to me. I couldn't even hate him.

One night he came home early and found me still in my robe, watching television. The house was a mess. Mrs. Willcock had taken a day off. Kyle was playing on the floor with his blocks.

"We have an awards banquet to go to tonight," Lawrence roared. "You knew I'd be here to pick you up. Look at yourself. You disgust me. Have you even fed Kyle today?"

I shifted a little in my chair. "I'm not going. Tell them I'm sick," I said.

"You most certainly are going!" he raged at me, pulling me to my feet. He pushed me to the bathroom and held me under the shower. I hit him with all my strength. He hit me back. I fell to the floor and sat there, the water soaking my robe.

Lawrence just stared at me. Then he said, "It's been months, Susan. Seth died. All of us die. I've given you all the time I'm willing to give you. You're my wife. You're Kyle's mother. It's time you stopped wallowing in your self-pity and started acting like a normal human being again."

Somehow I got up, dried myself off, and got dressed while Lawrence called a sitter. I had no will of my own. All I felt was a numb shame. I went to the banquet, but I don't remember anything about that night. I don't remember those final blurred hours preceding my complete mental and physical retreat from reality. . . .

I was completely locked inside my mind. I was vaguely aware of my surroundings. . . an institution of some sort. It was quiet and strangers would come in and talk to me. Someone fed me. I never seemed to move. I heard people's voices like dim echoes in my mind, but I couldn't make out what they said.

Then one day I saw the sun shining in a strange window, and when I went over to the window I saw a garden full of roses. Something inside me reached out, and I was sure Kyle was playing in that garden. "Kyle! Kyle!" I called.

I thought I was screaming, but later Dr. Morris told me I had barely been moving my lips. I started to have the strangest feelings. I felt like a vice was on my brain, and I was dizzy, trying to get it off. Sometimes I felt like a vacuum cleaner had sucked me into a light, white room and I heard people asking me things and I heard myself answering them.

Then one day I returned to the real world. Everything was strange, but I could remember everything. I asked Dr. Morris all kinds of questions. I found out Lawrence had brought me here and had only been back once to see me. The doctor said he had talked to Lawrence on the phone several times but he didn't want to tell me what he had said.

Dr. Morris explained what had happened to me. "You were grieving for a lost child and you had no support," he said. "When you reached your breaking point, your mind protected itself from further damage by blanking everything out. You are not insane, Mrs. Williams. You had an emotional breakdown, but you're well on the road to recovery now."

He was a very kind man. He waited until I was strong enough to handle more pain before he told me about his conversations with Lawrence.

"It's not going to be easy to face this," he said, "but I feel you are ready for it. Lawrence has told me he intends to divorce you and that he's going to fight to keep Kyle. He loves the boy very much."

"Have you talked to him recently?" I asked. "Is he still calling you?"

"I called him last week and told him you were just about ready to come home," the doctor said. "I'm sorry, but he doesn't wish to have you return to live with him. Are you able to handle that? Is there someone you can live with for a while? You really shouldn't be alone."

"I know exactly what Lawrence will do!" I said, ignoring the doctor's questions "He'll take Kyle so far away, I'll never see him again. He told me that once, when I was going to leave."

"People say things in anger that they really don't mean," Dr. Morris protested.

"No, he meant it," I insisted. "Kyle is the sun and the moon to him. He'll do anything he can to make sure I don't get him."

"How do you feel about that?" he asked. "I know you feel angry, but do you feel that Lawrence would hurt the boy in any way? Is he a responsible parent?"

"He'd never hurt Kyle," I admitted. "He's always been a good father. Kyle adores him. I know he'll be alright. I just don't want to lose him! He's my son, too!"

Dr. Morris was trying to prepare me, I knew. He wouldn't let me go until he felt I could cope with this new agony. My family was allowed to see me, and I gradually began to look forward to getting back out in the world.

From that time on, Lawrence didn't communicate with my doctor. Dr. Morris had tried to reach him but had no luck. Lawrence's company had clammed up, too.

"It looks like you were right about your husband, Susan," Dr. Morris said. "Perhaps you should plan on staying here a little longer . . . till you adjust."

"Time won't change a thing about this," I said. "The longer I'm here, the longer it will take me to come to terms with my real life. I'm ready. I want to go."

Lawrence had taken Kyle from me. He'd run like a coward from me. He'd dismissed my claim on him with a flick of his hand. The anger was what saved me from being badly hurt again. Clean, healthy anger. I took it out playing tennis on the hospital courts. I never wanted to see Lawrence again. If I did, I'd laugh in his face. He hadn't beaten me yet. I was alive and I was sane, much saner than he would ever be.

For the first time in my life, I understood that I was strong enough—and good enough—to make my own happiness, and I felt a new freedom. I was me. And I wasn't a bad person at all. I had a whole future ahead of me . . . a new life that was completely my own.

I still felt the pain of losing Seth. I never would stop hurting from the loss. But I knew that pain was a part of life, and I wanted to live . . . desperately.

When I got out of the hospital and went home, I found the house deserted. I called Lawrence's business firm and found that he had moved to Europe. He would be assigned permanently there, I was told. I was given his phone number.

I got through after about an hour. The same French woman answered the phone. "This is Mrs. Williams," I told her. "Please let me speak with Lawrence. It's quite urgent."

"Susan," he said a second later. "How nice to hear from you. Are you still in the nuthouse?"

"Don't, Lawrence. Where is Kyle?" I asked.

"He's here with me now. He's fine," Lawrence told me. "You'll be getting the divorce papers soon. Look, I am genuinely sorry for all that's happened. I'll take good care of him Susan. I'm going to marry again soon. She's wonderful with Kyle. He loves her very much. I'll give him the best. You know I will."

"You can't do this!" I exploded. "I'll take you to court. I won't give you a divorce. Don't take him from me, please."

"Do you want to put him through a long and ugly court battle, Susan?" Lawrence said icily. "I could easily prove you mentally unstable. I'd get uglier than that if I had to. Money buys a lot. I could find enough witnesses to swear that you were promiscuous. You won't win. Besides, there's nothing anyone can do to me here. The law can't touch me. So I'm afraid you'd be wasting your time."

"Will you at least let me see him?" I asked.

"I'd rather that you didn't . . . not right away, anyway. He's just beginning to adjust to his new surroundings. He hasn't seen you in three months. He's better off for the moment, getting used to his new mother."

"You're still the same," I said hopelessly. "You still enjoy being cruel."

"I don't know what you mean," he said. "I just want what's best for Kyle. You can write to him . . . when he's old enough to understand the situation. I won't keep him from you. Let him have a stable environment now. Let's not shift him from country to country. I promise I won't bad-mouth you with him. I'll just tell him you love him very much. Does that sound fair?"

Whatever Lawrence might be, I knew he cared deeply for Kyle. I wanted Kyle with me with all my heart, but I saw the sense in what Lawrence was saying.

"Would you send me pictures, Lawrence?" I begged. "You'd really let me come and see him when he gets older?"

"I will. I promise I'll be fair," Lawrence assured me. "I'm sorry we couldn't work things out, but I feel that this is all for the best. I'll give Kyle enough love for both of us. As for my obligation to you, I'm sending you a check in the mail. Put it in a trust for yourself. I don't want you to lack for anything, either."

"You didn't have to do that, Lawrence. I'm capable of making my own way," I said.

"I know you are, but I still want to do it," he insisted. "I know I wasn't the best husband in the world. I tried . . . in my own way. Just take care of yourself. Good-bye, Susan."

Shortly after that, I booked a flight to Augusta. I continued to see a therapist there, I was afraid that if I didn't, the loneliness might give me a setback. I got the divorce papers in the mail . . . and the check from Lawrence. A week later I got an album of pictures of Kyle. I started writing a diary to him, telling him about how I'd felt since the day he was born. I planned to give it to him someday.

I found out from my mother that Tim had been in touch with her. She'd told him all my troubles. "You were in the hospital," she explained, "and I'm afraid I was really upset and angry with Lawrence. I told Tim about your baby, and he felt so bad for you." "Did he say where he was . . . what he was doing?" I asked.

"No," she said. "I'm afraid I overwhelmed him, I was so upset. I didn't even ask why he had called."

I went to work at the same restaurant again, just singing and hostessing three days a week. The hours were all too empty. I volunteered at the hospital on weekends, in the children's ward. It brought back painful memories, but it gave me an emotional outlet, too. I gave those children all the love I had for Seth and Kyle.

I was restless. I saw all the young people at the restaurant and listened to their hopes and dreams. I hoped that they would follow them and not get sidetracked, the way I had.

I read Tim's old letters and thought to myself: *I wonder if he could still care.* It was just a thought, but it stayed with me. I started thinking about him and all the love I had let slip through my grasp. How I wished that I had married him. I realized now that I had loved him. Lawrence had been an unhealthy fixation. The longer I was away from him, the more I realized how I'd been almost hypnotized by him.

Kenneth came over and picked me up one night. "You and I are going dancing," he said. "I'm going to buy you a drink, and then I'm going to fix you up with someone. You've been alone too long. It's time for you to get back in circulation."

"Don't fix me up," I said. "I'll go, but don't fix me up. I don't want anything but the real thing. I couldn't take it."

That evening, I talked about Tim and Kenneth listened. When I was finished, he said, "That guy told me he still loved you six months ago. I got to wondering about him, and I called him in Sacramento. He said he'd never gotten over you. Why don't you call him?"

I was feeling slightly drunk and sentimental. I called Tim, but all I got was a recording saying the number had been disconnected. I danced with a couple of guys, but all I thought about was Tim. I was going to find him. I'd leave tomorrow. I just had to know where I stood with him.

I flew to Sacramento and rented a car. I felt a peace, looking at the mountains. I knew I was finally going to where I had belonged all along. I checked every little town for a Tim O'Brien. There were no O'Briens listed at all. As I drove on, the excitement got to me. How would he look? What would he say? If only he still loved me!

I finally stopped at a motel for the night. I was happy. I felt like I would burst with joyous anticipation. *Tim,* I said to him, *I'm coming home at last.*

The next morning I set out for Placerville. He had to have some family there, even if they weren't listed in the phone book. I stopped in a convenience store, ordered a cup of coffee, and asked the clerk.

"Sure, I know Tim," he said. "He used to live here with his mother. But she moved to Georgetown and he moved somewhere up in the mountains, I heard, fifty miles or so away. Why don't you go to the post office and see if they have a forwarding address?"

I headed right there and got the information I wanted. I even talked to a friendly postal clerk who'd been a pal of Tim's and had directions to the spot where he was building a cabin.

"I haven't seen it," he told me. "But Tim gave me a standing invitation to stop in. If you're planning to go there this time of year, you might not make it without a four-wheel drive."

I looked out at the sky. There were a few snow flurries blowing around, but it was mostly clear.

"I know this country," the man said. "See that cloud bank over the mountain? That's going to drop at least four feet of snow somewhere. And if you're starting out, I'd advise you to change into some warmer clothes, too."

Back at the motel, I changed into a ski jacket and some insulated boots. I couldn't wait to see Tim. I was less than two hours away. He had come to mean so much to me. It seemed like he stood for all the hopes and dreams and little-girl values I'd grown up with. He was all I had left from those days of bright ambition and honest love.

I followed the postal clerk's directions and eventually found myself in a high mountain valley. Sharp peaks bordered it on all sides, and tall pine trees studded the gentle slopes, reaching high into the open sky. The countryside reminded me very much of Tim and his quiet strength. This was his element.

"Take a right at the deserted barn," my directions read. "Go eleven miles on that road and turn left at the windmill. Follow that road until it forks. Then take a right and watch for an old school bus. If there's snow on the ground, you might have to walk the rest of the way. Follow the road up the hill. Tim's cabin is at the top."

I parked the car by the school bus and got out. The snow had begun to fall in huge flakes, and the wind had started to pick up. It swept through the trees with the mournful sound that only wind in the pines can make.

I turned my eyes toward the hill. In the distance, maybe a mile or two away, I could just make out a square shape . . . Tim's cabin!

I took a small suitcase and started up. The snow was getting deep. Already it was almost up to my knees. I'd made it just in time. It wasn't really cold, at first. I was even tempted to take off my jacket. The exertion of walking up the hill was making me too warm.

I was out of breath when I finally reached the cabin. A big dog started barking at me as I walked the remaining few yards to the door. "It's alright, fellow," I told him reaching down to let him smell my hand. "I'm a friend."

THE BEST OF MY THREE LOVERS

He whined as I knocked on the door. There was no answer. I shivered. The wind was much stronger now. I tried the doorknob and it turned easily in my hands. The house was dark and silent. I groped around for a light switch, but could find none. I took my lighter from my pocket and saw kerosene lamps on the tables.

By the soft glow, I looked at the beauty around me. The walls were glowing golden logs. The floors were covered with thick brown carpet. Massive timbers stretched across the high cathedral ceiling. A huge stone fireplace covered one wall. Over the mantel was a winter landscape I'd painted for Tim years ago. I sat down on the sofa and sighed. This was my home. He had built it for me . . . for us. My mother had told him about Lawrence's cruelty and our failing marriage, and he'd wanted everything to be waiting when I came to him.

I hugged myself in joy, then carried a lamp to the bedroom. I knew it would be blue and white before I opened the door. And it was. There was a blue coverlet on the bed and the carpet was deep blue. White curtains framed the windows.

I went to a smaller room and peeked in. It was a child's room. Everything was new. Little toys covered a shelf, and a rocking horse stood in a corner. *For Kyle, of course,* I thought. Tim had thought of everything. He hadn't known about Lawrence taking Kyle to Europe.

A lump rose in my throat, but I closed the door softly and went into the kitchen. Red brick floors, a wood stove, and peach ceramic tiles on the counters . . . it was a welcoming and warm room. "You knew I was coming to you," I whispered. "I love the house, Tim."

I lit a fire in the huge fireplace, then looked for something to eat. I hadn't eaten all day and I was famished. On impulse, I planned a dinner for two, with candles and wine, which I found in a root cellar off the kitchen. I had a stew merrily bubbling on the stove when I saw car lights coming toward the cabin and heard the roar of a powerful engine.

I rushed around making sure everything was perfect . . . the place settings, the candles. I couldn't wait to see the look on Tim's face!

The door opened, letting in a blast of cold air and a flurry of snow. "Oh, Tim," I cried, but then stared in dumb, amazed horror.

The woman I saw was as tiny and delicate as a flower. Her long black wavy hair was covered with white flakes. Her eyes were as dark as night, and she held a small boy in an exotic silk sling at her side. Tim stood in the doorway, stomping the snow from his boots. He looked up and saw me. An expression of disbelief was quickly replaced by anger. "What are you doing here?" he demanded.

"Who is she, Papa?" the little boy asked. "Is she your friend, Papa?"

The woman looked beyond me to the candlelit dinner for two. I gathered up my ski jacket and ran for the door. "I've made a mistake," I said. "I'm truly sorry. I didn't know—"

I ran into the storm while Tim called after me. "You can't go out in this weather!" he yelled.

In answer, I ran as fast as I could in the deep snow. *Oh, when will I ever learn? I did it again . . . I let myself be blinded by my romantic foolishness. If Tim doesn't love me, I have no reason to live,* I thought.

THE BEST OF MY THREE LOVERS

I sobbed and ran off the road into the trees. I ran and ran, falling and getting up. Then suddenly I thought to myself: *What are you running to? Why bother? There's nothing left for you. It's over. You've ruined your life. There are no second chances.*

I dropped wearily into the snow and gave in to the feeling. I was so tired of it all . . . the delusions and the false hopes and the pain. I would stay here. I had no responsibilities to anyone else. Kyle wouldn't even know me. He would love another woman as his mother. I would never find my place in his life again. So I listened to the howling wind and waited to feel the final numbness creep over me. Maybe the next life would be kinder.

As I drifted off to sleep, I heard a dog howling, far, far away. . . .

Strong arms lifted me up. "No," I screamed. "Leave me here. This is what I want. Please leave me!"

I felt a gentle rocking sensation, as if I was on a sea. Then I heard Tim's voice in my ear. "You fool! You fool!" he moaned.

Then I must've passed out.

When I awoke, the first thing I saw was Tim. He was sitting by a blazing fire. His shoulders were slumped. I realized I was in his cabin. He had come after me. I had on a warm robe and there was an Indian blanket spread over me. The house was silent. Tim stirred and turned toward me.

"I'm sorry, Tim," I said. "I chose the wrong man three years ago. I know it's too late now. Where's your family?"

"Sleeping," he said softly, pulling a chair up by my side. "I told them I'd sit with you until you came around. I'm sorry. It must have been a shock."

He took my hands in his. "Leyla is a good wife," he said. "She worked right along with me, building this cabin. I guess I've come to love her very much."

"Tell me about her," I said, tears welling up in my eyes.

"I met her in Baghdad," he began, "not too long after I found out you were getting married. I was so angry. I had always believed that someday you'd realize I was the right one for you. Anyway, I met Leyla and learned her story. She was pregnant with an American guy's baby. He refused to marry her, her family had disowned her, and she didn't want the baby. She was going to get rid of it.

"Maybe because of the crazy, angry mood I was in, I told her that if she would keep the baby, I'd marry her and take her to the States. She didn't believe me at first but after I found her a decent apartment and gave her some money, she began to trust me. When I got ready to come back here, she was waiting . . . practically ready to have the kid. She almost didn't make it back on the plane. She had little Jacob a day after we got stateside. He's really something. He's my whole world."

"I'm really sorry for the scene tonight," I said. "I hope Leyla isn't angry. I don't want to cause you any trouble."

"Leyla isn't a jealous person," Tim told me. "Things are not always what they seem."

I didn't know what he meant, so I simply said, "She's a lovely girl. I'm sure you'll be very happy. I'm so glad for you. You deserve everything—"

"You've been through too much, Susan," Tim cut in. "I'm still worried about you. You won't do anything stupid, will you?"

"No. I promise," I told him. "Life is too good. Just sitting here by the fire, talking to an old friend. . . ."

He looked at me for a long moment, and then he kissed me gently. I held on to him like I never wanted to let go, and then I pulled away. This was all I'd ever have of Tim.

He took my face in his hands and said, "I'll always love you, Susan. I'll love you till I go to my grave. Oh, Susan, what a mess we've made! But I could never leave Leyla. You love different people in different ways."

I looked into his eyes. I memorized them so I could lock them in my heart forever. Then I tried to lighten the mood that was building between us.

"I'm still hungry," I said. "Is there anything left to eat?"

I left the next morning, as soon as the roads had been cleared. Before I left, Tim had taken me for a walk to his special place on the hill. The clouds had passed. Everything was blue and white and shimmering. From the hilltop, you could see for miles and miles.

"You used to love to paint and write," he said. "Why don't you give it a try?"

"I'll find something," I told him. "I think I'll stay in the mountains, though. They've given me a peace I haven't known for years."

"Write and let me know how you are," he said. "You're welcome to come visit. Leyla is lonely. People up here haven't been the best in accepting her. She's not happy."

"Then she's a fool," I said. "She has you and her son and this beautiful world."

THE BEST OF MY THREE LOVERS

I squared my shoulders, hiked down the hill, packed up, and drove away. I drove where the urge took me. I stayed one night in South Lake Tahoe, and spent the whole next day just walking in the mountains near the ski lodge. I felt clean and refreshed. Suddenly I knew what I wanted to do with my life. I had enjoyed working at the hospital with the children so much. Why not go to nursing school? I had Lawrence's money to pay for the tuition. I needed to surround myself with other people's problems. I needed to be needed.

I went back to my room, feeling excited and adventurous. I called my mother and told her I had decided to stay in California and that I'd send for my things later. I was going to be on my own for the first time in my life. I wanted to prove to myself that I could make it on my own.

The next morning, I headed for Sacramento. I found a small apartment, then called the university. I found out there was a nursing academy in Sacramento and that the registration for the next class began in three days. I would have to send for my transcripts from the state university in Georgia today.

I was busy and happy once I started my classes. I studied at night and on weekends I volunteered at a children's hospital. I had one lonely moment each day—when I opened the door to the apartment and silence greeted me. But I began to enjoy the solitude, and I'd walk for long hours in the parks, watching the world go by.

I sent a card to Tim and Leyla, thanking them for their hospitality and telling them I was fine and what I was doing. I sent them my address. Tim wrote back telling me he was proud of me and sending a photo of the three of them. *Maybe someday we can all be friends,* I thought.

I got more pictures of Kyle, and a letter from Lawrence's wife telling me details of his progress. She said they were coming to Atlanta soon, and she would try to persuade Lawrence to let me see Kyle. That was something to look forward to.

I bought a guitar and learned to play it. I was so proud when I could play little songs for the children at the hospital. They loved it.

I did well the first quarter. Three years and I would be a real R.N. I was going to make it!

I made friends with some girls from school. We went out for pizza and to the movies. They'd talk excitedly about the guys they were dating. It was strange. I was only three years older than they were, and I'd already been married and had children of my own. I didn't think I'd ever go back to the dating scene. I felt too old and used up. I thought I could be happy with just my kids at the hospital.

One day I was singing to a little girl with leukemia named Katie Johnson. A young doctor stopped to watch. I knew who he was. I'd watched him work with the children. He was so funny with them, and so gentle. I admired him. All of the nurses were crazy about him, including me.

"Pretty," he said when I'd finished the song. "The music was, too. Buy you lunch?"

"No, thank you. I should study," I said, annoyed with myself for feeling so flustered.

"The mind works better on a full stomach," he said. "Come on. I don't like to eat alone."

We talked a while at lunch. I found out he was a

first-year resident and the same age I was. He was from a little town in the southern part of California. He had worked his way through school, and he wanted to be a pediatrician in a state or county hospital somewhere.

"Why?" I asked him. "There's not much money in that."

"Exactly," he said. "I'd like to treat whoever needs help and not have to worry about pleasing wealthy patients. It would give me a lot of freedom."

"I'm impressed, Doctor," I said. "I've seen you with the kids. You're pretty special."

"Call me Dan, please," he begged. "I've seen you, too. Today's the first time the schedule has been light enough to get to know you. I like your style. I can tell you really give your all to the children. Any special reason?"

"Yes, I guess I have a personal feeling for them," I said. Then I stopped, trying to decide whether to let this man see that much of my inner self at once.

"My sister died of cystic fibrosis," he said. "I always wanted to do something about it, but I couldn't. I guess that's what made me decide to become a doctor."

I nodded. "My little boy died. He was premature and he just couldn't make it," I said. "My other son is with his father. I loathe my ex-husband, but he does love Kyle."

"Wow, you've had a rough time of it," Dan said. "I admire you for not being bitter. You must be quite a lady."

Before I could answer, Dan's beeper went off in his pocket. "Duty calls," he said. "How about dinner Saturday night?"

"Don't expect much from me, Dan," I warned. "The only relationship I'm interested in is friendship."

"That's okay with me," he agreed. "See you Saturday. Meet me here at eight, and wear some old jeans. I'll take you to a place that has become my yearly escape from reality."

Saturday morning Katie Johnson died. Everyone in the hospital had been pulling for her for four years.

Dan met me in the cafeteria. He sat down on the chair across from me and put his face in his hands. "Sometimes you wonder if you do any good at all," he said. "I'm going to miss Katie."

"She was a darling," I said. My heart went out to him. He looked totally drained.

"She was a little trooper," he told me. "She should have made it. She gave it a good try."

"Want to skip our date? I'd understand," I said quietly.

"No, I really need to get my mind off this. I can't let it get me down," he explained. "I'm a doctor, remember?"

"You're a human being, just like all the rest of us," I said.

He grinned. "Let's go!" he ordered briskly. "I'll get a six-pack of beer on the way."

He took me to a huge carnival in the heart of Sacramento. We played all the little games at each booth and ate hot dogs and drank beer. Being part of the noisy, happy crowd was just what the doctor ordered. By the end of the evening, we were both giddy with laughter. Dan took me home to my apartment and we sat, with our feet propped up on the coffee table, watching TV.

"I'll make some coffee," I said.

When I came back from the kitchen Dan was asleep. I smiled and covered him up with a blanket, and then I turned in, too.

In the morning, coffee and scrambled eggs were waiting for me in the kitchen. "Sorry," Dan said, grinning. "I usually have better manners. I was just so relaxed with you."

"No problem, Doctor," I said. "We'd better hurry. Aren't you on at seven?"

He nodded, gulping his coffee. "Want to go sailing after work?"

I shook my head. "I've got a big exam Monday."

"Okay," he said. "Maybe next weekend, then."

But that night when I bumped into him, I asked him, "Can I change my mind?"

He laughed. "Sure, but I'm beat. So let's just grab a hamburger and watch some television. Your place or mine?"

He was good company. We watched television and drank a few beers. It was funny. We sat around like an old married couple, holding hands, sometimes not talking at all. He was so relaxed and undemanding. I liked him very much.

When the news came on, he yawned and stretched. "I better hit the road. Big day tomorrow."

"You don't have to leave," I said. "Stay over."

"Your couch gave me a stiff neck, lady," he scolded. "I better go home."

"You can sleep in my bed," I said, taking his hand. "We can keep each other warm. No strings, Dan. I haven't been with anyone since Lawrence. I want to know what it's like. I don't want to be alone tonight."

"I'd like that," he said, taking me in his arms and kissing me gently.

In the bedroom, we lay there, just holding each other and nuzzling our noses together for a long time. Then slowly and tenderly we began making love. There was a nice and steady flow to it that seemed a caring meeting of two people who were friends rather than lovers. I fell asleep on Dan's shoulder.

The alarm crashed into my dreams. Dan started to get up, but I held him next to me. "Just a few more minutes. You feel so good," I whispered.

He laughed and kissed me lightly. "Got to go, sunshine," he said. "See you tonight. Study hard today. I'll be wanting your attention after work."

I drifted back into a contented, dreamless sleep.

So it went for the rest of the quarter.

Dan and I kept each other company, and we made love together when we had time. There wasn't a dominance between us . . . I gave him as much as he gave me. We placed no demands on each other. We just enjoyed being together. When he had to work late I went out with my girlfriends or just relaxed at home. You would have thought we'd been married for years, we were so easy together.

I was just getting ready to turn in one night when the doorbell rang. Dan was at the hospital and was likely to be there all night. I looked through the peephole. "Leyla!" I said, unlocking the door. "Is that you?"

"Yes, it is me," she said, smiling. She had cut her hair and put on makeup. She had on a smart suit, and she looked very sophisticated and very American. "Do you like?" she said, turning around in a circle when she got inside.

"You look wonderful," I told her. "What are you doing in Sacramento?"

"I came to see you," she said. "I took a bus and then a taxi. I'm glad you still live here. I had to find you."

"Is something wrong with Tim?" I asked. "Is Jacob alright?"

"They are fine," she assured me. "Please, sit down. I want to talk very serious with you. I want to leave Tim."

"Oh, no!" I gasped. "What's wrong? I thought you were happy. I thought both of you were."

She shook her head. "I do not like the mountains," she began. "I have no friends. I'm very grateful to Tim, but I want—"

"What, Leyla? You have it all. You have a man who loves you, you have a wonderful little boy."

"I know. I know all these things," she said. "But I want to be with my own people. I want to live in a big city. I want to go to work and have my own money. I want to go to school and learn all about America. I don't want to be married anymore. I feel—I feel like I live in prison. But I can't leave Tim unless I give you to him. I know you love him. I love him too, but it's not the same. He gave me my life, but. . . ."

I put my arms around her. "Leyla, I can't just let you leave him," I said. "Life in the city is not so wonderful."

"It's what I want," she insisted. "I attended English classes in Georgetown, and I met many of my own people. They all have jobs. They all are happy. They are together. I am alone. I want to move there.

Tim thinks that I am in Georgetown now.

"I feel like I am a bad person . . . very ungrateful. But I cannot stay with this man. I do not love him. And he needs you. He stands on the hill and looks for you since you came. Go walk up the hill to him. Tell him I give him you and Jacob . . . in exchange for my freedom."

"If you leave Tim now, you might not ever get him back," I warned.

"That is alright," she said. "I am sure of what I want. So will you go to him? Will you take care of Jacob? Please, I must know."

"After you've told Tim what you want to do and have left him, I'll go see him," I agreed. "But I can't promise anything else."

She left and I sank down on the couch. Everything had been going so well. I had my work. I had Dan to keep away the loneliness. I would be starting my second year in nursing school after this quarter. I had finally found a place for myself in this world. And now this. Well, I didn't have to decide anything yet.

I went to bed and turned out the light, sinking into a deep and dreamless sleep.

I got a letter from Leyla two weeks later. "I am in Georgetown now," she wrote. "I am happy. I live with another girl from Baghdad and we work in a candy factory. You go see Tim now. He is very sad."

I was in the middle of my midterm exams. I put the letter aside and kept studying. But I did tell Dan about it.

"What are you going to do?" he asked. "You can't stop now, Susan. You have a life of your own. You're going to be a terrific nurse. Don't let anything stop you this time."

"Dan, would you mind not staying tonight?" I said. "I'd like some time alone."

"Sure," he answered. "I haven't been home in so long, it will be a good change of scene. Knock 'em dead on those tests tomorrow, kid."

When he left, I tried to study, but my mind kept wandering back in time. "I'll love you till I go to my grave," I heard Tim saying by the firelight.

I touched my mouth, remembering his kiss. I couldn't get him off my mind. I finally fell asleep on the couch, the open books falling to the floor in the night.

I passed my exams with very satisfactory grades. Dan picked me up, and we celebrated with dinner and good wine.

"You're going to make it, Susan," he said. "I never doubted you'd come out on top. Maybe we could be a team. I'd like to have you with me. We're good together. Want to add some strings to our relationship?"

"Not yet. I still want to take it as it comes," I said. "I'm out for a week or two. I think it's time I made that trip up the mountain. I have to settle things one way or another."

"Meaning?" Dan asked.

"Meaning I still have a lot of feelings for Tim. He's a wonderful man. He's warm and giving and gentle. . . ."

"I am all of those things," Dan teased. "And I'm here in Sacramento where you want to be. What would you do on a mountain?"

Then he turned serious. "Look, don't let the person you were in your past confuse you about who you are now. We all have feelings for old lovers, but

I don't think there's any going back. You may be remembering a person who doesn't exist anymore. He may be thinking of you as someone you're not. Just make sure it's real. And give me some consideration, would you? My ego is hurting!"

"We never made any promises, Dan," I said.

"I know," he agreed. "And I'm not trying to tie any strings now. You're a free woman, sunshine. If you really want this Tim guy, go for it!"

I grinned. Dan was special. I hated giving him up.

The next morning, I packed up and drove toward the mountains. I stopped lots of times along the way, thinking and remembering. I wondered if I really did see Tim as someone he wasn't. I certainly had changed. All those little-girl fantasies were dreams I smiled about now. I took life as it came and didn't question everything so much anymore. I had learned to live with myself.

I still felt that I owed Tim something for the pain I had caused him, but I didn't want that to get in the way of any decision I might make. If I took Tim back into my heart, I wanted it to be for all the right reasons.

As I turned off the highway onto the dirt road I'd taken to his place last year, my heart swelled. The high mountain valley was even more breathtaking in full sunlight. I could see why Tim would move here and never want to leave.

I stopped the car at the yellow school bus and started the climb up the hill. I couldn't stop myself from running. I reached the top and stopped, breathing heavily, crying and laughing. My eyes searched the meadow and at last I saw Tim. He was behind the house, chopping wood. He looked up and saw me. I started walking slowly toward him, my heart racing with joy.

He put down the ax and held out his arms. In that moment, I knew that he was all of my yesterdays and all of my tomorrows, and there was no way I'd ever leave him again. We stayed there holding each other for what seemed like forever until he led me inside the cabin. Between our kisses and crying, Tim managed to whisper in my ear, "You know, I built this all for you."

We came together and it seemed that it had only been days and not years since we'd been apart. The first time we had made love we were kids and unsure of how to handle what we were feeling. This time we were adults and embraced each other with a passion and certainty that neither of us had felt with anyone else.

That was eight years ago . . . the day Tim and I finally found each other. Our story didn't end, of course, with a tender embrace and vows to live happily ever after. There were problems and shadows from the past for both of us to deal with. For me, there was saying good-bye to Dan . . . packing up my belongings . . . canceling my classes; for Tim, there was seeing through his divorce from Leyla . . . arranging for custody of Jacob . . . setting up a support agreement for Leyla until such time as she married again.

But finally we'd done everything we could do to honorably correct all our mistakes and make amends for our sins and then we could at last get married and begin our wonderful life on Tim's mountain.

For Tim and me, it has been a beautiful, satisfying

relationship. For Jacob, it has meant having a loving mother and father—and two younger half brothers to play and grow with.

I still deeply regret my involvement with Lawrence and the loss of Kyle. He's a big boy now, and I pray every day for his happiness. Maybe someday he'll want to meet his real mother, and when he does I'll be waiting right here . . . with Tim by my side.   THE END

POSSESSED

As I stood waiting in line outside of the movie theater, I heard a voice call, "Emily!" I turned and looked to see who was calling my name. "Emily!" the male voice called again, and I saw a tall, attractive man moving toward me.

"Dave!" I exclaimed, my heart quickening.

He stopped alongside me, his eyes searching my face. "I heard about Samuel's death. I'm sorry," he said.

My throat was suddenly dry and full. I couldn't speak.

"How have you been?" Dave asked. I could see that he hadn't changed much since we had broken up eight years ago. He was broader, more mature, but he still had the same warm eyes, and the same shy, boyish smile.

"I'm fine," I murmured, tears threatening to well up in my eyes. "How . . . how are you? It's been a long time since I've seen you."

"I'm back in town," he said. "I've opened up my

own real estate office a couple of blocks from here. I worked late tonight and was walking past when I saw you in line." He paused for a moment, then added, "Justine and I are divorced."

"I'm sorry," I said. Then I turned to my friend Melissa. "Do you remember Dave Ellington?"

"Of course." She smiled. "How are you, Dave?"

After they'd exchanged hellos, he turned back to me. "It's nice seeing you again, Emily. Maybe we'll see each other again sometime." I watched until his retreating figure disappeared around the street corner.

"He's such a nice guy," Melissa said as we moved forward in line. "I've never been able to figure out why you didn't marry him."

I suspected that because she'd felt sorry for me, Melissa had asked me to go to the movies with her. It was the first time I'd been anywhere since my husband's death several months prior. When she first asked me, I was reluctant, but she'd refused to take no for an answer. "You can't stay cooped up in the house forever," she'd insisted. "Grief can drive you a little crazy."

As I sat down to watch the movie, I couldn't help but think how strange it was that on my first venture out, I'd run into Dave. Samuel had once told me that if anything ever happened to him, I'd be back with Dave before he was cold in his grave.

Dave and I had dated all through high school. Afterward he had gone off to college and I attended a two-year business school. Everyone took it for granted that eventually we'd get married, but then I met Samuel and fell madly in love with him. Handsome and dynamic, he swept me off my feet. By the time I was through school, I'd decided that Samuel was the man I wanted . . . and we were married.

Making an effort to forget the past, I turned my attention to the movie. But I couldn't concentrate. Instead, as usual, my thoughts returned to Samuel. I had been wildly in love with him . . . and totally dominated by him. He was charming and gentle most of the time, but he hadn't been an easy man to live with. He was possessive and insanely jealous, especially of Dave, whom he'd scarcely known. Maybe it was because Samuel sensed that all my friends thought I was making a mistake when I married him instead of Dave.

"What's with you?" I'd demanded once when he had made some derogatory remark about my old relationship with Dave. It was one of the few times when I'd stood up to Samuel. "I married you, didn't I? I love you!"

His death had been such a shock. So unexpected. He'd never been sick a day in the seven years we were married. Yet one morning as he was preparing to go to work he collapsed on the floor. Minutes later he was dead of a heart attack—at thirty-three.

Endless days of loneliness and missing him stretched before me as the terrible finality of his death sunk into my consciousness, filling me with pain. Night after night I lay in bed trying to sleep, but the moment I closed my eyes, Samuel's face was there and a horrible feeling of grief was in my heart.

I'd pray that wherever he was, Samuel was at peace. He had been a driven man. It was as if he was trying to prove to everyone that he was a better man, a better provider, than Dave or any other man could have been. And he gave me everything a woman could want: a beautiful home, nice clothes, plenty of expensive nights out. Everything except a baby. The doctor had assured us we were both all right, but somehow we just couldn't make it happen.

I suspected that Samuel resented my friends because they'd been Dave's friends, too, so I saw them while Samuel was at work or not at all. Although I'd had several job offers after graduation, Samuel didn't want me to work. After his death I had nothing to distract me from my grief . . . no job and almost no friends. Melissa, one of the few friends I still had was married and lived several houses down from us. I think it was because she lived so nearby that we were able to maintain a real friendship. A nurse by profession, Melissa was warm and compassionate. She mothered her patients and anyone else she could.

You've got to accept living alone, I told myself repeatedly on my sleepless nights. I tried to make my mind a blank, but it wouldn't work. If eventually I did fall asleep out of sheer exhaustion, it would be a troubled sleep filled with dreams of Samuel. Him walking toward me, his arms outstretched, but never quite reaching me. Dreams in which he was saying, "I know you married me, but it's Dave you're always thinking about. But you're stuck with me, Emily . . . forever!" Dreams in which I was calling out to him, denying his accusations.

Always, there was the memory of Samuel lying on the floor at my feet, clutching his chest while we waited for the ambulance to arrive. In my dreams, I saw the paramedic kneeling beside his body, about to tell me that Samuel was dead. But something stopped him from saying the final terrifying words. "I'm here, Emily," Samuel's voice spoke to me in my dreams. "I'll never leave you. You're mine."

Suddenly, my eyes began to play tricks on me. Samuel's face appeared over the images on the movie screen. I felt disoriented, hardly daring to breathe. His eyes peered directly at me, holding me captive. Slowly, the familiar feeling of Samuel's presence came over me, and I felt close to him and no longer alone. I welcomed the feeling. And then the image faded and the movie came back into focus.

Did Samuel somehow know that I'd just seen and talked to Dave? Did the dead know about things that happened to their loved ones left on earth? The thought was so disturbing I began to tremble. I knew it was crazy thinking. I pressed my hand tightly to my temples and held them there as if to stop my thoughts. But try as I would, they wouldn't go away. The feelings inside me were too big, too powerful. It seemed that Samuel's eyes were watching me accusingly and a sudden eerie feeling filled me.

"Emily, are you all right?" Melissa whispered, leaning over to me.

"I'm fine," I lied. Then I concentrated all my willpower on banishing the thoughts from my mind. It was useless. Samuel's face reappeared just as before. *This is utterly, ridiculous! Samuel is dead,* I told myself. Yet I was consumed with a sense of foreboding.

Apparently Melissa sensed my uneasiness. "Are you sure you're okay?" she whispered.

"I—I'd like to leave if it's all right with you," I whispered back. Then I stood up, moved into the aisle, and almost ran out of the theater. Outside on the street, I halted and tried to catch my breath. The warm night air, the sound of the traffic, and the flickering lights seemed to bring me back to reality. Bewildered and shocked at my own behavior, I struggled to get hold of myself.

"What's wrong?" Melissa questioned me with a look of concern on her face.

"I'm sorry," I apologized. "Would you mind if we went home?"

"Of course not," she said softly, linking her arm in mine.

As we drove home, Melissa suggested that I go away for a while. "Visit your parents," she urged. "Get away from everything that reminds you of Samuel."

I shook my head and stared out the open car window. The cool night breeze lightly caressed my hair. I knew Melissa meant well, but it wasn't that easy. I was aware that I would only take my grief with me, no matter where I went. I had to live with it, try to cope with it. But how?

When Melissa dropped me off at my house, she offered to come in with me. But I assured her it wasn't necessary. Once inside, I crawled right into bed. But it was a long time before I fell asleep.

Then I awakened suddenly. I'd dreamed that Samuel was standing at the foot of my bed. I sat up, shaking violently. I had to clasp my arms about myself to control my trembling. Finally, I pulled the blanket around me and sat huddled there with my knees drawn up under my chin. It's only a dream, I told myself over and over. Still, I couldn't put it out of my mind. I could feel Samuel's presence in the room.

The next morning, when I opened the closet door to find something to wear, the sight of Samuel's things . . . which I'd been unable to get rid of and were still hanging beside mine, frightened me. Somehow, giving away his belongings seemed even more final than watching his casket being lowered into the ground. For the first time, my unwillingness to dispose of his things seemed more than just a weakness. Now it seemed to be an indication of some mental problem. If I was to get control of my grief, I had to let the dead die.

After breakfast, I boxed up all Samuel's things and took them to the Salvation Army store.

Several days later there was a knock on the door and when I opened it, Dave stood in front of me. "Hi," he said with a grin. "I thought I'd stop by and say hello." He paused expectantly as I stood motionless. My hand froze to the doorknob. "Did I catch you at a bad time?" he asked.

If you ever see him again, I'll know it. The words . . . Samuel's words . . . echoed in my mind. "You look a little upset," Dave said. "Is something wrong, Emily?"

I stepped back hesitantly. "Come in." I motioned toward the sofa. "Sit down. Can I get you a cup of coffee or something?"

"Whatever you have is fine with me." Dave smiled.

My hands shook so much as I filled the two cups of coffee that it sloshed out into the saucer.

"How have you been?" Dave asked as I sat down across from him.

I looked down into my cup. "Being alone is hard to get used to."

"I know," Dave agreed quietly. "It was hard for me to get over Justine after she left me." He paused. "I've often thought about you, Emily." He looked slightly embarrassed, as though he'd confessed some dark secret.

"I didn't mean to hurt you," I said apologetically. "But Samuel sort of swept me off my feet."

"It's okay," Dave assured me. "You don't have to explain. I recovered. Enough to get married. Unfortunately, Justine and I couldn't seem to make a go of it."

"I'm sorry," I murmured, not knowing what else to say.

"Justine deserved someone better than a mixed-up guy like me," he went on. "Forgive me if I go too far in what I'm about to say, Emily, but I've never stopped loving you." His eyes gazed at me searchingly. I averted mine and stared down at my hands clasped tightly in my lap. "I'm sorry," he apologized when I made no response. "I shouldn't have said anything yet. It's too soon for you."

He paused, then added, "I feel as if we've been given a second chance. This time, hopefully, it'll turn out right."

"There's nothing to forgive or to be sorry for," I told him. "I've thought about you, too, Dave. I've always felt guilty about the way I treated you." I stood up and went over to the window and stared out into the park across the street. "That doesn't mean I didn't love Samuel. I did. I still do." It was as if I was compelled to speak those words, perhaps to convince myself more than to convince Dave.

"I understand," he said softly. When I turned around, our eyes met and I felt the tension of the attraction between us. "But Samuel is gone and that doesn't mean you can't ever love anyone else," Dave added.

I looked at him, anguish in my eyes. "Please, Dave. I don't think we should be talking like this so soon after Samuel's death."

"I didn't mean to push," he said, getting up from the sofa. "I think I'd better leave for now."

As I walked him to the door I felt faint and I caught the back of a chair for support.

Dave took hold of my arm. "Emily, are you all right?"

I gripped the back of the chair. "I—I don't know. Ever since Samuel died, I've had this strange feeling. I feel as if he's watching me."

"You're just under a lot of stress," Dave reassured me as he led me to the sofa so I could sit down.

"Samuel always resented you," I blurted out. "I could never fully convince him that I loved him, no matter how I tried. Once he told me that if something happened to him, I'd be with you before he was cold in his grave. I thought it was a ridiculous thing for him to say. But here we are . . . just as he predicted," I finished in a hushed tone.

"You've got to put the past out of your mind," Dave insisted. "Samuel is dead. You've got a right to begin a new life. There's nothing wrong with you and me seeing each other again."

"But it's too soon," I protested. Suddenly I began to cry helplessly. He sat down beside me and pulled me into his arms. I clung to him momentarily. Then I pushed him away and stopped the tears with the back of my hand. "Please go. I'd like to be alone."

Dave looked at me with an expression of sadness on his face. "I'll call you in a couple of days."

After he was gone, my mind was in a turmoil. I was still grieving over my husband, yet I'd allowed another man to hold me in his arms. What was the matter with me? I was filled with confusion . . . and fear.

The next few days passed slowly, as usual. I wandered aimlessly about the house. I looked forward to seeing Dave again, but at the same time I was apprehensive. I considered looking for a job, as Melissa had suggested I do, but I couldn't seem to make myself open the newspaper to check the help-wanted ads. Samuel had had plenty of life insurance, and he'd left me fairly well off.

Then one evening a week later, Dave stopped by again.

It was a balmy summer night, and because I was afraid that the intimacy we'd experienced the last time we'd been together might happen again, I suggested we go for a walk in the small park across from my house.

His eyes were warm as we sat down on the park bench. "How have you been, Emily?" he asked. I knew what he meant to ask was if I was getting over Samuel.

"I'm trying," I answered.

"Good for you." He smiled. "What do you do to keep yourself busy? Do you have a job?"

I shook my head. "Samuel didn't want me to work." I tried to blink away the tears that began to form in my eyes. "I'm sorry. I just can't seem to pull myself together."

"Oh, Emily." Dave reached out for me and pulled me close. I clung to him. Then he took my face in his hands and kissed my cheeks. When his lips touched mine gently, I didn't pull away for a long moment.

"No!" I cried out, drawing away from him. "I can't do this." *Samuel will be angry,* I thought frantically to myself.

"What's wrong?" he asked, taking my hand in his. "You're shaking life a leaf."

"I don't know," I mumbled. "I can't explain it. I keep thinking Samuel knows . . . that he's watching us."

"Samuel is dead," Dave said gently, as if he was talking to a bewildered child.

"I know. I know," I said tearfully. "But I can't seem to . . . I keep dreaming about him. I keep seeing him in my dreams."

"Maybe you should talk to someone about it," Dave suggested, his voice weighted with concern. "Get some counseling."

"I'm not crazy," I said almost angrily.

"I know that," he told me hastily. "But you're obviously having a bad time accepting what's happened."

Dave walked me home, and after he was gone I thought about what he'd said. Maybe I should talk to someone. I remembered Pastor Carington, the minister at the church where Samuel and I had gone quite often. He'd always seemed warm and friendly.

The next afternoon when I rang the parsonage doorbell, Pastor Carington ushered me into his study. He made me feel instantly at ease, and I soon found myself telling him about my confusion, my feeling that Samuel was watching me, and about Dave.

"Your distress is understandable, Emily, since this man has reentered your life so soon after your husband's death. You and Samuel seemed so close," Pastor Carington said quietly, his hands folded in his lap. "But God wants us to be happy. I'm sure the answers will come to you if you pray to Him." He paused and smiled. "He probably won't whisper in your ear or shout it from the clouds, but if you listen carefully, your answer will come to you."

"Why do I feel that Samuel is still here . . . that he doesn't want me to begin a new life without him?" I asked.

"I suspect it's because you feel guilty for having feelings for another man so soon after your husband's death," Pastor Carington replied. "But maybe it's God who's bringing you and this man back together. And it's not a sin."

"I didn't say I thought it was a sin," I protested.

"But it's in the back of your mind, isn't it?" he asked. "You think it's wrong that you're so attracted to Dave."

"Tell me how to stop feeling that way," I pleaded.

"Pray for guidance and your confusion and anxiety will eventually pass. And your dreams will stop," he assured me. "If it's God's will that you and Dave should be together again, accept it and be grateful that you've found each other after these years apart."

"How will I know if I'm doing the right thing?"

"If it feels right in your heart, it will be right," he told me.

I pondered his words for several minutes. Then I

stood up and smiled at him. "I feel much better. Thank you so much."

Pastor Carington took my hand in his and pressed it warmly. "God be with you, Emily."

His words had made a profound impression on me. When I'd come to see him, I'd felt as if my life was reeling out of control. Now I felt less confused and looked forward to the future.

For the next several nights, my sleep was free of frightening dreams of Samuel. I felt more relaxed and happier than I had in months. I was even able to watch television again without my mind wandering from the story and back to when Samuel had been alive.

One night I fell asleep on the sofa watching the late movie, but later, when I woke up enough to climb into bed, sleep eluded me. I rolled and tossed restlessly for what seemed like hours. The more annoyed I became with my inability to go to sleep, the wider awake I became.

Finally, I got up and took two aspirin. They were of no help. I still remained wide awake. Disgusted, I climbed out of bed once again and went to my open window overlooking the park. The night was bright with a full moon. I could smell the dewy freshness of the night, almost hear the rustle of the leaves as the breeze filtered through them.

Suddenly the curtains billowed out, and I shivered and got back into bed. I tried once more to go back to sleep, but it was useless. I sat up. It was an insane idea, but maybe if I got up and went to the park, I would eventually get some sleep.

No! I told myself. *It's crazy to get out of bed in the middle of the night and go wandering around out-*

side. But the more I thought about it the more the idea grew. What was wrong with it? The park was relatively safe. And it was just across the street from my house.

I crawled out of bed, combed my fingers through my hair, and pulled on a blouse and a pair of jeans. Then I slipped out of the house and across the lawn to the park.

In the moonlight, I saw the bench where Samuel and I used to sit. The same bench where Dave and I had clung to each other just days ago. My heart leaped into my throat and my hand went to my mouth. There was a man standing by the bench!

Samuel! It must be Samuel, I thought. As if mesmerized, I walked toward him. He turned in my direction and held out his arms to me. I closed my eyes and walked into his arms. He tightened them about my waist.

"Emily," he whispered huskily. Then he was kissing me wildly. Passionately. Our bodies were pressed together, our arms locked around one another. Finally we broke apart. I struggled to catch my breath. And then I saw his face.

"Dave!" I exclaimed.

"Yes," he answered. "Who did you think it was?"

"Where did you come from?" I demanded. "What are you doing out here?"

"I got this sudden urge to see you, but I didn't quite have the courage to ring your doorbell at this late at night," he explained. "So I parked my car and walked over here where I could look up at your bedroom window, if nothing else. Why are you out here?"

"I couldn't sleep," I told him. I felt as if we weren't

in the park together by chance. It was as if some strange force had drawn us.

Dave took my hand and we walked toward the house in silence. We entered the back door, and I led him inside. We stood apart momentarily, staring at each other in the moonlit kitchen. The passion that had been kindled in the park was still with us drawing us together like a magnet. We were in each other's arms.

"Emily, I—" He broke off. Taking me by the hand again, he led me down the hall into the bedroom. We lay down on the blanket, trembling against each other like leaves in the wind.

Dave was kissing me, his lips moving down my throat, pressing hotly into my flesh. He kissed my ears, my eyes, my cheeks. His hand slipped down my shoulder . . . lower and lower still. The effect was immediate. I had never felt so full of urgent desire. The sensations Dave was creating in me were far more vivid than I'd ever experienced. My body felt electric.

"I love you, Emily," Dave murmured in a husky voice. "I've never stopped loving you."

My fingers stroked his neck, sifted through his hair. Then we were wrapped in each other's arm. Gently, tenderly, he began to make love to me. . . .

"I love you," he whispered again afterward. "I'm not going to let you get away from me this time."

The words sounded beautiful, and I fell asleep with them ringing gently in my ears while feeling the warmth of being held in his arms.

The morning sun was beginning to cast a warm light into the bedroom when I awoke. I sat up and peered down at Dave, who was stretched out beside me in the bed where Samuel and I had made love so many times. I thought about what had happened, wondered what had drawn Dave and me to the park. Had Samuel been right when he had accused me of still being in love will Dave?

Then the old torment was back, messing up my mind. If Dave and I were to have anything together, would I always wonder whether my thoughts and feelings were for him or for Samuel? And if they were for Dave, would I always feel guilty about them? How long would I go on being haunted by Samuel?

Quietly, I got out of bed and showered. Then I dressed and went into the kitchen. A short time later, Dave came in and placed his hands on my shoulders. "I don't know exactly how things came about last night, Emily, but I'm glad they did," he said tenderly. "I think something is telling us that we should never have broken up, that we belong together. Don't you?"

I shook my head in confusion. "I don't know. There are so many ghosts."

"There won't always be," Dave reminded me softly.

"I'm not so sure," I said.

His gaze held mine. "Didn't last night mean anything to you, Emily? We can have something good if you'll let it happen."

I could tell he was hurting, and I looked I away, filled with conflicting emotions. "I really care about you, Dave. But it's too soon." How can I have any kind of relationship when I'm still being tormented by my dead husband?

I closed my eyes. "It's all so crazy. I don't know

what to do!" I was torn between a ghost and the flesh-and-blood man beside me.

"Samuel was so possessive of you while he was alive that you're having difficulty pulling away from him even now," Dave said patiently. "He insisted on knowing your every thought, your every move. He had no right to do it then, and he has no right to do it now."

"How dare you talk about Samuel like that!" I burst out, angered by Dave's words. "Samuel was a wonderful man. He loved me very much. And I loved him!"

Dave took hold of my arm as I turned away. "I didn't mean to hurt you, Emily. But I can't stand to see you do this to yourself. Melissa is worried about you. I'm worried about you."

So Melissa had been talking to Dave about me, telling him about my marriage to Samuel! "Please go," I told Dave. Then I pulled away from him and walked out of the room.

"Emily," Dave called after me, "you've got to let him go!"

A month went by without my seeing Dave again. *Maybe it's for the best,* I told myself. It gave me time to be by myself and come to terms with Samuel's death. And I knew that I had to before I could think clearly about Dave and me. I wished that what had gone on hadn't taken place. I didn't want it to happen again until I was at peace with myself . . . and with Samuel.

At times I was angry with myself and Dave for the intimacy we had shared. I wondered if I would ever forget Samuel. I kept trying to practice what Pastor Carington had told me, and I found that praying eased my anxieties.

I also finally found the courage to check the help-wanted ads. I found a job available that I was interested in, but I had to cancel the interview at the last minute because I wasn't feeling well. Being sick was unusual for me, and I worried about it.

One morning Melissa stopped by, and we sat across from each other at the kitchen table sipping our coffee. I was staring into my cup and trying vainly to ignore the churning in my stomach.

"You look positively green," Melissa said, staring at me curiously.

"I'm fine," I assured her quickly. Then, sighing heavily, I admitted, "Well, that's not exactly true." I knew I could confide in Melissa. "It's probably nothing, but I'm almost three weeks late getting my period. I've never been late before in my life."

"I suppose it could still be the shock of Samuel's death," she reasoned. "That happens sometimes."

"I know," I agreed. "But why didn't it affect me before this?"

She shrugged. "I don't know. But one thing we do know is that you certainly can't be pregnant."

"Of course not," I began. But before the words were out, the realization began to dawn on me, and I was filled with a sense of frightened surprise.

Melissa's laughter rang out. "You should see the expression on your face, Emily! Don't take it so seriously. I was just kidding. How could you be pregnant when your husband has been dead for six months?" She paused and our eyes met. "Unless there's someone else? And I know there can't be," she rushed on.

I flushed. "I . . . well, I—"

Melissa held up her hand. "This is none of my business. You don't have to tell me anything if you don't want to."

"I have to share this with someone," I said. I told her about the weird dreams I'd been having, about my visit to Pastor Carington, and about finding Dave in the park and what happened afterward. As I spoke, I realized how strange it must sound to someone else. In fact, it even began to seem to me that I was relating something out of a movie or a novel . . . a story about someone else. When I finished, Melissa remained silent for a long moment.

"Those dreams must be very disturbing to you," she said finally. "But meeting Dave in the park in the middle of the night by sheer accident sounds very romantic." When I didn't comment, she asked, "You aren't on the Pill?"

I shook my head. "I've never been on it. Samuel and I always wanted children. I tried for seven years to get pregnant and nothing happened."

"But only one night with someone else? I mean, the chances of your getting pregnant, especially since you didn't before. . . ." Melissa trailed off and shook her head in disbelief.

"There's got to be another reason why I haven't gotten my period," I insisted.

"Maybe you'd better see a doctor," Melissa advised. "It could be any number of things. These crazy dreams you've been having could be upsetting you more than you realize." She paused and studied me. "Emily, what if you are pregnant?"

That question had been tumbling over and over in my mind for the last several minutes. "I can't be," I said. But despite my denial, the possibility was creeping into my mind.

A week later, when I was still feeling nauseous and my period still hadn't started, I had to face up to the fact that something was definitely wrong. Not wanting to go to Dr. Anderson, the doctor Samuel and I had always seen, I made an appointment with a doctor affiliated with another clinic.

I sat at home impatiently the next day, waiting for the doctor's office to call with the results of my tests. "What did you find out?" I asked apprehensively when the nurse finally called late that afternoon.

"You're going to have a baby, Mrs. Rodriguez," she told me happily, unaware that I'd been a widow for over six months.

"Are—are you sure?" I stammered.

"Quite sure," she told me. "Congratulations!"

The fact that I was pregnant hit me like a blow from a sledgehammer. I sat riveted to my chair after I'd hung up the phone. All I could think of was the irony of the situation. For years I'd wanted a child. I'd done everything possible to get pregnant, but nothing had happened. Now, six months after my husband's death, I was pregnant after one night with Dave. It was ridiculous, even funny, but I felt more like crying.

"I'm going to have a baby," I repeated over and over. It was incredible. When I hadn't become pregnant, Samuel's disappointment had been even greater than mine. What would he think if he knew I was pregnant now? The thought was so devastating I dropped my head into my hands. "How can this be?" I cried out. "Samuel, please understand how it happened. Please forgive me." But I knew he wouldn't understand or forgive anything concerning Dave and me. He never had while he was alive, and he wouldn't now.

Oh, why had I given in to my desire for Dave that night? I knew when I told him about the baby, he would insist that we get married right away. For an instant I considered not telling him, but I knew I must. Yet how could I marry him when there were still so many memories inside me? I didn't want to hurt him again. I couldn't hurt him again.

If only I could be certain that Samuel would be happy that I was going on with my life. But I knew how he would feel. Especially if he was aware that the man I was with was Dave.

The feeling that wherever Samuel was, he knew about the baby and was angry, followed me the rest of the day. I wondered if I could make amends by not telling Dave about the child. By cutting him out of my life again. But what about the baby? Did I have the right to deny the child its father?

That night, after tossing and turning for hours, I finally lapsed into a troubled sleep. And then the dreams came back . . . more terrifying than before. Samuel's angry face loomed before me. A pair of burning eyes stared at me. They were Samuel's eyes, brimming with accusation and hatred. A hollow voice hissed, "You cheater! I was right about you and Dave. But you won't get away with it. You didn't give me a child, and you won't have his, either. I'll see to that!"

I woke up screaming. Over and over, I reminded myself that it was only a dream, but it didn't help. Samuel had said he'd see to it that I never had Dave's baby. Now a new fear entered my mind and I began to shake uncontrollably. "Please, Samuel, let me go!" I pleaded into the darkness of the night.

"Oh, Emily!" Melissa exclaimed when I told her about my dream the next day. "Your morbid sense of guilt is getting the best of you!"

"I can't help it!" I cried. "I can't seem to escape from the feeling that Samuel is watching me, condemning me."

"I understand your guilty feelings about not having a child before," Melissa told me. "But did it ever occur to you that the reason you didn't get pregnant with Samuel could have been his fault and not yours? When a woman doesn't conceive by a man she's been with for years, and then becomes pregnant by another man after one night with him, it looks pretty darn suspicious for that first man."

"But both of us saw a doctor," I argued, annoyed that she was blaming Samuel for our inability to have children.

"Did you both see a doctor at the same time?" she questioned.

"Samuel couldn't get off work, so he went later," I said after a minute's thought. "But he told me the results of his tests. There was nothing wrong with him."

"Could he have lied to you?" Melissa asked softly.

My eyes flashed with anger. "How can you even suggest that Samuel lied to me! Why should he?"

"Because he was afraid he might lose you," she stated in a quiet voice. "You know how possessive he was. How jealous. Why, he even resented your friendship with me and wanted you to end it."

Reluctantly, I had to admit that what Melissa said

was true. Still, that didn't mean Samuel had lied to me.

Melissa took my hand in hers then. "I'm not trying to hurt you, Emily, but I can't stand to see you so depressed, blaming yourself for something that may not have been your fault at all."

I swallowed the lump that had formed in my throat. "I know you mean well," I told her as I clung tightly to her hand.

"Honey, you were a wonderful wife to Samuel. But he's gone and your life has to go on. You have to think about the baby you're carrying," she reminded me.

Tears misted my eyes. I went over to the window and stared out. Melissa was right. I had to go on. But how? If only I could rid myself of Samuel's condemning presence!

I wondered what had made Melissa suggest that Samuel had lied about his ability to have a child. I knew she was never fond of him . . . she, like all the others, had thought I was making a mistake when I married him. But I knew it wasn't like her to say something hurtful . . . not unless she really believed it was true.

Suddenly I could see Samuel's angry face before me . . . just like in my dream . . . full of hatred and threatening the baby I now carried. I turned back to Melissa, full of fear. "Samuel wants to hurt the baby! He's going to do something terrible." I burst into tears.

"Emily, you'd better get such ridiculous thoughts out of your head or you're going to have a breakdown," Melissa warned me sternly, placing her arm about my shoulder. "Paul's going to be out of town this weekend. Why don't you and I go up to our lake cabin?" she suggested. "Maybe getting you away from here will help. We can lie in the sun, go for boat rides, picnic in the woods."

"I don't know," I began hesitantly. Yet I could scarcely bear the thought of spending another sleepless night haunted by terrifying dreams.

"I won't take no for an answer," Melissa persisted.

At last I agreed, and the idea of spending the weekend at the lake with my friend helped somewhat. But as the week progressed, my nightmares about Samuel and the baby grew more frightening and more frequent. I dreamed constantly that as punishment for my betrayal of Samuel, my baby would be born with some horrible deformity. I was afraid to sleep for fear of dreaming.

Too tired to think straight while I was awake, I did my best to thrust all thoughts of Dave from my mind. I felt that if I didn't have anything to do with him, Samuel would forgive me. But I was afraid that Samuel was aware of what I was thinking as well as my every move. I felt completely exposed and totally possessed.

Sunday afternoon I was walking along the shore, feeling a little better after two days of Melissa's company, when I sensed someone's presence. I panicked.

"Emily!" a voice called.

I halted and glanced back fearfully. Then I saw who it was. "Dave!" I gasped, seized with both joy and dismay.

Hurriedly, he walked toward me. When he reached me, he caught me in his arms and held me tightly against him. I clung to him momentarily as he kissed me.

Finally I pulled myself from his arms and stepped back. "How did you know I was here?" I asked apprehensively.

"Melissa mentioned that you were spending the weekend up here with her," Dave said.

"She told you to come up here?" I asked, a trace of annoyance edging my voice.

"No. She didn't know I was coming. I didn't know it myself. I suddenly had the feeling that you needed me. Emily, I've been trying to get hold of you for the past week, but you wouldn't answer the doorbell or the phone. What's wrong?" His voice was insistent.

"Didn't Melissa tell you that, too?" I retorted, angry with her for telling Dave I'd be here with her.

Dave frowned and shook his head. He placed his hands firmly on my shoulders. "Are you going to tell me what's wrong?" he demanded.

"I—I'm pregnant!" I burst out, my voice trembling.

His eyes widened and his grip on me relaxed. "You're what?"

"I'm carrying your child," I told him, and he reached for me again. I pulled away. "No, please."

"But this is terrific!" he exclaimed.

I smiled sadly and turned away.

Dave reached out and turned me back to face him. "Or don't you want our child?" he questioned me.

"Of course I want it," I answered, my voice barely audible.

Dave took me by the hand then and led me to a fallen tree near the shoreline. We sat down on it side by side.

"Tell me what's going on," he insisted. "I'm not going to leave you alone until you do."

"Samuel is very angry with me because I'm going to have your child," I began. Then I told him about my dream.

There was compassion in his eyes, but anger in his voice when he spoke. "Emily, will you get off this guilt trip! Samuel is dead. Gone forever. But I'm here . . . right now. I love you, and I think you care about me, too. Don't feel guilty about it. I'm happy. Can't you be, too?"

I stared at him as if I was in a trance. "Samuel is angry because I didn't give him a child." I began to tremble again, and Dave placed his arm around me. I jerked away. "Don't touch me!" I cried out. Somehow I had to make him realize that I couldn't have anything to do with him or the baby would be harmed.

He stared at me in confusion. "Why not? I love you, Emily. I want to marry you."

I looked at him dully. "That can't be. At least, not yet."

"Why not?" he demanded. "You're carrying my child."

"It can't be because of Samuel," I tried to explain. "Why can't you understand that?"

"What?" Dave yelled in disbelief and anger. "Samuel can't do anything to us!"

"Not to us, to the baby," I said defensively.

Dave seized me by the shoulders and shook me. "Listen to me, Emily! A ghost can't harm anyone."

"Samuel can!" I shot back.

"You can't believe that. This obsession of yours is making you sick. It can't be good for the baby, either," he added.

"Please go," I said sadly, touching his face with my fingers.

Dave studied my face for a long moment. "All right, I'll leave. For now. But I'm not going to allow you to do this to yourself or to us."

I heard the determination in his tone and wished that I could be so certain of myself. Dave stood up and began to walk away. I hated what I was doing to him, but I couldn't help it. If only he knew how much I wanted him to stay, how much I needed his strength. But I knew if I relented in the slightest, he would insist on staying with me, and I couldn't take that chance.

As I watched Dave walk away, I longed to call him back. But I was afraid that Samuel would hear. Tears began to slide down my cheeks.

Much later, when I returned to the cabin, Melissa asked if I had seen Dave.

"I sent him away," I said quietly.

"Why?" Melissa immediately asked.

"Because. . . ." I mumbled.

"Because you're afraid of a ghost!" she said angrily. "Somehow you've gotten this crazy idea that you've been unfaithful to Samuel. He wanted to own you body and soul while he was alive, Emily, and you're still letting him do it."

I stared at her, surprised by her anger. *And she's right,* I admitted with a deep sigh of resignation. But it really didn't matter. I was totally overpowered by Samuel's possessiveness . . . whether he was dead or not seemed to make no difference.

She studied me with anger still in her eyes. "If you aren't careful, you're going to lose the baby. Or is that what you're trying to do? Sacrifice the baby to appease an imaginary ghost you think you've wronged?"

I was horrified by her accusations. "How can you say that?"

"I'm sorry." Melissa put her hand on my shoulder. "But, Emily, someone has to get through to you before it's too late. You've got to face up to the truth. It's the only thing that will free you."

Is what she's accusing me of doing true? Am I a victim of my own morbid guilt? Over and over her words echoed in my mind. I recalled what Melissa had said about the possibility of Samuel being sterile, of his having lied to me. The realization suddenly came to me that if Samuel had been sterile, he was the betrayer. Then I could stop blaming myself for failing him. How could he possibly be angry with me for not giving him a child if he had been incapable of fathering one? I had to find out the truth. I had to go back to the doctor Samuel and I had both gone to, Dr. Anderson.

As soon as I got home from the weekend trip, I called the doctor and made an appointment to see him Tuesday afternoon.

"You've lost a lot of weight since I last saw you, haven't you, Emily?" Dr. Anderson said when I was seated in his office.

I hadn't noticed the hollows in my cheeks or how loosely my clothes fit until I'd glanced in the mirror while I was dressing for this appointment.

He peered at me questioningly. "Haven't you been feeling well?"

"I need to ask you something about Samuel," I said haltingly.

"I see." He frowned. "You realize that a patient's medical records are confidential."

I nodded, but my sanity and the welfare of my unborn child were at stake. "I have to know if Samuel was sterile. I must know," I said. And then I explained why.

Dr. Anderson studied me for several moments. "Ordinarily, I wouldn't do this, but since it's your husband you're inquiring about and since he is, he has passed away. . . ."

He pushed a button and asked a nurse to bring in Samuel's file. As he checked the pages carefully, I began to feel uncomfortable, as if I was prying into something too personal. I sat on the edge of my chair, holding my breath.

"Well?" I demanded when Dr. Anderson glanced up.

"Samuel was sterile," he said.

I gripped the arm of my chair. "Are you sure?"

When he nodded, I slowly sank back into the chair. How could he have lied to me all those years? He had known I blamed myself for our childlessness.

"Did he know about his sterility?" I questioned Dr. Anderson.

"Yes," he said.

I covered my face with my hands and began to cry. For a moment, I hated Samuel for permitting me to feel so inadequate all those years when he'd known all along that he was to blame for our not having children. Then as I dried my eyes, I thought, *Poor Samuel. He must have suffered so much because of his insecurity!* He hadn't told me about his sterility because he believed it would have made him less of a man.

I returned home, at peace with myself for the first time since his death. That night and the nights to follow were free of nightmares.

A week later, when I opened the door and saw Dave, I tried to contain the excitement that was building up inside me "Come in," I said with a smile. "I've given you a hard time, haven't I?"

"Well . . . yes, you have," he agreed with a wary grin as he sat down on the sofa.

After I explained again about the fear that had tormented me and what I had done about it . . . what I'd found out about Samuel . . . he asked, "Does this mean that we can be together at last? Are you telling me you love me?"

"I guess maybe I always have," I answered. "I loved Samuel, too, but in a very different way. A way that never was too good for me."

With a note of caution still in his voice, Dave asked, "Does that mean you'll marry me?"

"Yes, Dave. Yes, I'll marry you!" I told him.

A boyish grin covered his face. As I went into his outstretched arms, there was a feeling of rightness about it, and I remembered Pastor Carington's words: *If it feels right in your heart, it will be right.*

And nothing had ever felt so right to me. Samuel's ghost was finally gone. In its place, my heart was filled with Dave's strong caring love.   THE END

SWEET-TALKING HEARTBREAKER

When my husband, Phillip, came home Friday night with his pay, I went to Mother's to give back the twenty dollars I had borrowed at the beginning of the week for groceries. I felt so guilty. I laid the bill on the kitchen table and pulled over the cup of coffee she offered me, tears blurring my vision as I spoke. "I wonder if anything will ever work out for Phillip and me, like it does for Tanya."

Mother's face was full of understanding as she sat down. "Jenna, you and Phillip are having a streak of bad luck. It will end one day. None of us know what's ahead in the future. We just have to keep our faith and be thankful for what we have."

I nodded and thought about our children, Christopher and Lisa. They were more important than all the money in the world, but I still yearned to have less of a struggle making ends meet. I wasn't skilled like Tanya. I didn't go to business school when I graduated from high school. I married Phillip right out of high school. That was what all my friends were doing, getting married, settling down.

I was just leaving when Tanya breezed into Mother's house on her way home from work. She looked so lovely, so confident in her leather jacket and expensive slacks. She was excited because she and her husband were taking a three-day vacation. She also told us about her plans for a longer vacation in the fall.

My eyes passed Mother's. "It must be nice," I managed to mumble, and then I left. Resentment burned through me as I noticed my car was almost out of gas again. Tanya could fly all over the country and I still couldn't go out to a movie!

When I got home Phillip was holding Lisa in the living room. The dishes were piled in the sink and the table was wiped off. "How's your mom?" he asked.

I tossed my jacket on a chair and stared at him. "She's fine. I told her to hang onto the twenty because I suppose by the middle of next week I'll have to borrow it again." I watched the expression on his face change from relaxed to tense. "Tanya stopped in, too. They're flying to the Jamaica for three days and in the fall they're going to New York City. It hasn't been three months since they went to Niagra Falls. And we can't go to the movies!"

He looked away. "I know. But this won't be forever, I promise."

"Phillip, if you hadn't quit working at the insurance company we wouldn't be this bad off. And you wouldn't be working seventy hours a week at the garage."

He didn't respond to my remark, maybe because he knew it was true. I washed and dried the dishes.

Phillip gave Lisa and Christopher their baths, and we both tucked them in bed. We read them a bedtime story.

Then we went into the living room, and I sat down on the couch. Phillip sat beside me, putting his arm around me. I stiffened up and said, "Please, Phillip. I don't feel like being close."

He withdrew his arm and asked, "Why, Jenna?"

I closed my eyes over the stinging tears and answered, "I don't know why. Maybe because I'm so tired of this hopeless situation we're in. This cramped apartment, being broke, sometimes hungry. I think about Tanya and my friends. None of them live like we do!"

Phillip got up and walked over to the window. He stared out at the darkness. "I know. Don't you think I know that? But, Jenna, you wanted to get married right after graduation. I asked you if we shouldn't wait, if you wouldn't regret it if you didn't go on to school. Remember?"

The telephone rang and I answered it. It was Frank Fischer, a man who worked at the garage with Phillip. He wanted to speak with Phillip. I never liked Frank. He was always in trouble, paying fines, sitting in jail for one thing or another.

They talked for a while, then he cuffed the phone receiver and looked at me. "Do you mind if I go out with Frank for a while?"

I shrugged. "Why would I care what you do?"

That night, when Phillip returned home, he came into bed and moved close to me. He smelled of liquor and there was a slur in his voice as he said, "Come on, Jenna unwind. Give me a little loving."

I pushed him away. "I don't want you to touch

me! I don't want you near me."

There was silence before he sighed heavily and whispered, "Jenna, why did you marry me?"

"I don't know why, Phillip. I really don't. Believe me, if I had it to do over, I wouldn't have."

He moved away. "That's what I thought."

Two days later he came home with an extra three hundred dollars, which he tossed on the kitchen table. His eyes met mine, and he stared as he said, "You can take it. It's for you. I earned it."

"How could you earn that much in two days?"

He walked past me into the bathroom, speaking as he moved. "I did some deliveries after work for Frank."

I followed behind him. "What kind of deliveries?"

"Listen, Frank has a lot of connections. He's making good money now. Soon he's going to quit working at the gas station and just run his own little enterprise. It's kind of like a catalog business. His uncle has a horse ranch, and Frank sells items for rodeos, that kind of stuff. As soon as he can, he's going to hire me."

Something inside me said: *Don't believe him! Phillip is making deliveries all right, but it isn't anything for rodeos or horses.*

"Phillip, you wouldn't do anything dishonest, would you?" I asked, yelling above the sound of running water.

He hesitated and then answered me. "I wouldn't do anything to hurt anyone. I just want to see you happy. I want you to have things like Tanya, like your friends."

Tears spilled out onto my cheeks. "Phillip, don't do anything that you think is wrong. Not for me, not for anyone."

I put the money in a jar in the cupboard. Weeks went by, and he kept bringing additional money home. I used half of it for household expenses and the other half I put in the jar. It was like a bank account. It was my security.

Tanya and Jack, her husband, had been to Jamaica, and she stopped at Mother's. She said they'd had a wonderful time, but now she was anxious to get back to her job. She was going to have her own office in the new bank building. She was proud and enthused.

She looked at me and said, "Jenna, when the children go to school, you should take a course at the technical college. It will give you something to do during the day and you'll learn a skill so you can work and get some better things."

My throat was thick when I said I might do that. I tried to hide the bitterness I felt as I put on my old jacket. I observed the way Tanya was dressed . . . so smart and sharp. As I was going out the door Tanya said to stop in and see her when I was uptown. She'd take me to lunch. I said that would be nice. But it wouldn't be, because I wouldn't be comfortable going to her swanky office.

On the way home, I drove to the gas station where Phillip worked because I needed some gas. Kipp Jenkins sauntered out and asked, "Are you looking for Phillip?"

I told him I needed gas, and asked him where he was.

Kipp shrugged. "Who knows? Maybe out looking for another motorcycle. He wants to trade in the one he has."

His words struck through me like a knife cutting into my heart. I stared at Kipp, numbed by his words. "Another motorcycle?"

"Yeah, another cycle. You didn't know about the one he keeps here, I bet. The one in the back of the garage."

Kipp was telling me something he thought I should know. I told him to put ten-dollars' worth of gas in the car and I got out and walked inside the shop. Sure enough, parked against the wall was a large motorcycle. My heart pounded, as if I were meeting a rival.

Kipp came over and stood beside me. "Listen, I didn't tell you to cause trouble, but I figured this was something between Phillip and Frank Fischer. Like the boat he has docked on the lake. I'm a family man myself, and with what I make here, I couldn't buy a fishing license, much less fun equipment. Frank's bad news, but Phillip goes along with everything he says."

I paid Kipp for the gas and drove home. My neighbor, Betty, who lived upstairs, was watching Christopher and Lisa. We exchanged baby-sitting favors; sometimes I kept her baby. I thanked her and picked up Christopher and took Lisa's hand.

Phillip came in late, after eight o'clock. He looked tired as he tossed his jacket on the kitchen chair. "I'm really tired. It's been a long day."

I faced him squarely and said, "Yeah, it's been a long, long day for me. I went to the gas station, Phillip, and I noticed your cycle. It must be nice to have."

His face darkened with anger and his mouth twisted angrily as he shouted, "Well, don't ever think I have to report everything I do to you because I don't and I never will! There's a lot that you don't know and you'll never know! You can walk out of here anytime you want. It sure won't bother me."

His words hurt me. Although I thought I didn't love him, I must have cared enough to want him to need me. Tears filled my eyes as I walked away. "Oh, I can't leave, Phillip, you know that. Even if I really wanted to, I can't leave."

I listened as he walked to the window. He sighed with resignation and said, "I wouldn't want you to leave. It's just that everything seems wrong; nothing is right. Is it wrong for me to want a few things like other people have? Is it more wrong for me than for you?"

"No," I answered in a quiet voice, "it's not wrong, Phillip. What is wrong is that you have them and I can't understand how you can afford them. And why would you do it without even telling me? After all, I'm your wife and I thought husbands and wives didn't keep secrets."

"Let's not fight, okay?" he said. "You've got a little more cash these days and things should be looking up."

I said okay, because maybe I didn't want to face the full truth. Maybe I already realized that whatever Phillip was doing to earn extra money was not legal.

When I came home from town a few days later, police cars were parked in my driveway. My heart pounded wildly as I entered the porch and Betty came out to meet me.

"The cops are in the shed. They never came into the house, but doesn't Phillip use the shed? Isn't he the only one that ever uses the shed?"

I nodded because it was true.

My mouth was dry when I asked in a trembling voice, "What have the police done, anyway?"

Betty looked concerned. "I don't know, they've taken a few things out to the car. I don't know what's going on. Maybe you should ask."

I asked her to keep the children and I walked outside and around to the path that led to the shed. They were speaking in low voices. I stood inside the open door. I introduced myself and asked, "What are you looking for?"

One of the policemen turned around and faced me. "We have a search warrant." I nodded and said it wasn't necessary for me to read it. He continued to glare at me. "Your husband is in a lot of trouble. A whole lot of trouble."

I asked where Phillip was and he said he was at the police station with Frank Fischer.

When I went into the house, Betty followed. I sat down and sobbed. "I don't know what to do, where to turn. I don't even know what Phillip has been accused of doing."

Betty suggested that I wait until her husband came home. He could go with me to the station, and she would watch the children. I thanked her. Betty went upstairs to fix some coffee and said I should come, too. But as soon as she left, Phillip came in. He was pale, and I could see that he had been crying. He avoided looking at me and went straight for the cupboard where I had the money.

"I know the cops were here. I'm in a lot of trouble, but Frank has this lawyer and he got us out of jail. I've got to give him what I've got—the cycle, the boat, and this cash. I'd die in jail, Jenna."

I sat down on the kitchen chair. "Phillip, what did you do anyway? And why?"

He appeared astonished. "Why? So you could have something. I knew I'd never make it working at that stupid job. I never dreamed Frank was dealing in stolen merchandise. Now I lost my job, and you, haven't I?"

I didn't say anything. I put Christopher in my lap and watched Phillip as he raced around the house. Soon he left, striding out the back door without a word, letting it slam shut.

He never came home that night. The next afternoon he walked in and announced, "I've talked to the lawyer and he plea bargained for me. Since it's my first offense he got me off. I'm not sticking around here, I'm leaving. Look at it this way . . . you're going to be a lot better off without me. There are a couple of factories that are hiring east of here. I'll try to find a job, and as soon as I get some money together, I'll send some. I talked to the lawyer about a divorce. It's all set up. All you have to do is go down and see him. His name is Thomas Caine. He's in the bank building where your sister works. You know, Queen Tanya." His voice was wavering. Tears flowed from his eyes as he turned his face from me.

"I'm sorry, Jenna. Sorry I was so dumb. I always loved you, but for a long time now I knew you didn't love me. There comes a time when a person has to face life squarely and my time has come. Somewhere down the line I'm sure there's some nice, secure guy for you. Someone that will be a husband and a father to our kids. Someone that will be what you deserve. . . ."

He walked to our bedroom, packed his clothes, and left. He said he had a ride to the city, and then he was gone.

I cried myself to sleep that night.

The next day the local paper's front page listed all the charges made against Frank Fischer. Frank was in the county jail, and it was noted that Phillip had been arrested but, because it was his first offense, he would be let off if he testified against Frank.

It was just getting dark when the landlord came. He was a stern man and wanted to know if we would be able to keep up the rent payments because he had read about what had happened to Phillip.

I said I would have the rent and that Phillip wasn't aware of what Frank was doing. He didn't know anything about the stolen merchandise.

"Oh, that's what they all say. Every time they get caught, they're innocent as a newborn babe. Phillip had to know that the tires he stashed in my shed were hot. They were from the garage where he worked!"

Shame washed over me like I had done something wrong. I was going to tell him that Phillip had left us but I'd have broken down if I talked. So I just said good-bye and closed the door.

I bathed the children and fixed them a bedtime snack. Mother called. She'd just bought the paper at the grocery store and read about Phillip. She said she could hardly believe it!

I knew how proud my folks were and what this would do to them. I started to cry, and Mother said she was sorry. She was going to pray for Phillip. Then I knew I'd have to face Tanya, too. It was like dominoes falling, my heartache touched them all.

The rent was due in five days and I only had fifty dollars. Betty told me to apply to Social Services for emergency funding. She was pretty sure they would give me something to tide me over, at least until I could get on a regular welfare fund. Betty volunteered to watch the children.

I went to the Social Services offices and filled out forms and answered questions. The processor pursed her lips together and said she supposed I would qualify for assistance.

When I left the office I felt like a thief. Guilty and humiliated.

I stopped at the store for milk and bread. When I came home I noticed Tanya's car in the driveway. How I dreaded facing her!

Betty had gone upstairs and Tanya was sitting at the dining room table with a cup of coffee. The apartment smelled of her expensive perfume. She looked at me and asked about Phillip's whereabouts. I said I didn't know.

"And what are you supposed to do in the meantime?" she asked pointedly.

Hot tears burned my lids. "Tanya, I don't know. But I don't need you on my back on top of everything."

I put the milk in the refrigerator and felt my whole body trembling. I wished I could die! It would have been easier.

"What are you going to live on?"

I couldn't see her face through my tears. "I went to Social Services and I'm going on public assistance. I don't plan to be on assistance the rest of my life, but until I can earn some money, I'll have to do it. I know it shames you, but I have to think about the children. We have to have a roof over our heads and something to eat."

Tanya walked away and stood at the front window. For a long time we didn't speak. I was crying and Tanya stood silently. When she turned around, she shrugged and said, "You can come and stay with us, at least until you can get into another apartment. I heard at the bank that the Oceancrest Apartments will be available next month. They're subsidized housing and a lot nicer than this place. It's for people like you, single parents."

I swallowed hard and wiped my face dry, pulling Christopher up on my lap, soothing him with my hand. I said, "Tanya, I don't want to do that." I couldn't imagine my family living in her posh home.

She looked tense as she was summing it up in her mind. "I know, it won't be easy for any of us, but you really don't have much of a choice. I want to help you, even if I am uncomfortable doing it. You are my sister, after all."

Social Services had given me some emergency money and I offered it all to Tanya, but she said she'd take just enough to cover the water and electricity that she figured we would use. The rest she said I should use to pay bills and buy groceries.

Dad and Jack moved everything out of the apartment. Tanya insisted we put most of our belongings in storage except our clothes. Some of the children's toys were brought to our parents' house. Tanya didn't want her home cluttered up any more than necessary.

Their house was large and elegant. Jack and Tanya had the bedroom downstairs, and the children and I had the entire upstairs. There were three bedrooms upstairs and two bathrooms so we weren't crowded. There was a television set in the one bedroom, so we didn't have to be in their way during the evening. During the day we had the downstairs to ourselves.

I put all of Tanya's exquisite figurines and plants up so the children couldn't knock them down. I cleaned the house and Tanya told her cleaning lady she wouldn't have to come until we moved out. I did her washing and ironing, and if there was something special she wanted baked or cooked I'd prepare that, too.

They didn't dine at home often, but on Jack's birthday they did. Flowers came to the house and a birthday cake from the bakery. That day Tanya left instructions for setting the table with her best linen and silver, candles, and goblets. She also left me the entire menu to prepare.

I did everything to perfection, but I felt sad. I kept wondering about Phillip—he could be dead as far as I knew! I thought about the birthday parties we had shared, nothing as elegant as this, but there was always a thrill sharing a birthday cake and opening some small gift. Every day brought some remembrance of Phillip. Sometimes it was the children, the way they looked, an expression on their faces or the way they seemed to be missing their daddy.

I had the children upstairs long before Jack or Tanya arrived home. This was their special evening, and everything was ready. As I walked up the steps to our rooms, I felt envious and resentful. *Why should Tanya have everything? Because she's smarter!* I thought.

A little after nine o'clock Jack called up the stairs. "Jenna, come on down and have some birthday cake."

I was surprised at the invitation because Tanya always emphasized that even though we were living in her house we were not to infringe on their personal life.

I went to the door and looked down. "Tanya left. It's my birthday and I don't care to spend it alone," Jack told me.

I checked on the children and went down. The candles had burned low, the music filled the dimly lit rooms, and Jack handed me a glass of wine. His eyes met mine and then he said, "Tanya had an important business engagement. Her work comes before anything or anyone, including me."

I sipped the wine and sat down. When Jack came and sat beside me on the sofa, I mentioned that the table needed clearing. His hand touched my arm and sent shivers of excitement through me. I walked away, not wanting to feel the way I felt. I had a longing to be held in someone's arms again. It seemed a lifetime ago since Phillip held me.

I cleared the table and put the dishes in the dishwasher. All the while Jack watched me quietly, his eyes filled with yearning.

I was uncomfortable. "Couldn't Tanya have rearranged the meeting to another time?"

Jack moved closer, pulling me to face him. "Listen, she's so wrapped up in that job, that even if it were life or death she wouldn't take one minute from it. Tanya doesn't need me at all! We're in the same boat, only she has money and Phillip was broke. Maybe you and I can work things out to satisfy our own needs." His hands fumbled nervously with the buttons on my blouse as he led me to their bedroom.

I told him no, but I said it in a weak voice. For a moment I forgot that this was my sister's husband and my sister's house. I forgot everything, except the feeling of a need for love, which was greater than right or wrong, greater than anything else. "Take me, Jack," I whispered.

Jack was gentle and loving; his lips held mine, warm and tender. A warmness stirred inside me, one that I had not felt in a long time. Our bodies came together passionately, filling the void of being deserted by our spouses. As our hands raced over each other's bodies, we let go of our familiarity and reacquainted ourselves as lovers. His heart pounded against my heart, and for a time there was the wonderful feeling of being needed and desired.

He was holding me in his arms, telling me how Tanya had always cast him aside, how she valued her position and status above everything else in the world. He said it hurt to be at the end of her priorities. He was dressed and we were sitting in the darkness of the living room when he told me that Tanya had aborted two of their children. He wiped tears from his face and admitted that that was the beginning of the end for them.

Jack glanced at me, murmuring, "It's crazy, how I feel about Tanya. I still love her! But it doesn't make any sense to me. I lover her, but I hate her, too. She's hurt me more than anyone will ever know, yet I desire her. I don't think our marriage will last any more than yours and Phillip's. It's just a matter of time, I guess."

Jack built a fire and we sipped wine and listened to music in the glow of the flame. It was so cozy; the scene was right, but the players were wrong. I felt a twinge of guilt and regret, but it was so wonderful to be near him, to feel his body near mine and his lips kissing me.

It was almost two in the morning before I went upstairs to bed. As I lay awake I thought about Jack downstairs waiting for Tanya to come home. When she did come in, I heard them speaking in soft tones, and then everything was silent.

The next day, Tanya came in my bedroom before she left for the office. She looked at me with searching eyes. "Jack says you were down for a piece of birthday cake last night. Did you have a party of your own? I noticed the wine was almost gone."

My face felt hot, but I shrugged her question off casually. "I had one drink. Jack must have been nipping by himself. Too bad you can't spend more time with him. I think he's lonely."

For a moment she frowned, and then suddenly she replaced that expression with a confident smile, tossing her head so that her hair shimmered on her shoulders. "Oh, Jack isn't lonely! He likes being free as much as I do."

She turned abruptly and left, leaving a trail of perfume behind her.

That day Mother offered to watch the children so I could go out and register for a secretarial course at the local community college. The refresher course was only six months, and Tanya thought I could easily get a job at the bank.

I was having coffee with Mother and my grandmother, Nanna, filling them in on everything I found out at school. I was excited. It was like a new beginning for me. If only I could stop thinking about Phillip and Jack and what had happened the night before.

Mother's voice went on and on, cutting into my thoughts. She was saying how lucky I was to have a sister like Tanya. She was someone that knew what to do about everything. Wasn't it charitable for her to take me in and give us a home under her roof? And Tanya was the person who got my name on the apartment complex list, who encouraged me to go to school.

Nanna kept watching me with her searching eyes. She stirred her tea and mumbled, "Have you ever tried to find Phillip?"

Tears came suddenly, and a pain shot through my heart. I couldn't look at her directly. "No, Nanna, I haven't the slightest idea where he is. I haven't heard a word from him. I guess if he had wanted us to know, he'd have been in touch. Under the circumstances, I guess we're all better off this way. Phillip could never get a job in town after what he and Frank did, and we'd had no way of moving away. I think he's glad to be away from any responsibilities. We were too young to get married. It was a mistake and it's over now. I don't want to think about it or about Phillip, either. Okay, Nanna?"

Mother fixed her eyes on a piece of coffeecake, but she was speaking to me. "Jenna, are you and Phillip divorced? Dad and I were wondering."

I resented her question and I snapped back, "Mother, Phillip left word with his attorney to set up a divorce. I never contacted him and he never contacted me. I guess we must be married, but it doesn't mean anything. It's just a piece of paper. Any time I want a divorce all I have to do is call the attorney."

Mother couldn't drop it, she had to comment again. "Well, maybe when Phillip gets on his feet he'll come back for you and the children. I always liked him and Dad did, too. Sometimes I think he did what he did because he wanted you to have everything, and there was no way he could get it for you. He really loved you, Jenna."

No one was home when I drove in. The house was quiet, and Tanya hadn't left any messages on the counter. I turned on the television to a show the children liked to watch.

It was almost seven when Jack came home. He was going through the mail as he entered the kitchen. His eyes met mine and the excitement mounted inside of me, just remembering the night before.

"Hi, Jenna," he said. "I guess we're going to be alone again tonight. Tanya called me. She was flying to Chicago this afternoon. Next week she's going to be in Nevada. Good thing I won't have to be home alone every night."

He picked up Lisa and started playing with her. In the meantime, I was trying to deal with my emotions, trying to smooth out all that had been said and done the night before. I was filled with uneasiness.

Lisa and Christopher were in the tub when Jack came up behind me and put his arms around me. Holding me close he said, "Jenna, it's a good thing we have each other."

Thoughts of Tanya and Phillip washed through

me, and tears flooded my eyes as I turned around and looked into Jack's eyes. "I know I have to move before we get into something we can't back out of. Before I really care for you."

His face went sober as his hands dropped their hold on me. He looked away. "Why is it wrong for us to have feelings for each other? Or even a relationship? Phillip and Tanya abandoned us; we didn't leave them."

I was crying and Jack put his arms around me. We didn't speak. He just held me tenderly with gentleness.

That night when the children were in bed sleeping, I walked down the stairs at his beckoning call. I went into his arms and his bed, and I belonged to someone again. He kissed me gently, and we found ourselves embraced in lovemaking more tender than the night before. We took our time enjoying every moment and every part of each other. Before we knew it, the sun was beginning to rise.

The next day, as soon as Jack left the house, I bundled up the children and went downtown. I went to the building complex Tanya had told me about and knocked on the manager's door.

Robert Cooper, the apartment manager, opened the door reluctantly. I explained who I was and asked him if he could give me an idea when the apartments would be ready for occupancy.

He shrugged. "I don't know. My wife and I are lucky we even got in when we did. I told your sister that you'd be one of the first to move in. She's pretty anxious for you to have a place of your own."

I left without a firm date, but with a promise he would call as soon as he knew something for sure. I knew I had to get out of my sister's house!

I ran into my ex-neighbor, Betty, at the grocery store. She seemed so glad to see us. Betty picked up both of the children and said we had to come over for lunch one day soon. Her eyes held mine as she asked, "Have you heard from Phillip?"

I shrugged and felt a pang of pain shooting through my heart. Tears came as I remembered in a flash how he'd looked the last time I saw him, that night he said good-bye. I looked away. "I haven't heard anything. I have no idea where he is, but I'm sure he wants it that way or he'd have contacted us. Phillip said we shouldn't have gotten married so soon after I graduated. I guess he was right, the way things turned out."

Betty commented, "Well, Phillip was a pretty nice guy. Maybe in the beginning he didn't know that Frank was doing anything illegal. One thing is for sure, Phillip really loved you and the children. I bet he still does. He just doesn't want to hurt you any more."

My throat was tense and hurting. I was really trying to forget Phillip and get on with my life. I told Betty about going to school next semester and hopefully getting a job at the bank.

I don't know how I would have gotten along in the next weeks except for the hope of the future, the apartment, and going to school.

Tanya was never home, except to change clothes and flit through the house. I made sure we went upstairs when her car came into the driveway so that the children and I were not in the way.

One night, after she and Jack finished eating, she came up to my room and knocked softly. She came in and sat on the chair by the window. I felt my face getting warm as her eyes met mine.

"When do you plan on moving?" she asked in a firm voice.

I felt so guilty. It was as if she knew about Jack and me. I explained that I had been to see Mr. Cooper and that he had promised as soon as an apartment was available he would notify me.

She glanced away. "Jack seems different toward me, distant. I love him and I wouldn't want you or the children to come between us."

I almost cried when she said that, but I managed to say, "Tanya, I wouldn't come between you and Jack, you should know that." I lied and it was almost easy. She didn't know how lucky she was to have a man like Jack, to have everything that she had! When she stood up to leave, she moved slowly. I said, "Tanya, maybe you should spend more time with him. Maybe he feels your job is more important to you than he is."

She walked to the door and opened it, hesitating without further comment and smiling that smug expression she used to get when we were younger . . . putting me in my place as she looked down on me. Maybe that's why, that night, when she went out, when I was in Jack's arms and in her bed, I felt a special measure of satisfaction, knowing there were some things that Tanya had that I could have for the taking.

The day that Mr. Cooper called and informed me that the apartment was ready, I cried. I don't know if it was from relief or regret. It meant we would be leaving Jack. The dream was going to be over and the nights would be long, lonely, and empty.

That was the day that Jack came home with flowers. He entered the kitchen with a grin on his face and his eyes were searching mine. "These are really for you, but, of course, you'll have to put them in one of Tanya's vases and leave them on her table. But you will know that they really are from me to you . . . with love."

The children were playing in the living room. I started to cry, my heart pounded hard, and I looked away from Jack. "Mr. Cooper called. The apartment is ready and we can move in this weekend."

Jack turned around, but not before I noticed the sadness on his face. "We'll have tonight and tomorrow night. Tanya is going to be gone for two days. She called my office. I didn't want her to go, but nothing I say means a thing to her. It's always some big deal, something more important than being with me. No wonder I'm falling in love with you!"

Jack held me close in the broad daylight of my sister's kitchen.

That night, after the children were asleep, we had a candlelight dinner. Jack held my hand in his, the moment was magic, tinged with an aching restlessness. He kept saying he'd come around to the apartment to see us; it wasn't going to be over. I was just going to have a whole new future.

The next afternoon Mother called. She had talked with Mrs. Cooper at the grocery store and she mentioned that I could be moving things to the apartment. I felt my face getting hot. I resented her quizzing me . . . or was it just conversation and I was feeling guilty?

"Mother, Mr. Cooper said we could move on the weekend. I'm not going to move my things while the workmen are still there."

"You could come for supper tonight. Nanna said she would like to see the children."

"Mom, some other time. Jack is bringing home pizza and ice cream. He wants our last night here to be special."

"I'd think he'd be glad to have his house to himself. It sounds like a regular family party. Tanya is out of town, isn't she? She's always working. I know you've resented everything she has, but now you can see it hasn't come easy, she's earned everything in that house."

What's she trying to say? I wondered. Tears burned my eyes as I commented, "Mom maybe I have been a little jealous of Tanya, but I don't resent her, and, yes, I can see she has devoted her entire life to earning money and buying things. That's fine, that's her choice, and maybe her mistake."

After I hung up, I went upstairs to pack. I kept reminding myself that this should be an exciting time. We were moving into a new apartment, and for the first time everything would be new and nice.

Jack came upstairs. His eyes met mine and he opened his arms. "Stop packing for now. Come down and be mine one more time."

His words sent an agonizing thrill and desire through me. I followed him down. We were in bed, he was making love to me, kissing me, holding my face in his hands, saying he loved me over and over again.

I was lost in the moment of ecstasy when suddenly the lights went on and the world stood still. Tanya had come home!

She was screaming and began hitting Jack. He

was trying to dress as I held the sheet around my body, numb and scared.

She glared at me, dropping her hands at her side, and said, "I don't know which I want to do more . . . kill you both or just myself."

"Tanya, you were never here—we were both lonely," I cried out in a voice that sounded strange.

Her eyes were filled with hatred as she yelled back, "Is that a good reason to crawl into bed with my husband? I took you in and this is the thanks I get!"

Jack was dressed, and as he came around to reach out for Tanya, his face was wet with tears of regret.

She turned abruptly and muttered she would never come back to this house again. Then she ran out of the front door into the darkness.

Jack glanced at me, muttering that he would bring her back. But I had better get out of sight, maybe go to my folks.

I was lugging my things out to my car when Jack came driving down the street, returning to the house. My heart felt heavy and a premonition came to me . . . Tanya wasn't coming home again!

I returned to the kitchen and waited. When Jack came in, his face was wet with tears and his lips moved automatically as he spoke the news. "Tanya is dead! She drove straight into the bridge abutment. Jenna, there was no way I could have stopped her. She died instantly."

I looked away as the words became reality and grief consumed me. "Jack, I killed her! We had no right to do what we were doing. My children were sleeping upstairs and Tanya was away. What was I thinking?"

Jack walked into the other room. He was dealing with his own pain, and somehow that didn't include me.

I'm not sure how we got through the funeral. I made it up to the front of the chapel to gaze down at Tanya in her coffin. I wanted to touch her hand, but I couldn't bring myself to do it. As I sat down beside Nanna, truth flooded through me, guilt and shame, this was the price I had to pay for what I had done!

I didn't want to move into the apartment, but I couldn't stay with my folks. There was no place I wanted to be, no place for us on earth! Dad and Jack moved everything to my new apartment, and Mother came over to help me put things in their proper places.

I sat down at the table and Mother started a bath for the children. I gazed numbly around the room. It didn't feel like home with everything so new and nice. It was more than I deserved. Hot tears flowed down my face and anxiety blotted out reason. Nothing would ever be right again. I wished that I would have been the one to die.

Mother had the children tucked in bed. She fixed coffee and poured us each a cup then sat down across from me. "Jenna, you are going to school, aren't you? You do remember that Mrs. Simpson down the hall will come and sit with the children."

I stared at her, but her words sounded far away, like they were coming from a distance.

The words stuck in my throat. "Mom, I can't go to school. I can't do anything. I'm not Tanya, remember?"

She jumped up nervously and went to the sink,

running water for an unknown reason and muttered that she knew that.

I kept watching her as she wiped the counter over and over, so she wouldn't have to face me.

"Mom, I wish I had died instead of Tanya. It would have made more sense, been easier on everyone."

Mother turned around and glared at me, her face set and her eyes holding tears. "Isn't it enough that we've lost her? Don't you think we've had enough pain? You have two children who need you and need your love. You have a nice apartment, a chance to go to school to better yourself, and Mrs. Simpson down the hall is willing to care for the children. And you wish you could have died! It wasn't your time! God wants you to live, but not this way, not wallowing in your self-pity. You better wake up, Jenna. Dad and I have our hands full with Nanna and all her problems. You've got to stand on your own two feet."

I wanted to tell her about Jack and me. I don't understand why, but maybe I could have felt free of the sin. In a small voice I said I'd try, that I was sorry I had disappointed her again.

Two days later I was standing in line for registration. I was recalling her words, but thoughts of Phillip, Jack, and Tanya kept haunting me with memories of the last time I saw each of them . . . the way they looked, what they had said to me. It was all there like an old movie, only it was real and it was painful.

I never saw Jack, but Betty called and said she heard he was working out of town. Someone said he was so distressed about Tanya's death and the way she'd died . . . deliberately driving into the abutment. Her words shot through me like a hunter's arrow and I gasped and inquired, "Who says that, anyway?"

Her voice became regretfully low. "Everyone, Jenna. But I didn't mean to say it. And maybe it isn't true."

The next morning I woke up feeling very ill. Immediately I remembered the last time I'd felt that way . . . it was when I was pregnant. I turned my face into my pillow and knew that fate had trapped me playing my own game with life.

That day after school I drove past Jack's house. His car was in the driveway and I pulled up to the curb and got out. My heart pounded hard as I approached the house. My legs felt wooden and I felt like I was in some kind of a dream. I couldn't be returning to Tanya's house on a mission like this!

I rang the doorbell many times, hearing the sound of its echo again and again. Finally, there was the sound of footsteps, and he opened the door abruptly.

His hand dropped at his side and he muttered, "Jenna. . . ." He opened the door wide and invited me in as he apologized for the mess. He had let the housekeeper go because he wasn't home much.

He said he would fix some coffee. I sat down at the table in the dining room as tears flooded my eyes and memories crowded my thoughts. Everywhere there was something of Tanya, even now, in the midst of the mess. And there was memories of Jack and me . . . sitting by that table, dinner by candlelight, with cut flowers and wine, music softly wafting through our lovemaking.

He came in with two cups and saucers. Our eyes met and locked. The old thrill was gone. There was no spark of magic or love. Just pain. Thoughts of Phillip crowded in filling me with lonesomeness for him.

"I hear you're in school and I'm glad. It means a lot to your folks. You know how they worry. Your mother says you're every bit as intelligent as Tanya, you just never had her drive."

I looked down, tears spilled onto my skirt. "I was never like Tanya, Jack. Not in any way."

He didn't react to my statement, but went for the coffee. He poured us a cup and dropped a bag of cookies on the table. He sat down and blinked back the tears. "I was going to stop in and see you and the children. I didn't know if you'd want me to or not, so I decided to let you make the first move. Whatever was best for you."

Suddenly I wondered what I was waiting for. I blurted it out. "Jack, I'm sure I'm pregnant. I don't know what to do."

His face turned pale, and I heard the sound of a helpless gasp coming from deep inside of him. He slumped back against the chair, as if he'd been shot.

"Do your folks know?"

I told him no one knew. I hadn't told anyone because I wanted to talk to him first.

He got up and walked to the window. "What do you want to do? Do you want me to marry you?"

I looked away. "I'm still married to Phillip. I can't have an abortion, I know that, Jack. I just don't know what to do. It will kill my folks."

I just wept and Jack stood still, with his back to me, engrossed in thoughts of his own. I didn't feel he was distancing himself from me, he was just thinking. Finally, he turned around and sat down again. Looking at me, he spoke with quiet resignation as he said, "There's only one thing to do. One right thing to do. You divorce Phillip and we'll get married and move away, so we can start over. I like you a lot, Jenna, I like the kids. It will be all right. I always wanted a child with Tanya, but I guess that wasn't meant to be. I'll love this baby. I'll be good to all of you."

Jack was such a wonderful person that a part of me loved him. It wasn't the same sort of love Phillip and I shared, nor was it the love I thought I felt when we were having an affair. Jack was just a good, unselfish, caring man.

I was at Mother's the next Saturday afternoon. Dad had the children outside with him, and Nanna was taking a nap. Mother was kneading bread and talking. Trying to be casual, she told me that someone said that Phillip was in town. "You haven't heard from him, have you?"

My heart started beating like a drum, pounding hard. Perspiration wet my palms and tears filled my eyes. "No, I haven't. But I can't imagine that he's in town."

She shrugged and turned around swiftly, her eyes meeting mine. "I thought I'd mention it because if it is true, what are you going to tell him? If he comes around and finds out about you and Jack. . . ."

I couldn't believe Mother knew about us.

She waited for me to speak. Finally, I looked at her and said it. "I'm pregnant with Jack's child, and we're going to be married. We're going to move to the city and make a home for the baby and the children. I can't ever bring Tanya back or do anything to change what has happened because it's all over and done. I just pray that God will forgive me, forgive us, that some day you will find it in your heart to forgive us, too."

Mother pulled a chair out and sat down dropping on it, sighing, like she was consumed with weariness. She leaned back and asked, "When were you going to tell us? Were you ever going to tell us before you picked up and left town?"

"I was hoping for the right time. It never came. I guess Jack and I would have come over some night and told you. I don't know. It isn't a happy announcement, not like sharing good news."

"Do you love Jack?" she asked pointedly, staring at my face.

I shrugged, tears kept streaming down my face from an endless source of pain. "I respect him, I like him. He's a good person, Mother. He really loved Tanya but you know, she was away so much. He was lonely, like I was lonely. It's no excuse I know, but that's why we were together. I never could take her place, I know that. Not with Jack, or with you and Dad, or with anyone. I don't even think about it so much anymore, about trying to be as good as she. I can't be and that's it."

When Dad came back with the children, we left for the apartment. I was torn inside, hurting, with so many loose ends in my life. At least now Mother knew, it was out in the open.

When the children were in bed, the telephone rang. It was Betty calling. "I saw Phillip at the grocery store," she blurted out. "He asked about you, and I told him that you had this nice apartment and that you were attending school. I didn't know what you'd want him to know."

I was thinking I'd like to see Phillip one more time.

SWEET-TALKING HEARTBREAKER

Maybe to talk to him, to tell him that I was sorry about the way I had been with him, expecting so much, giving so little. Maybe I needed to tell him about Jack and what happened with Tanya.

I thanked Betty for calling, and when I hung up I called Jack. I told him about Phillip being in town, and then he admitted that he knew because Phillip had called him when he heard about Tanya.

"I wanted to tell you, but he asked me not to. I don't know why. I felt that I should honor that request." Jack's voice was void of expression, like he felt guilty.

Jack seemed far away, he wasn't in the mood for small talk. I said I was tired and he said he was too and that was the end of our conversation.

I had just gone to bed when the buzzer from the security door sounded. I rushed out of bed to answer it. It was Phillip! He wanted to come up for just a few minutes.

Excitement raced inside of me, tears came as I reminded him how late it was. He said he was aware of that, but he was leaving town early in the morning, that at first he wasn't going to see us, but it didn't seem right to leave without a word.   •

I released the door lock and ran to brush through my hair and dab lipstick on my lips.

When I came in the kitchen, he was standing there looking prosperous and well. Better than when he was my husband and living with me.

We both had tears in our eyes, neither of us could hold them back. Nervously, I offered him a chair and put some coffee on. His eyes were following me.

I poured us coffee.

"I was wondering if I could look in on the kids.

Under the circumstances, it's probably better if they don't see me. I'm sure they're used to not having a dad around."

"You could have written to them, you know. Nothing stopped you from writing, did it?" I asked.

He shrugged. His mouth twisted as he whispered, "Jenna, I thought you'd want it that way. You were pretty sick of me and how we had to live. I knew it was no use me trying to set things straight with you after the cops came to the house—especially with Tanya and the whole family feeling ashamed. I knew I had to prove myself.

"I was going to look you up when I came to town, but I got in late. I asked your mother, and she said you and Jack are getting married. Seems kind of strange to me, but that's your business." He fixed his eyes on me. "But that doesn't stop me from still loving you, Jenna. Guess I'll always love you— whether it's right or wrong."

Then he got up then and said he'd look in on the kids. He stood in the hall for a long time and when he came out he was wiping his eyes. He walked right past me toward the kitchen door, and I stood like I was frozen to the spot where I was standing.

I wanted to be in his arms and to feel his lips again, to feel his body next to mine. He was a man now, with all childish things put in the past. I kept staring at him and he didn't move. Then I leaned against the cupboard and let the tears rush down my face.

"Phillip, there's so much I'd like to tell you. But I don't dare. I don't dare let you put your arms around me because I couldn't let you go again. I couldn't tell you about when Tanya died and how lonely Jack and

I were. I wouldn't want you to leave hating me. . . ."

There was a sound that came out of him, like pain from down deep inside. He crossed the room and pulled me close, holding me so tight I could barely breathe.

When I was finished he didn't release me, he just put his hand on my head and said he'd take the baby and give it his name if I wanted us to be a family again, this time a real family, like it should be. It would be up to Jack and me.

The next day Mrs. Simpson came to watch the children, and I met Phillip at a restaurant downtown. Then we went to see Jack. I had called him earlier and told him that Phillip had been to the apartment and we wanted to come and see him. He said he wasn't surprised and he sounded relieved. When we got to the house, Jack was straightening things up. It was awkward but amicable. I told Jack that Phillip wanted us to stay married, and I asked him how he felt about that, with the baby on the way.

Jack said that was fine with him. His eyes met mine and he said, "You know Jenna, we'd have done all right married, but we both know that we never loved each other the way you should love someone you marry. I'm glad for you that everything worked out."

Next Phillip and I went to see my mother. At first it seemed that Mother was disappointed, like she felt there was no end to the problems I was going to bring her.

Then Phillip glared at her and said, "Just for once in Jenna's life, can't you say you're happy for her? Can't you wish her well, give her your blessings?"

Mother looked at me suddenly and opened her

arms. I stumbled into them like a child wanting for forgiveness, seeking love. It was the first time I ever remembered her reaching out for me.

"Jenna, if you're happy then I'm happy for you. You can stop blaming yourself for Tanya's death . . . for a long time she was coming over, lamenting her unhappiness because she was in love with a married man she was having an affair with. I had promised I wouldn't tell, but it's time now to set you free. That night he told her it was all over. She was going home to Jack to try to make their marriage work. Finding Jack with you was too much of a shock."

I realized then that my sister must have been devastated to find us together . . . when she expected Jack to be waiting for her! The double . . . or triple . . . rejection must have been too much for her to handle.

Mother touched my face with a cool hand. "Tanya was always the attraction, but you were always the good little girl. I love you, Jenna. You're still a good person, just like when you were little. I hope you forgive me for not telling you sooner, but I just couldn't. It seemed unfair to Tanya, but now I realize that it was you that was treated wrongly and I hope you can forgive me."

Phillip, the children, and I moved, and he got a job with an insurance firm, the same one he had started with. We have a nice home, and as far as anyone knows we are just an average family, a nice young couple with a new baby boy.

Last Christmas we received a card from Jack via my folks. He wrote that he was going to be married in the summer. I was happy to learn that he had finally found the love and happiness that Phillip and I share. THE END

ONLY LOVE
REMAINS

I heard the front door slam and yelled, "If you track grease and mud onto my kitchen floor again I'm going to break your neck!"

My son came creeping up behind me where I knelt in front of the gaping sink cabinet. He had my head in the crook of his elbow before I could react.

"Who's going to break whose neck?" he teased, his young voice, just making its transition to manhood, was deep and intimidating.

"You may be a big boy now, but a pro-wrestler you are not," I ribbed him, trying to pull his arm from my neck.

"I can body slam you." Jason squeezed some more.

He was strong for a fourteen-year-old and was about six feet tall. He was going to be just like his father, long and lean and hard as a rock.

"Jason, I will pinch a hunk out of your leg if you don't let go," I warned. I reached behind my back and tried to pinch his leg. It was like trying to pinch a brick wall.

"Pinch! Go ahead and pinch me," he growled in my ear.

"I'm going to report you for parent abuse," I threatened.

"Shoot! They would give me a Medal of Honor for putting up with you. You're the grouchiest mother in town." Jason began to mock me in a high, shrill voice, saying, "Don't track grease on my floor. Did you wipe your feet? Don't slam the door."

"If you don't turn me loose in three seconds, no phone privileges till you're twenty-five years old," I threatened.

"Now that would be child abuse," he accused.

"I'm starting to count right now," I warned. "One, two—"

Jason started laughing and continued to hold me tight.

I stopped counting. "Just for that I may take more drastic action, like no radio or guitar privileges."

"Oh, no way!" he objected. "You sure know how to win a fight. Besides being a grouchy mother, you cheat and that's not a very good example for me. I might grow up to be a crook and it would be all your fault."

Now I laughed and began counting again. "Two and a half—"

Jason let go, and I sat down on the floor.

"Now get up," he taunted.

But each time I started to sit up, he would grab my shoulders and pin me there.

"Jason, when I get up from here I'll get you with the broom handle," I said with a determined voice.

"You think so, huh? You're tough when you're on

the floor," he teased, laughing again.

Suddenly a voice from the doorway asked, "Should I call the police?"

Jason let me go, startled by the masculine voice.

"Please do. I'm being tortured by my brute of a son."

My son's young cheeks turned pink. He was embarrassed that he'd been caught playing around with his mother like a child.

"Come on in, Patrick," I invited as I slipped my foot back into the shoe I had lost in the scuffle. "You remember my son, Jason?"

"Sure, I remember him. He looks just like Brian. I haven't seen him in awhile, but I would've known him anywhere."

They shook hands, then Jason used quick thinking to leave the room. "Excuse me. I need a shower," he said, gesturing to his dirty clothing. He'd been tinkering with his old junk car all morning.

"Jason, wait. Patrick may need to cut the water off," I told him.

Patrick had come to repair the kitchen drain that had been dripping for weeks. Jason and I had tried our hand at it, but we finally gave up and called Patrick McMullen, the town's only plumber.

"Nah, that's okay. I only need to shut off the valves beneath the sink. The rest will be fine," he assured me.

So Jason went for his shower and Patrick dug into his tool kit.

"If that stuff is in your way, I'll move it," I offered. I never realized how much I had stored in that cabinet until I was clearing it out to make room for the repairs. It was all over the place.

"It's fine. All I need is enough space in front to crawl around in." Patrick was on his knees, his upper torso inside the cabinet, his head twisted upward to survey the problem. I couldn't figure out how his body could make all the different positions at one time.

While he worked, I sat at the breakfast bar and watched. We talked about the work he needed to do to repair the damage to the sink's drainpipe. I gave him permission to do what he thought was necessary.

"Your son has sure grown up, hasn't he?" Patrick asked.

"Yes, soon he'll be fifteen years old," I replied wistfully.

"They grow up fast, don't they?"

"I saw Leslie and Tiffany at the grocery store the other day. If they hadn't been with your mom, I wouldn't have known them."

"Yeah, they're nine and eleven now." Patrick hesitated, then added, "I don't know how I could've taken care of them if it hadn't been for Mom."

I was sorry I had mentioned his little girls. I could've kicked myself. It was as if I had brought them up on purpose. I would never have done it intentionally. I knew how devastated Patrick was when their mother abandoned them. They had been just babies, two and three years old. Patrick's mother took care of them, and she wasted no time in letting everybody in town know just what her no-good daughter-in-law had done.

Patrick had gone away to the city to be an apprentice plumber. He met Veronica while he was living there. They got married and he brought her back to our little town, pleased and proud to show her off.

But Veronica hated life in a small town. There were no parties, no nightclubs. She detested housework, grocery shopping, and more than anything she disliked being pregnant. Losing her figure was something she hated. It ranked second, though, to caring for babies.

When Veronica got pregnant two years after little Leslie was born, she was furious. She'd actually wanted to have an abortion, his mother had told me one day at the market. But Patrick had pleaded until she gave in when he promised he'd never let it happen again.

Things were never the same after that. Veronica sulked and whined. The housework was never done. The babies were uncared-for. Patrick's mother came over every few days to help her or they might have never received the little attention they did get.

One day Veronica left the little girls with their grandmother. Apparently she then went home, packed her bags, got in the car, and never looked back.

Patrick came home to find a note scratched on a paper towel. She never apologized or tried to cushion the blow. She only told him he was to get a divorce because she was never coming back, and that he was welcome to the children.

Many thought that Veronica did Patrick a tremendous favor by leaving. Opinion was that no matter how hurt and rejected he felt, he was better off.

Patrick had been a handsome teenager. All the girls in school liked him. He was popular, but he was never real serious about anyone until Veronica. And then she turned out to be a horrible wife and mother.

I was immediately sorry I thought of her in that way. It wasn't a Christian thought. But I didn't have many Christian thoughts lately. I hadn't in almost two years now. I'd lost my ability to believe when my husband, Brian, was taken from Jason and I so quickly and cruelly.

Brian was such a good man. I'd loved him since I was fifteen. We married when we were only nineteen years old. He was a mechanic. While most people frown on that work as dirty and menial, Brian loved it. He knew everything about cars. He had a feel for repairing them. He'd never had a formal education in auto mechanics, but he'd taken several courses to gain knowledge where his natural ability needed a boost.

He had his own garage and a large group of faithful customers. He was always overrun with work. Eventually Brian hired two assistants and he made a good living for us.

It was flu season and Brian was working long, hard hours at the garage. He came home greasy and grimy and exhausted. One night after scrubbing himself free of all the grease, Brian sat at the table and just stared at his dinner.

"Aren't you going to eat?" I questioned him. He usually ate like a horse after a long day under the hood of a car.

"I'm not hungry." He half smiled. His hazel eyes were dull and he had an unusual pink tinge to his cheeks.

"Are you getting the flu, Brian?" I knew how it had struck our little town . . . hard and without warning.

"Nah, honey, I'm just tired. I've really been going at it for days now," he reasoned.

He made excuses, but I didn't like the way he looked. I went to the cabinet and got a couple of aspirin and insisted he take them. Even though he put up a meek fight, he finally swallowed them.

An hour later he was back in the kitchen eating cold fried chicken and coleslaw. For the rest of the evening he was his same old self.

When Brian snuggled against me in the night he felt like a chunk of red-hot coals, but he seemed to be sleeping well. I finally fell asleep, but I slept fitfully.

I awoke suddenly. Something had startled me awake. I jumped from the bed. It was Brian. He was sick in the bathroom.

I got a cool wet cloth and held it against his brow. By then he was exhausted. At daybreak his temperature was rising higher. I was scared to death. I'd never seen him sick before, not really sick like he was now.

I called the doctor as soon as he reached his office and explained Brian's symptoms.

"Sounds like the flu to me," he surmised, and decided to call a prescription in to the drugstore. Brian was also to have bed rest, take aspirin, and drink plenty of fluids . . . the oldest prescription in the book.

Brian got steadily worse. He was burning with fever. I used alcohol to bathe his hot skin, but in only a few hours he lay quiet and unresponsive. I called the doctor again. He sent an ambulance this time. I prayed silently while I waited. I also called a neighbor to stay with Jason. By the time the ambulance arrived, he had begun to thrash around in the bed. Brian moaned and held each side of his head. He must have been in so much pain.

He fought the ambulance attendants when they arrived. He was completely out of his head and began to scream from the pain. Even after they administered an injection to relieve some of his agony, they were forced to use restraints to keep Brian on the gurney.

This was not like Brian. He was a gentle, loving, caring person, not loud and talking like he was now. He cursed the faces he didn't even look at. His glazed eyes were staring into a space far away . . . only he knew where.

At that point I began to notice unusual swelling in his face. Then his head seemed to grow. Twelve hours later I didn't recognize my own husband.

Spinal meningitis, the doctor had diagnosed. It had caused pressure on his head and he was wild with pain, incoherent. Medicine could not stop the pain, only take the edge off, the doctor explained. He gave Brian massive doses of medication. It didn't do a thing. This sick, hurting, human being, who was my husband, was unrecognizable . . . his looks, his character, his actions.

The frustrated, exhausted doctor finally told me it was a matter of time. He didn't see how Brian could survive. If he did he would be no more than a vegetable. He would never be Brian again. The illness had already killed his brain. Death would actually be a blessing. And the sooner the better.

I was already in shock and this news turned me to stone. I felt like a mummy. Inside I cursed. Outside I said nothing. Inside I cried. Outside I never shed a tear. I did not think God, if there was a God, would allow this to happen to Brian. He was a man who'd never harmed a soul. A man that had only given, never taken. A man that belonged to me. My man! Jason's father. I screamed at the God I'd always believed in and mentally vowed never to believe in anything again if He took Brian from us.

God never heard my pleas or my bargaining. Brian died, not peacefully as he had lived, but in a hell that no human should have to know.

Something inside me died, too. When I looked into his disfigured features I felt a strange sense of relief to see that the agony was gone, that the pain had finally ceased. Despite the fact that it had taken my husband, my lover, my friend with it. The eerie claws of death had torn him from me hatefully and cruelly. I would never forget. How could I? It was a horror I hope never to face again.

Jason and I had to take medicine as a precautionary measure. But I just wished I could die. I would have if Jason hadn't needed me so desperately. He'd adored his father, walking in his footsteps, following him everywhere, idolizing him. Brian had loved it. He never tired of Jason's endless questions and tagging along. He was a proud father. They had loved each other, and something just as important, they had been buddies.

Twelve-year-old Jason was unable to understand how his father could be so well and thirty-six hours later be so dead. He hadn't known death up until that point. He cried his heart out and all I could do was hold him and love him.

I had no explanation for him. No words to comfort him. I was lost myself. My heart had a crack wide and deep, a chasm like a canyon. Brian's death was more than I could bear. Death . . . I wanted death. I needed it. But my son had no one but me, and so I survived for him. Only for him.

Jason was my feeble hold on reality. He was my guide wire, my anchor. I lived for him. From the day we'd lain Brian to rest in the cemetery on the hillside, surrounded by many vibrant trees, their leaves glowing in the warm bright sunlight of late autumn, I lived for my boy.

The hours were long but they turned into days, and the days into weeks, then into months. I sold the garage to Brian's employees, but they still welcomed Jason's visits like they had when his father had been their boss. Jason grew and accepted his father's death.

I didn't accept that fact, but put up a good front for my only child. At night, when he was safely asleep, I let my bitterness flow. Tears soaked my pillow and the sheet felt the grip of my hands as I tore at it in anger.

I grieved. I was bitter. I was sad. I hated this loneliness. Sometimes I ached to hear his voice, to feel his touch.

But I kept going. I did what good parents do. I attended PTA meetings, football games, baseball games, and Boy Scouts. I was father and mother and friend to Jason. We teased each other. We had playful fights like we were having when Patrick arrived. We'd done pretty well alone, better than I could have imagined.

Jason was no mama's boy. He was rough and rowdy, but he knew when to be a gentleman. Each day that passed he grew more like his father in actions as well as looks. I was proud of him and I adored him. I knew someday he'd leave me and find a wife. He'd love her as his father had loved me. I envied her, whoever she'd be. He'd make her very happy.

And I knew his father would be happy to see him so relaxed and at ease with life, so adjusted to his loss. Jason spoke often of his father, and I hurt inside when he did. But I kept the pain hidden and shared his thoughts.

I wasn't as willing to accept things as my son was. I doubted I ever would be. I missed Brian as much now as I ever had. I felt the pain, sharp and deep, every day of my life.

My grief was actually my salvation . . . as strange as that may sound. I held on to it so I could remember everything about Brian: the good and the bad, the beginning and the end. I treasured the time we'd together, over a dozen years of marital bliss. Those memories were my treasure, my jewels, and I counted my bounty every day. . . .

Patrick turned the water back on, checked the pressure, and watched as his handiwork proved itself. He wet his hands under the flowing water. "Could I have a squirt of that soap on my hands, Sarah?" he asked.

"Sure." I took the bottle of dish detergent and squeezed some into his cupped hands.

I watched as Patrick worked the soap into a lather. He worked it with his hands into his cuticles, up his forearms, to his elbows. My stomach drew into a gripping knot as I watched his strong hands twist through the cleansing suds . . . just the way I'd seen Brian do so many times when he had washed away the morning's work for a hurried lunch. It was funny the little things you were never conscious of ever seeing that came back so clearly when you lost someone.

Patrick jarred me back to reality, asking, "Where are your paper towels?"

I put the liquid soap on the countertop and removed several paper towels for him.

"Thanks for letting me wash up in your sink, Sarah. I don't like to ask to do that, but I have to pick the girls up and drop them off at the ballpark."

"Are they cheering or playing?" I asked.

"Not cheering!" He laughed loudly. "My girls are the biggest tomboys I've ever seen. They think cheerleading is for sissies. They'd rather play baseball." He wasn't complaining, he was bragging.

"Have a seat, Patrick, and I'll cut you a piece of chocolate cake," I offered politely.

He glanced at his watch. "I do have a few minutes, and it is awfully hard to turn down homemade chocolate cake."

I placed the wedge of cake before him. "You want tea, milk, or soda?"

"What's cake without milk?" He grinned boyishly.

"That's what Jason has with his, too." I poured him a large glass of milk and got a soft drink for myself. I sat down facing him across the small breakfast bar.

Patrick was a strong man. He was tall and broad shouldered. He also looked much younger than his age. I knew he was close to forty. His eyes were deep set and he had thick, dark lashes. Veronica had been crazy to walk out on him. He was a good man, he worked hard, and he adored his girls And he was a very attractive man, too, I was noticing.

"This is delicious." He took another bite. "I don't get very many home-baked goodies." He laughed heartily. "I never was much for baking."

I smiled at his remark, but I felt sorry for him, and for his little girls, too.

"Are you going to the spaghetti supper at the school next Saturday?" he asked between bites.

"Yes, I promised them I would help with the bake sale."

"Well, Sarah, if you bake a cake like this one, you'll be sure to sell it. I know I'll sure bid on it!"

"Then I'll bake one. That's Jason's favorite, too," I told him.

"He's a good-looking boy. Must get plenty of attention from the girls at school," Patrick joked.

"I can remember that you had plenty of female attention yourself when you were in high school."

"You remember back that far?" he asked, grinning. "You must've been a baby."

"Thanks for the compliment, but I'm only a few years younger than you. I'll be thirty-four years old soon."

"You're still a fledgling," he teased.

"I don't feel it." I shouldn't have said that.

"I know. You've been through a lot. It sure can make the years seem like they're longer, can't it?"

I watched his eyes turn to steel as he spoke. Then he immediately changed the subject. "Does Jason play baseball?"

"No, he's not much of a sportsman. He loves his music. He plays the guitar and he's into cars. That boy is just like his father. He could tinker on an old car all day."

"A chip off the old block, huh? He sure looks enough like Brian."

"He does. And he has Brian's good nature, too," I agreed. "He's a little on the playful side and a little awkward when it comes to showing affection, but it's his age. That scene you saw when you came was a show of affection, believe it or not!" I laughed. "He pinches, tugs, teases, and roughhouses instead of kissing and hugging like he did when he was younger. He's such a good kid," I went on proudly. "He makes good grades, doesn't get into trouble, just likes to play his guitar, listen to his records, and talk to his bird."

"Bird?" Patrick repeated.

"He has a parrot named Gabby. They talk in their own language sometimes for hours with Jason lying on his bed, the music blaring, and Gabby perched on his arm or chest," I explained. "But there's a little blue-eyed blonde that's been getting some of his attention lately."

"Oops! Better watch out." Patrick laughed.

I felt a pain in my heart. I knew it wouldn't be long before Jason would be on his own. It was a subject I never dwelled on very long. It made me extremely anxious to know that one day I'd be alone.

Patrick gathered his assorted tools, packed them in his box, and prepared to leave.

I held the door for him, because his arms were full of gear.

Then I remembered. "Oh, Patrick, I'm sorry. How much do I owe you? We got to talking and I forgot to pay you. It'll only take me a second. How much?"

"I'll send you a bill," he told me.

"No, I insist on paying today."

"Sarah, please, I really wish you'd let me bill you. If I lose a check, my books get all fouled up. I'd rather get the check in the mail, then it will be right where it's supposed to be when I need it."

"Well, if you really mean that," I said.

"I wouldn't say it if I didn't." Patrick made his way to the van put the tools in the back door, and closed it with a bang. "Thanks for the snack, Sarah. See you at the school supper," he called.

"See you there, Patrick." I waved and went inside.

I baked cakes all day on Friday. I was exhausted when the eleven o'clock news came on. I plopped down on Brian's old recliner and watched the local TV news.

I'd baked four cakes for the cake sale. I wondered if Patrick would really bid on the chocolate one. I fell asleep before I got to see the weather report, and that's what I wanted to hear in the first place.

Jason was clattering in the kitchen, making himself a midnight snack, and he woke me up. I stumbled to the door, blew him a kiss, and went to bed.

The spaghetti supper was better than the one the year before. And the turnout was better, too. Jason and I'd arrived early, so I could help set up the booth for the cake sale before we ate. Just as we were beginning to eat, a troop of people approached our table.

"May we sit here?" It was Patrick's mother, Annette.

"Sure, Annette." I motioned toward the empty seats and they set their loaded trays on the table. She was with Leslie, Tiffany, and her husband John.

"How are you all doing?" I greeted them.

"Almost late. We waited for Patrick, but he wasn't

home when we left. I suppose he got busy with a job and couldn't leave it." Annette barely stopped to breathe as she talked, and she was unfolding napkins, buttering bread, and helping her family as she chattered.

"Patrick never knows when to quit. He works night and day. I've tried to tell him all work and no play makes Jack a dull boy." She laughed. "But he just grins and says, 'Jack has to make a living.'"

She went on with more funny stories, and I tried to listen to her, but I kept thinking someone else would buy the cake. And for some reason, I didn't especially like the idea of it going to someone else.

"Mom, I've finished," Jason said then. "I think I'll go find some of my friends."

"Okay, honey, have fun." I watched him walk away. I was proud of my son. He was tall and lean, hard as young timber. His dark blond hair was long, almost to his shoulders. He didn't care that his friends had short, neat cuts. He wanted long hair. It went with his guitar and loud music. I knew he'd grow out of it, so I let him grow his hair long. But that wasn't all that was growing. There was a pretty good bit of peach fuzz on his upper lip. It was almost impossible to believe my baby was becoming a man. It frightened me more than a little.

"Where's Jason going?" Leslie questioned.

"Leslie McMullen, you eat like a lady," Annette reprimanded her granddaughter, who had just splattered sauce on her clothes. "Use your napkin."

"Aw, Grandma, I hate acting like a lady. I'm not one, anyway," she complained.

"You're correct. You aren't a lady . . . yet. But I want you to start acting like one."

Leslie disregarded the lecture and pulled a long string of pasta into her mouth.

Annette shook her head and barely hid the grin that almost burst through. I winked at her understandingly and finally answered Leslie. "Jason went to join his friends."

"Lucky him," she grumbled. "Grandma makes me stay close to her."

"Perhaps when you're almost fifteen, she'll change her mind. By the way, how old are you?" I asked her.

"I'm eleven, going on twelve. In four months," she said proudly.

"I'm almost ten," Tiffany chimed in.

I looked at Patrick's two girls. They were going to break a few hearts before too long. Just as soon as the tomboy stage was over and they discovered makeup, clothes, and boys!

Annette and I talked until it was time for the auction. First, there were door prizes to be drawn for, speeches to be made, and awards to be presented. Then came the big moneymaker: The cake sale.

Last year Linda Warner's cake had gone for seventy dollars! Her husband had bought it because the men ganged up on him and ran the bid up as high as they dared. It was all in fun and the money was really a donation to both the school's pep club and band. All of the cakes went for high prices, and the two clubs benefited from the fun and generosity of the townspeople.

The professional auctioneer, Jake Johnson, was babbling away in his mumbo jumbo calling that was hard to understand. He'd taunt the bidders and shame them into higher bids by threatening to buy the cake himself.

The cakes were going fast. The three I'd made, besides the chocolate one, had brought sixty-five dollars combined. I was sorry Patrick wouldn't get his chocolate cake. I'd have to bake him one and give it to him.

Finally, my chocolate cake was the only one left. Jake, obviously feeling full of mischief, started the bid at thirty dollars! He said he loved chocolate cake and rubbed his rotund belly. A bid echoed higher to spite him, and all at once madness prevailed. The bid was actually up to eighty-five dollars, I guess because this was the last cake.

"Going—going—" Jake called.

"One hundred dollars!" A voice jarred the silence.

A roar of cheers rose from the excited crowd.

"Sold!" Jake bellowed. "Sold to our town's only plumber for one hundred dollars!"

Everyone applauded, and a loud voice yelled out in fun, "No wonder he charges so much to fix our drainpipes!" The cheers and whistles began again.

"Come and get your chocolate cake, Patrick," Jake ordered.

My heart was thudding like a jackhammer. My face was flushed beet red. My ears were ringing like a bell. I wasn't sure my knees would support my body. Why would Patrick do such a thing? He had to work hard for his money.

I felt terrible. I was afraid he felt obligated to bid too high for the cake just because he said he wanted it. I was so sorry they ran the bid up on him. Patrick was a good sport, but a hundred dollars?

Patrick got a lot of slaps and handshakes as he walked through the crowd to claim his cake. He really was a handsome man. He was in jeans and a gray sports shirt, and his eyes were bright and happy.

Patrick wrote the bookkeeper a check, then held his prize high in the air. He licked his lips as the crowd hissed and yelled, loving his antics.

A yank on my arm broke my concentration. "Mom, can I ride home with the guys?" Jason asked.

I looked at him worriedly. "Now, Jason," I began.

"Mom, please. We'll be careful," he promised. "We're only going to stop by the diner for a snack."

I didn't want him to. I wanted him to stay with me. I didn't want him to grow up too fast. But I gave in.

"Be home before midnight," I said firmly.

"Thanks, Mom. I will." He squeezed my arm lovingly. "You don't mind driving home by yourself, do you?" he asked.

"No, Jason. You go on and have a good time. I don't mind at all. Just be careful."

"We will." He gave me a happy smile before disappearing into a crowd of teenage boys.

Everyone was beginning to leave, and people were congratulating me on raising the most money for my cakes . . . a total of one hundred and sixty-five dollars. I couldn't believe it!

I never even got to see Patrick. He was surrounded by his buddies who were ribbing him, trying to buy his cake for outrageous amounts. Of course, they were teasing, but he refused their offers with humorous answers that drew loud peals of laughter.

I felt guilty, embarrassed, and thrilled all at once as I suddenly realized just how attracted I was to Patrick.

Annette and John McMullen were getting ready to leave, and Leslie and Tiffany, who were staying at their home overnight, were chattering happily. I bid them good night and walked slowly to my car.

I almost jumped out of my skin as a man stepped from the shadows.

"You're not running off, are you?" a deep voice asked.

"Patrick, you scared me to death!" I held my hand over my racing heart.

"I'm sorry, Sarah," he apologized. "I thought you heard me. Are you all right?"

"Yes." I breathed deeply. "Now that I know it's you." I laughed awkwardly. "But I should be afraid of you. Anyone crazy enough to pay that much for a cake could be dangerous."

"I had no choice. When I walked in the bid was already there. I couldn't let anyone else have my cake at any price," he said with a smile.

"I'm sorry. I would've made you another one," I told him.

"But it wouldn't have been nearly as much fun. Besides, the money went to a good cause."

"It was too much," I protested.

"I don't feel bad, so don't you." His voice mellowed. "I'll tell you what you can do for me. I'll let you buy me a cup of coffee."

How could I say no after what he'd done? Still, I did hesitate.

"I'll even let you drive me in your car," he said, aware that I was feeling uncomfortable. "It's the least you can do," he teased.

I gave in. What was wrong with sharing a cup of coffee? "I haven't been out much lately. Where to?"

ONLY LOVE REMAINS

I was hoping he wouldn't say the diner, since that was where Jason and his friends were going. Why that mattered, I don't know, but it did.

We ended up going to a quiet little café on the edge of town. It was practically empty. I felt young again, like a kid on her first time out. I was nervous and unable to hide it from Patrick.

"This your first time?" he asked.

I didn't answer.

"You haven't been out since Brian died, have you?" he persisted.

For a second I was angry at him for bringing up Brian. I composed myself before I answered, "No."

"No wonder you're so nervous, Sarah. I'm a harmless guy. You're safe with me." He smiled so easily.

"I know you're a nice guy. I'm just being silly." I felt completely embarrassed.

"No, you're not silly. You're being human." His eyes dropped to his coffee cup. "I know, Sarah. I've been there. I felt like a little boy. I was lost, didn't know what to say or how to act."

He was staring right at me now. I could feel my eyes tearing up, and I tried to blink them back.

"Veronica left a mark on me. A deep scar that almost ruined me." He was still watching me as he went on. "At least Brian didn't drag you and Jason through the mud when he left you. I may be out of line, Sarah, but I could've buried her much easier. I'm sorry."

He took my shaky hand gently in his. "I mean it. To know she died loving me and the children would've been better than knowing she could just walk out on us."

Tears scalded my eyes. I felt so strange. I never knew anyone could hurt worse than I did. But Patrick had hurt worse than me, and he'd survived. How had he managed that? How did he live through the horror and pain of rejection and humiliation . . . the still, lonely nights that dragged by like a never-ending hell?

"Hey, lady, how did we get on this subject?" He took a napkin and dabbed at my cheeks. "Smile, Sarah. I feel like a heel."

"Don't," was all I could manage to say.

"You sure are pretty. Even when you cry," he teased.

"Hush, Patrick." I grinned in spite of myself.

"You are pretty."

I grinned again.

"Say 'thank you, Patrick,'" he prodded. "If you don't I'll take it back."

"Don't you dare. I need all the compliments I can get."

I really did feel good about Patrick's words. I needed to hear kind words, personal compliments. My well had been dry for so long. It seemed like forever since Brian had kissed me, touched me, whispered sweet secret things to me. I missed those things. I always would.

"Let's get out of here," Patrick said suddenly. He flipped some money on the table and we headed out the door.

He intended to open the car door for me and our arms made contact. Just a brush of flesh to naked flesh, with no explanation for what followed. Patrick's arms enveloped me, his strong hands pressed me to him, and our lips came together.

The kiss rocked me. It made me reel. It made me want Patrick McMullen. Later it made me ashamed that I could desire another man the way I had Brian. My body had been willing, but my head had over-ruled.

Patrick didn't apologize. He didn't need to. It was my fault, too. And when we got back to the school parking lot, I walked him to his van. He said good night and touched my lips with his fingertip.

I drove away, my body in a turmoil of emotion. My mind was angry with my body's betrayal. I'd desired Patrick. I actually wanted him to make love to me. I did then and I still did as I drove home.

And I did when I lay in the darkness of my room . . . in the bed I'd shared with Brian. I actually ached for Patrick. Wrong or right, it was true. I wasn't proud of the fact, but I was honest enough to know it was undeniably true.

During the next few weeks, Patrick called several times. After his girls were in bed and Jason was in his room, we'd talk long hours about our lives, how we handled the hard times, what we wanted for our kids. We talked about the weather, sports, and mundane things, too. Neither of us wanted to end the conversations, but we steered clear of personal feelings. And especially about the night of the cake sale.

Patrick asked me out several times. He was polite and understanding when I turned him down. I used trivial things, and I knew he knew they were trivial, but he'd accept them like a gentleman. He kept trying but I wouldn't give in. I wasn't afraid of him, but I was scared to death of my own feelings.

I was cooking dinner when Jason grabbed me

from behind in his favorite hammerlock. He stood behind me with his arm locked, but he didn't put any pressure on me. I did what I had missed doing, I kissed the part of his forearm that tilted my chin upward. He didn't shy away as usual, but he let go and asked, "Mom, why don't you give Patrick a break?"

I turned to face him. "What does that mean?" I hadn't known Jason had paid any attention to our phone calls and long conversations.

"He's got the hots for you." His voice was serious.

"I beg your pardon." I swatted him with the towel I had in my hand.

"What I mean is, he likes you. Why do you think he calls you all the time?"

"That's ridiculous, Jason. He just calls to talk," I insisted.

"Hah!" he mocked. "Mom, why don't you just go out with him sometime?" He hesitated. His young face turning serious. "He's real nice, Mom. All the guys like him. They think he's cool. And he's got a mean body."

I looked at him questioningly.

"That's good. I wish my body was built like his. Do you think my pecs will ever be that big?" Jason flexed his muscles and grinned. "Boy, I bet he could really put a hammerlock on you."

"I am about to put one on you if you don't let me finish dinner," I told him curtly.

"That will be the day!" he smarted off as he left the room. He yelled back from down the hall, "Don't play so hard to get, Mom. He might quit calling."

I couldn't believe what my son had just said. He was encouraging me to see a man! How could he

162

when he'd worshipped Brian? He'd idolized his
father. Had he forgotten him already? I hurt inside
for Brian. I was disappointed in Jason. He should
have more respect for his father's memory.

As I began to clear the table, Jason came back
into the room and asked, "Mom, are you mad at
me?"

"No, Jason. Why would you ask that?" I said
casually, but I didn't look at him.

"I think you are because of what I said about
Patrick." He sounded sad.

I headed toward the kitchen. "It's not that. It's just
your—"

He stopped me. "I know. It's Dad. Mom, listen,
you can't die just because he died."

His voice almost broke my heart. It was shaky
and so full of emotion.

"I loved Dad," he went on, "and I will never forget
him. Now he's not here anymore, but I still do things
and have fun. And I'll keep on doing them because I
know he would want me to."

"You're absolutely right. That is exactly what he
would want you to do," I agreed. I kept my back
turned. Tears were gathering in my eyes and I didn't
want him to know.

"He'd want you to, also." He stumbled over the
words. "Mom, he'd never want you to be lonely."

"I'm not, son. I try not to be."

I began to cry softly, and Jason came to me and
put his arms around my waist and leaned his head
on my shoulder. "Think about it, Mom. You're still
young. Someday I might go away to college. Or get
married."

He was trying to act casual, but when Jason went

to his room, I knew he was in deep thought. He was playing one of what I called his mood songs.

My fourteen-year-old son was preparing me for his absence. He was trying to take care of me before he had to leave. He didn't want to leave me alone.

I covered my face with the dishtowel then and cried like I hadn't in months. . . .

It wasn't easy for me to talk to Patrick after that night. I always had Jason's words on my mind. He wanted to see that I was taken care of. Well, I didn't need a baby-sitter! I could take care of myself. I didn't need Patrick. I'd managed without Brian and I'd make it when Jason eventually left home.

It wasn't long before I stopped talking to Patrick completely. Jason asked me about it and I told him to mind his own business. We'd never had words before, but this time we were both stewing.

"You sure have been acting like a bitch lately!" he yelled as his bedroom door slammed shut.

Like lightning, I streaked down the hall after him. No son of mine would ever say such a thing to me! I was furious. I yanked at the doorknob. It was locked.

"Open this door, Jason!" I demanded.

In response, he turned his music up louder.

"I'm not going to let you get by with that. You're grounded for a month," I shouted.

I still wasn't satisfied, though. For the first time in my life, I really wanted to slap my son. So I banged on the door until my fists were sore. If Brian had heard our only child call me an ugly word like that, it was hard to tell what he might've done. If Brian had been here, Jason wouldn't have said it.

ONLY LOVE REMAINS

That made me feel like it was my fault. I had failed. Somewhere along the line, I'd shirked my duty as a mother. I'd let Brian down, myself down, and, worst of all, I'd failed Jason. Next thing, he would be drinking and staying out late. I let my imagination go wild . . . drugs, jail cells, then prison bars. All I saw was a path of destruction for my little boy. He was doomed.

I didn't sleep that night. I thought and thought some more, each thing worse than the other. My nerves were shot, and I felt drained.

I didn't even hear Jason slip away to school the next morning. And when he came home that afternoon, I'd calmed down some. I didn't say anything, though. He got a snack and went straight to his room to do his homework.

This went on until the weekend, talking only when we had to. I kept sulking and he let me. I also kept thinking: *Just wait till he wants to go to the mall with his friends or to a movie. I'll show him I mean what I say.*

Jason cleaned his room on Saturday and mowed the lawn. Then he spent the rest of the day in the workshed out back, tinkering on the old car that he'd jacked up and was rebuilding. He came in at dinnertime, showered, ate, and went to his room.

I was watching television. The noise from the TV was low, so I could hear Jason talking to Gabby. I purposely made a trip down the hall to check on him. He was propped against the headboard with the bird perched on his forearm, and they were chattering away. I knew then he wasn't going to ask to go out. And it was a good thing he didn't, because I had a speech ready for him.

Around ten-thirty the phone rang. I froze. I knew who it was . . . Patrick.

"Mom, telephone," Jason called.

I pretended not to hear.

He walked down the hall. "It's for you," he told me.

"I'm not talking on the phone tonight. It's my bedtime." I stomped off to my bedroom and hurried to get into the shower.

There was a knock on the bathroom door.

"Aren't you going to talk to him?" Jason called.

"I'm in the shower," I called back. I didn't say it aloud, but I never intended to talk to Patrick again. He'd helped turn Jason into a smart aleck with a rude tongue. I wished I'd never become friends with Patrick McMullen. I hated him for interrupting my serene family life. Jason and I were just fine until he came along.

Jason and I gradually began to talk and things got back to normal. The incident the night we fought was never mentioned. But for four weekends, he stayed home and never once asked to go out or to have friends in.

I felt guilty after the first week, thinking I had reacted hastily. Then I calmed my guilt by saying to myself that he'd gotten what he deserved. So I let the punishment stand, hoping my son would learn a lesson on how to keep a civil tongue. I couldn't let a mere fourteen-year-old treat me like that. Not now and not ever . . . not even when he was fifty! I was determined.

The calls from Patrick stopped. I never saw him, but I saw the girls and Annette McMullen often. We always chatted about this or that, yet Patrick was never mentioned. They probably didn't know that he and I had been friends; more telephone friends than anything else. I was glad they didn't know, no matter what we had been to each other.

The first weekend after Jason's grounding was up, he went to the movies to see a double feature of horror shows. He and his friends rode their bikes since they weren't driving yet, and I knew he'd be late since it was a Saturday special.

It had been so long since Patrick called, that I forgot and answered the phone when it rang. I usually left that to Jason because he got more calls than I did. Right away I knew I'd goofed. It was Patrick!

Instead of saying hello, he asked, "Where's Jason?"

"At the movies," I answered coolly.

"Oh, he's out of prison now?" Patrick commented.

I didn't like his condescending attitude at all. "That's between Jason and me," I replied curtly.

"Don't you think you're being a little rough on him?"

"Don't you think you're out of line? He's my son and my responsibility," I said defensively.

"Yes, he is. And you sure are tightening the apron strings." His voice burned my ear like a spark from a firecracker, setting me off. "Patrick McMullen, that is none of your business!" I snapped, my blood boiling.

"Someone has to stick up for the kid. He doesn't have anyone on his side," he said, sounding strange as he stood up for my boy.

"He doesn't need anyone to stick up for him. If he hadn't called me a dirty name, he'd never have been grounded. He never got what he deserved. I should have slapped his smart mouth," I added.

"Sarah, I can't believe you!"

I stopped him. "Well, I couldn't believe he called me a bitch, either." I was talking loud. My voice was high pitched and trembling.

"Have you ever thought maybe he was right? That you were acting like one."

"If you dare call me that name you will be sorry!" I don't know what I would have done, but I wouldn't let Patrick get by with it, either.

"I would never do that. But you're taking his meaning all wrong," Patrick argued. "What he meant was that you were nagging or fussing all the time. And from what he tells me, that's what you have been doing lately."

"This discussion is over, Patrick. Don't call here again." I hung the phone up quickly. My insides were churning. I was still furious with him for interfering in our lives.

The phone rang again. I didn't answer. It rang and rang and rang. Finally, in a rage, I grabbed it from the hook.

"I told you not to call here again!" I yelled.

"Mom, what's wrong?" Jason asked with a startled voice. "Are you okay? Is something wrong?"

"No, honey, I'm fine," I lied.

"Where were you? The phone rang and rang," he said.

"I was in the bathroom," I lied again.

"I was going to ask permission to stay over at Sam's house. All the guys are. But if you're upset, I'll just come home." His voice was filled with concern.

"No, Jason, you can stay at Sam's. I'm fine," I assured him.

"You sure you'll be okay, Mom?"

"Yes, Jason. You have fun and don't keep Sam's parents awake all night."

"We won't," he promised. "See you in the morning."

"Night, honey," I said.

"I love you, Mom," he whispered faintly.

I didn't know if he didn't want the boys to hear, or if he was just being shy. "I love you, too," I told him.

I was in a turmoil of emotion. Jason and I were on rocky ground and I didn't know what to do about it. I needed him, he needed me . . . but we needed less of each other. Was I keeping him too tight to my apron, like Patrick had said? I'd never had to deal with a teenager before. I didn't know how. I'd never even had a brother. I didn't know what boys went through. I didn't know if I didn't understand Jason, or if I was simply being overprotective.

Being a parent wasn't easy. Being a single parent was even harder. But being the single parent of a teenage son was both terrifying and hard. What if I did fail him? What if I did hold him back? I was so confused.

If only Brian were here! He would know exactly what to do. He always had. He was great to have around during a crisis. He'd been so levelheaded and patient. I missed him so much, and I needed him desperately to help me with my mounting problems with Jason. It seemed to get all out of proportion when I thought of it. I tried to keep it from my mind, but it loomed there, ever present, confusing me. What was I going to do?"

Suddenly the doorbell rang. I immediately panicked. I felt sure that something terrible had happened to the boys on their bicycles. I opened the door prepared to see the police and hear the horrible news. What I saw startled me just as badly. It was Patrick—all six feet of him—looking handsome and very intimidating.

My arms went limp by my sides. In an exhausted breath I asked, "What do you want?"

"You," he said, dead serious.

I was too stunned to manage a reply. I stood there dumbstruck and straight as a stick.

It seemed like forever before Patrick ended the silence, asking, "May I come in?"

"Please, just go away," I said shakily.

"No," he refused gently. "I can't."

He came in and closed the door behind him. And when he reached for me, I went willingly into his arms. I knew it wasn't Patrick I was angry at, it was the truth behind what he said and at that moment I just needed to be held. After a few moments Patrick kissed me gently, and then passionately. I shivered and knew that I not only needed to be held but loved in a way I hadn't in so long.

Sometime later, I don't know how much later, he carried me to my bedroom. Time was nothing . . . it vanished like thin air. Our kisses lay on each other's bodies like a flower floating in the water . . . gently flowing along with the waves.

Hours later we lay back exhausted and I fell into a deep sleep and dreamed of Brian. We were young again and desperately in love. We had managed to save ourselves until our honeymoon, and it was heaven. I could see his eyes filled with love for me.

His young face full of desire. I felt his hands against my skin. His kisses burned my flesh, my lips, as he loved me. Brian was so healthy and young. So alive. How could he be dead? He'd never died! He was here. He always would be. I snuggled close to his body, feeling his warmness next to me.

A noise jarred me from my dream. I awoke trembling and astonished. Brian wasn't there! He hadn't been. It was only a dream. And he never would be again. At daybreak Patrick left reluctantly.

"Oh, God, what have I done?" I sobbed aloud, clutching the pillow to me. I had spent the night in Patrick's arms, then slept with my husband in my dreams. I was ashamed that I could have acted so loosely with Patrick, giving in so easily. He hadn't persuaded me. He didn't have to. I was all too willing. Starved and eager, I'd shared my bed . . . the same bed Brian and I had shared . . . with Patrick.

I heard another noise. I knew it was Jason. He was home, probably with a friend.

He peeked through the crack in the opened door and asked, "Are you still in bed, sleepyhead?"

I never slept this late and he knew it. "I watched TV until the early hours and slept in since you stayed at Sam's," I fibbed. "Are you hungry?" I asked, trying to regain my composure.

"I ate already. I scrambled some eggs, but I didn't wash the dishes," he told me.

"I'll wash them, honey, don't worry. I'm going to shower and I'll be right out."

"Don't hurry, Mom. The guys and I are going to play some football out in the back."

"Have fun," I managed to say, relieved that they had plans to leave the house. I didn't want to face anyone now.

The boys laughed and stomped their way out-side. When they were gone, I got into the shower. Then with hot water and soap I tried to scrub my sins away. My skin was red when I got out, but the guilt was still there. To my way of thinking, I'd com-mitted adultery. I'd slept with another man and he wasn't my husband, even if neither of us were mar-ried any longer.

I was exhausted and ashamed by my night of lov-ing. But I couldn't get the feeling out of my mind. I'd wanted Patrick. I'd needed him. I'd made love to him willingly. And much to my shame, I'd enjoyed it. Truthfully and honestly, it had been wonderful.

How can I think that? What kind of person am I? I can't ever let it happen again. I'm too strong to give in again. I know I am. I don't need a man. I'd had one, the best, and that is all I need, I thought.

I went back to my old ways. I wouldn't talk to Patrick when he called. I always had some trumped-up excuse. I didn't even dignify him with an explanation. I didn't know what he thought and I didn't care. I told myself I was protecting me and Patrick at the same time. I reasoned that I was somehow keeping Jason, Leslie, and Tiffany safe from hurt and embarrassment.

This had continued for a couple of weeks, my refusing to see or talk to Patrick. It was Friday, and I'd shopped all afternoon. Jason needed new jeans, I needed odds and ends, and I'd to pick up a CD for Sam's birthday. I was in the lingerie department, looking for a new bathrobe, when a baby-blue gown caught my eye. I picked it up, but then put it back. It was too revealing for me.

I wandered around in the department, but my eyes kept straying back to the gown. Finally I made my purchase and left the store as if the devil were chasing me.

It was getting near dinner when I pulled into the driveway and saw Patrick's van parked there. *What was he doing here?* I wondered. I almost backed out, but I knew Jason would need the CD I had picked up for Sam's birthday party tonight.

As soon as Jason saw me come through the front door he said, "Mom, where have you been? It's time for me to leave." He hardly breathed as he went on. "Did you get the CD?"

"Yes, I did, son," I answered.

"Where is it?" He searched through the bag I was holding.

"It's in the car with the other shopping bags," I told him.

"I'll get them."

He rushed out and before I even had a chance to take my shoes off or gather the nerve to see why Patrick was there, Jason returned with the CD.

"I've got to go, Mom. We're going for pizza and I'm going to be late. I'll see you around noon tomorrow, okay?" he said as he ran out the door. "See you later, Patrick," he called.

"Okay, Jason," he answered from down the hall.

What's he doing? I wondered. Then I finally made myself walk down the hall to see. Patrick was gathering his tools from the bathroom floor.

"What happened?" I asked.

"Jason called. The tap was broken and flooding. He was afraid the water would reach the carpet. I rushed over and changed the tap," he explained.

"Jason cleaned the water up, I fixed the break, and everything is fine now."

He picked up his tool kit, then walked away as if I wasn't even there.

"How much do I owe you?" I followed him.

"I'll send you the bill," he told me quietly.

"Like you did the last time?" I said. "You've yet to send me the first one."

He shrugged. "It must've gotten lost in the mail. It happens sometimes."

He headed for the door, stopped, and you could have knocked me over with a feather when he said, "You know, Jason did it."

"Did what?" I wasn't sure I wanted to know.

"Broke the tap on purpose." He turned to face me.

"Why would he do a thing like that?"

"I can tell," Patrick said.

"How?" I wanted to know.

"A faucet doesn't twist itself off. They might spring a leak and drip, they might rust and become hinged, but that spigot was twisted off with a wrench."

"Why would he do a thing like that?" I just couldn't believe it.

"Think about it, Sarah." Patrick was watching me, obviously nervous.

I sat down on the easy chair, unable to believe my son had vandalized our home. "Why?" I repeated.

"You know why," Patrick insisted.

"But I don't. Honestly," I told him.

"Us," Patrick replied.

"Us? Why?" I still didn't understand.

"It was a way to get me over here," he explained.

174

"He wouldn't do that. I know he wouldn't," I disagreed.

"Then I know him better than you do. Because it is obvious that he wants something to happen between us—"

"Well, he can keep on wanting!" I interrupted. I was humiliated and furious. "He's in a lot of trouble."

"Why, Sarah? Why are you going to punish him? He's trying to help you do something that you don't have the guts to do yourself."

"I beg your pardon?" I flashed him an icy glare.

"You don't have the guts to let us have a chance," he accused me. "Jason was only trying to arrange for us to be together, hoping something would click."

"Something's going to click," I shot back. "The lock on his door! When he has to spend a lot of time there for this little episode."

"You're wrong, Sarah," Patrick said flatly.

"Don't tell me I'm wrong. I'm his mother! I'll be the judge of that." I was so angry now I was shaking.

"Why are you so angry?" He came nearer.

"I'm not angry. I'm furious! Jason did something wrong and you think it's all right. I am boiling over with anger . . . at him and at you."

"He was just trying to get us together," Patrick repeated, sticking up for Jason again.

"If you were a fireman, would he have burned the house down?" I said sarcastically.

"Now you're exaggerating. He's not dumb. He's just young and worried about you. Calm down." He stepped even closer.

"I'm not excited. I'm mad. I'm really mad."

"Because your son has more guts than you do?" he stated.

"What's that supposed to mean?" I wrung my hands. They were trembling and moist.

"You want me, Sarah. You need me and you won't admit it. He was only trying to make you realize that."

"I don't need you, Patrick McMullen. You are out of your mind. Just because I made a stupid mistake and let you stay here, you think I need you?" I was really worked up. "Well, I've got news for you. I don't need you. I don't need any man."

"Liar," he accused. "Make excuses, deny it, yell, tell yourself you're right. But then, explain this!" He picked up the flimsy nightgown from the floor where Jason had let the box fall when he was rummaging through the packages for Sam's gift. The gown was there on the floor, the box askew.

My face burned like a flash of fire and my thudding heart beat double time. I couldn't find my thoughts. I couldn't answer. All I could do was stare, stunned and thoroughly embarrassed, at the nightgown.

"Sarah," Patrick said gently, "it's all right to feel emotions for someone else. It's okay if you desire a man. It's a perfectly normal feeling."

I turned my back. He was hitting me where it hurt. The truth was the hardest thing to face. And I wasn't ready to face this truth. Everyone was pushing me, but I wasn't ready for this.

I stiffened as Patrick touched my arm lightly. He removed his hand quickly, sensing my reaction.

"I've been there, Sarah. I know. It really isn't different for a man. I've faced what you have, only I was filled with the shame that I hadn't been able to hold on to my own wife. Veronica left me and never looked back. I had to worry if any woman would ever want me," he went on. "To really want me forever and ever. To want me to hold her, kiss her, and touch her. To share my bed, my home, my life. I've been to the brink, Sarah. It's shaky and frightening. It isn't easy. But it passes. It really does . . . if you allow it to."

I bit my lower lip hard to keep from crying. My eyes were flooded with tears that I fought to control. Was Patrick right about all of this? I knew I did feel guilt. I didn't feel free enough to have a life after Brian. He was my life, a wonderful life, not just a memory.

"You can love again, Sarah," Patrick continued. "Just let it envelop you and guide you. Don't hold it back. Life is too short. You of all people should know that. You had Brian one day and he was gone the next. What you had was real, it was good, it was more than that, I'm sure. You should never forget your life with Brian, but you can't live in the past forever." He took a deep breath and said, "There's the two of us now . . . you and I. You may not admit that to yourself, but it's true."

I shook my head. I didn't want to hear this. It was not what I wanted. I didn't want change. I wanted time to stand still.

"The night we shared was real, Sarah. It wasn't a one-night stand. Not for you and certainly not for me. It was the beginning. We can have a new start," he said quietly. "If you'll let it happen."

Patrick drew in a deep breath. He'd made a long speech. He'd done all the pleading and encouraging he could do. The ball was in my court and I chose to keep it there. I couldn't talk about it. I wouldn't let myself. I was too overwhelmed by his words and my feelings to react.

Apparently he knew how I felt. Wanting to put me at ease, he began to tease me. He picked up the gown, saying, "Wow! This really is sexy." He grinned slyly at me. "Did you buy this for me?" His grin broadened. "I like blue."

I glared at him, hiding a smile. Then I yanked the flimsy gown from his hand. I was unable to hide the fact that I was no longer so angry. Patrick was slowly but surely wearing me down, or winning me over was a better way of putting it. I was ready to be won, I suppose. I was ready to begin my life again . . . a new beginning.

Patrick edged closer to me, and still closer. His hands eased along my waist, traveling around to my lower back where he gently pulled me toward him.

I didn't move quickly, but I didn't hold back. I put my arms around his neck. I held onto him and I felt at home in his arms.

We didn't let desire complicate our reunion. We enjoyed the pleasure of being close, just holding each other with easy movements, gentle caresses.

"Forgive me, Patrick," I finally said.

His fingers played up my back. "For what?" His voice was breathless.

"For being stupid," I whispered, kissing his neck lightly. I felt him shiver from my touch.

"It may have been stupid, I won't argue that, Sarah. But if it was, you certainly aren't alone. There are a lot of lost and lonely people. As of tonight, there'll be two less." He kissed my hair. "Right?"

I nodded yes, and Patrick pulled me even closer.

Right or wrong, Patrick and I stole another night. This time I gave over fully to everything inside of me and opened up to Patrick body and soul. I wouldn't feel guilty for finding love again, everyone deserves to be loved and give love. We talked and planned and loved the hours away. His caresses and kisses were tender but passionate. I finally felt free beneath his touch.

I never questioned Jason about the broken faucet. I also never received the two plumbing bills from Patrick. And I never wore the blue gown . . . there was no need for it.

We began to do things together. I went to Leslie's and Tiffany's ball games. We had Sunday afternoon hikes and family picnics. The girls liked me, Jason was crazy about Patrick, but the three kids took a little longer to adjust to each other. The got along alright, but it was when Jason asked us to keep the girls out of his hair, I knew he had accepted them. When Leslie and Tiffany began to stick their tongues out at him and tease him about his girl-friend, I knew they'd accepted him also. We were becoming a close-knit group, though Jason wasn't always with us. But he was growing up, and he needed his privacy, too.

Patrick's parents were happy for us, and they welcomed Jason into their warm company. He took to them immediately.

One night Patrick took all three children with him, leaving me to wash the dishes alone. I assumed he had business to attend to and they were helping him. I didn't especially like them leaving all the cleaning to me, but it was the first time they had ever done it, so I didn't make a fuss.

It was late when the four of them returned. I was on the sofa deep into a gossip magazine when they came barreling into the house. There was fire dancing in four pairs of eyes as they surrounded me.

"What's going on?" I sat up and glanced from one to the other. Three young heads turned toward Patrick, all faces smug and on the verge of erupting into excitement.

"We have a proposition for you, Sarah," Patrick began. "Jason, Leslie, Tiffany, and I have decided we want to be one big family. And we want you to be the mother and the wife."

I was thrilled. I loved their way of doing this. I loved them. I could never have dreamed of a better proposal.

"What if I don't want to be a wife and mother to four people who run off and leave me with a mountain of dirty dishes and a messy kitchen to clean?" I joked.

"Aw, Mom!" Jason fussed.

"We did it for you!" Leslie said.

"Uh-huh, we went to get you something," Tiffany put in.

Finally Patrick intervened. "It's okay, kids. I've got my nerve up," he said, taking a small velvet box from his pocket and handing it to me. "Do you want me on my knees or what?" A smile flashed, wicked and teasing, across his face.

"On your knees," I ordered with a smile.

And he did a dramatic scene on his knees before me that had the kids in stitches. They squealed and Jason laughed when he placed the ring on my finger and kissed my hand. The diamond was much larger than I would have chosen, but it was beautiful and I was keeping it . . . forever.

"Party's over. Everyone in bed," Patrick ordered. The girls were staying the night. Patrick would stay until dawn, leave, and then he would come back again.

After the kids were in the bed, Patrick and I necked on the sofa like teenagers. When we were sure they were asleep, Patrick asked me to marry him again. Not on his knees, just sitting beside me with my face cupped in his hands. We confessed our love for each other, and we made plans for a simple ceremony.

"Let's do it soon, please," Patrick said anxiously, and I couldn't have agreed with him more.

Two weeks later we were married. Annette and John McMullen kept the kids during our honeymoon. Our little town was minus its only plumber for two whole weeks.

Brian is still with me . . . a sweet, sweet memory. And Patrick didn't take his place. He has a place all his own. And I am his completely, with no guilt, no shame. I can't change the past by trying to hide myself in memories. My eyes are wide open, aimed straight ahead. I'm ready for my new life with Patrick. We don't foresee Easy Street ahead, but we don't anticipate anything we can't handle together.

Patrick and I had each loved before and lost our loves in different but no less painful ways. But now we'd found each other. We had many trials, mostly on my part, but we were together and that was what mattered. I thank God every day that Patrick and Jason didn't let me give up, that they kept at me until I was able to get on with my life and accept the love I was being offered. And I love this man, my husband, more and more each day we share together.   THE END

THE DARK PATH IN THE WOODS

I knew something was wrong that morning when Kathy came to the little clothing and gift shop I ran out on the highway. Kathy was my husband Randy's sister and we'd lived across the road from each other for years. I never had a sister, but if I did, I couldn't have had one any better than Kathy. She was seven years older than Randy, who was just a few months older than I was.

Kathy had been like a mother to all the kids in her family after their mother died. She'd worked in the fields along with all her other responsibilities. Then, when Randy was twelve and the youngest was about school age, their father died. Kathy had the whole burden of taking care of the farm and raising her siblings. Somehow she and her young husband, Peter, had kept the kids together and got them raised. They were very poor but it didn't seem to matter.

Kathy wasn't very well now . . . no wonder, hard as she'd worked all those years. She'd held down a job at the shirt factory and cooked and worked on the farm and in the garden even when her own two boys were little. We all had it better now. All our kids were nearly grown and we had nice houses and good lives that we sometimes forgot to appreciate.

"What's wrong, Kathy?" I asked.

Her eyes met mine and she shook her head. "Donna, I hate to tell you this, but I can't *not* tell you either," she said.

We were alone in the store.

"What's wrong, Kathy?" I repeated.

"I was uptown at the supermarket and I ran into Kathryn on her way out. We talked for a while and then she left. Then I heard some boys about her age talking. Oh, Donna, I hate this." She stopped.

I got a cold feeling around my heart. Kathryn, our oldest daughter, slim and tall and lovely, had been married two years now. We hadn't wanted her to marry that young . . . just eighteen, but there'd been no stopping her. Her husband, Jason, was a good boy, from a prominent local family.

I searched Kathy's tired, sad face and told her to go on.

"The boys were talking about seeing her parked out in the woods with Jason's father," Kathy blurted. "They'd been working for him planting the week before, and then one of them told the others that Kathryn had met him every day and they'd go off into the woods."

"Clint?" I asked. Kathy nodded and I felt sick.

Clint Henderson owned and farmed the whole bottom for miles, one of the few farmers making any money. Mostly he raised cotton and soybeans in those rich, dark fields between strips of thick woods left as windbreaks and to hold the soil against erosion. Clint also owned, or at least controlled, the feed mill. Actually, his wife had inherited it, along with her brothers, from her father. They'd bought out her brothers or made some arrangement and Mary Ann had run it for years.

I liked Mary Ann, my daughter's mother-in-law. She was a few years older than I was and her family had money, but she was a nice person. She worked hard running the mill, at least doing all the bookwork. She was never snobbish or anything like that, and she'd been nice enough to Kathryn.

Her husband, Clint, was likable, too, and was probably the most prosperous farmer in the county. Maybe that was why nobody ever said much against Clint, even though everybody knew that he was the worst skirt chaser around.

As far back as I could remember, everybody knew that Clint went out on Mary Ann. There'd been a lot of talking from time to time, when he'd gone with first one woman and then another. I hadn't really paid any attention to it because back then Kathryn was small, Jennifer hadn't been born yet, and Randy and I were busy just trying to make a living for ourselves. We certainly had no connection with the Hendersons.

After awhile, I guess people got used to how Clint was and didn't even bother to comment about it much anymore. I remembered hearing he'd broken up one couple and that another divorcée had supposedly had his baby, but she'd moved somewhere up North. Clint and Mary Ann had four boys and they all lived together in their nice big house like nothing in the world was wrong.

THE DARK PATH IN THE WOODS

Randy and I hadn't wanted Kathryn getting serious with anybody at sixteen, but it happened almost before we realized it. Jason was eighteen and a senior when they started dating. He was a football player and not really as good looking as his father was, but he resembled him a lot. They both had the same easy grin and a sort of disarming way about them. Jason liked to hunt and fish, so he and Randy hit it off, and before long he was at the house every day.

Neither Randy nor I had graduated from high school . . . both of us had to go to work before we had the chance. But we'd tried to impress on both of our girls the importance of an education. We even told them we'd help them find a way to go to college if they wanted to go.

Kathryn was smart and made good grades. We hoped she'd go on to college and learn to make a better living than she would in the shirt factories where most of the women in our area wound up. But suddenly her mind was only on Jason and getting married.

We tried to talk her out of it, or at least until she'd looked into going to college. But after Jason graduated and started farming with his father, she had no interest in school. Her grades fell and nothing her father or I said seemed to make any difference. We talked to Jason, telling him how much it meant for us that Kathryn finish high school.

He nodded. "I understand," he said. "I guess I'd feel the same way. It's just that we're so in love, we want to be together. If we got married, she could still go on and finish high school. A lot of girls get married in high school. But we'll do what you think is best. I don't want to go against you in any way."

He was such a nice, polite boy and able to support our daughter, we knew that. It was Kathryn who argued and demanded and cried and pleaded.

"Why? I don't understand," she said. "Jason and I are sure we want to get married. We know what we want. We've made plans. It's not just some infatuation I'm having with some boy I met last week! There's no reason to wait. Jason's folks said we could use the little white house until we get a house of our own built. Jason has cattle and fields his dad lets him farm for himself. He makes a good living."

We couldn't deny the things she said. Our only argument was that she was too young. After awhile we saw that her grades were failing and she was angry with us all the time. If we didn't let her marry Jason we'd wind up losing her anyway. So we gave in on the condition that she'd attend the nearby community college for at least one year.

Mary Ann and I arranged a small but pretty wedding and they were married the day after Kathryn graduated from high school. Randy and I had bought a secondhand car for Kathryn the summer before, and we gave them that. Jason had a good pickup truck. The Hendersons said they could live rent free in a small frame house on their property about a mile from their own.

We gave them Kathryn's bedroom set and bought a new queen-sized bed to go with it. Mary Ann and Clint gave them an old living room set they had. I found a table and chairs at a garage sale. Kathryn and I sewed kitchen and bedroom curtains. Mary Ann bought them living room drapes. There was a stove and refrigerator already in the house.

Kathryn's friends had a shower for her and Jason's aunt had another one, and then Kathy wound up giving her a personal shower. The young couple was off to a good start. Kathryn was a glowing bride and Jason a proud husband.

Even though Kathryn bounced in and out of our house or my store nearly every day, it was several weeks before I learned that she'd dropped out of the community college. It was our twelve-year-old daughter Jennifer who let it slip. Immediately, I wondered if Kathryn was pregnant. I was torn between wanting a grandchild and hoping that Kathryn and Jason would have time to grow up a little themselves before they had a baby. But when I asked Kathryn, she shook her head.

"Oh, no I'm not pregnant," she said. "We're going to have our own home before we start a family."

"I know you're not going to school," I told her.

She hung her head. "I'm sorry, Mom." Her eyes turned solemn and pleading. Randy, too, had always been able to melt me with that look. "You just don't understand. I can't concentrate on schoolwork while I'm thinking of things I should be doing at home . . . planning supper or wondering how I'm going to get the laundry done. And it's like I'm too old for the other kids in school. All they do is drink and party and talk about who they're hooking-up with."

In a way I did understand. Kathryn kept their little house spotless and cooked meals that Jason bragged about endlessly. The summer before school had started she'd planted an amazing garden of vegetables and braided a rug for the living room floor of the drafty little house. She carried wood for their heater in the winter and ran the store for me a few days when I had the flu. She'd broken her promise to us that she'd get some sort of a college education, but we just couldn't be too angry with her for it. Then she went to work for Mary Ann in the office at the feed mill, so we figured she knew what she was doing.

Now after what Kathy told me, I was ready to cry. "Kathy, I don't want to believe what you're telling me," I choked.

She put her arm around me. "I know, Donna. Maybe it's just an ugly story. You know how it is with talk around here, the terrible things people will say. There's probably nothing to it. But if those boys were talking about it in the grocery store. . . ."

I nodded. "You can bet the story has already made the rounds," I finished for her. She nodded.

"Maybe there's some explanation," I said, more to myself than to her. "Maybe the whole thing is innocent. Perhaps Kathryn and Clint had a reason for meeting. . . ."

"They probably did," Kathy chimed in.

After she left I kept going over and over it all in my mind. I'd seen less of Kathryn lately than any time since her marriage, though that didn't mean anything. But she'd stopped working, too. She had tired of the feed mill after nearly a year and started working in a real estate office. But she'd become dissatisfied with it after a few months and quit.

I was surprised when she quit because she'd been so impatient for a home of her own and disappointed that she and Jason hadn't been able to start building yet. She'd complained about that, so I thought she was anxious to work and save towards building.

Jason's parents had given them a nice piece of land near the fields. Jason farmed, but there had been two bad years in a row . . . one summer would be too wet and the next too dry. Cotton and soybeans hadn't done as well as they'd hoped. Kathryn complained about Jason spending too much money buying cattle, and the calves they'd sold hadn't brought as much as they'd hoped.

I couldn't decide what to believe. Surely Kathryn wouldn't take part in such a thing. Clint was older than Randy, though I had to admit he didn't look it. He was a handsome, muscular man. He'd been so generous and seemed so concerned that the kids get off to a good start. Of course, he was always kidding and teasing Kathryn whenever I saw them together, but that was Clint's way. No matter what he'd done in the past, surely he wouldn't go after his son's wife!

No, I told myself. *Such a thing can't be. There has to be some innocent explanation or else the whole thing is nothing but a terrible lie someone's made up.*

Still, there were little nagging doubts that ate at me. There was no denying that Kathryn was angry and disappointed at having to keep living in that little frame house. The first spring she'd planted flowers around it and a vegetable garden, too. The next spring she hadn't bothered with flowers.

"I'm not doing another thing for this house," she'd complained. "As long as I go on fixing it up, Jason thinks I can go on living here."

She had planted the vegetable garden, though, and we'd helped them get a freezer to put up food for the winter. But this spring she hadn't even planted vegetables.

Once I asked her if she was looking for a job. "I'll let you know when I get around to it," she had answered curtly.

Randy had hinted to me that Kathryn and Jason might be having problems, since we saw so little of them anymore. Of course Jason was busy with fieldwork and he'd cut wood through the winter for extra money. Randy and I had talked about Kathryn's disappointment over not having their house started yet. Randy wasn't very sympathetic.

"Remember that apartment we lived in those three years in Jackson?" He grinned. I remembered. We'd gone there before Kathryn was born because Randy and his brother got good paying jobs in Jackson when there was nothing in Alabama. I'd worked in a factory and we'd saved every penny we could to pay off our land back home. I'd worked until they made me quit because I was pregnant.

Our apartment was so cramped we had to move the dresser out into the living room to make room for a crib in the bedroom. The heat and cold and mice and roaches . . . it'd been terrible. But we struggled through, enduring it for the home we'd have later.

Back then, Randy and I could live on peanut-butter sandwiches and be happy together. We just wanted better for our girls, and we'd made it better. We came back and built our home, both of us working.

After Jennifer was born, my friend Brenda offered me a partnership in a shop she was opening. I could work three days a week and have the kids with me if I wanted, and Randy was all for that. So I'd gone into the store with Brenda. We didn't get rich, but we made grocery money and I got all the girls' clothes and my own wholesale. I'd enjoyed the store and being able to have more time for my family, too.

I tried to decide whether to tell Randy about Kathryn. I never kept secrets from him, but this, if it were true, would break his heart. He adored our two girls and they were as close to him as they were to me. And he'd be angry, whether it was true or not. He'd be furious! He'd want to get to the bottom of it. Would he go see Clint? And what about Jason . . . what would he do if he heard that rumor?

I tried to think what to do, the whole thing growing in my mind. In a community the size of ours, there were no secrets. If those boys were saying that, true or not, it would soon be as well known as if it had been printed in our weekly paper. Sooner or later, after everyone else was talking about it, someone would tell Randy or Jason, or even Clint and Mary Ann. A scandal like that didn't just die down and go away easily.

I decided not to tell Randy that night. I was off the next day. I'd go see Kathryn or call her to come over. I'd talk to her, and we'd try to find out what had given rise to such an awful rumor and maybe decide on a way to handle it.

The evening dragged and I had a headache, so I took some aspirin and went to bed. Randy let me sleep in the next morning, but I was still up before seven. Jennifer slept later in the summer when she didn't have to catch the bus. I put off calling Kathryn. I knew she often went back to bed after Jason left. I made up my mind to call her midmorning and to be calm.

I called her at nine when Jennifer was in the shower, but nobody answered the phone. She could be out hanging clothes on the line, I decided and tried again twenty minutes later. There was still no answer.

Jennifer wanted to go to a girlfriend's house and for once I was glad to be free of her. I took her to Lisa's and then drove the seven miles to Kathryn and Jason's place. The pickup and Kathryn's car were both gone. The little house looked more neglected than usual. The grass needed cutting, and there was a plastic bag of trash on the front steps and some soda bottles and cans strewn about.

I tried the door. It was unlocked, so I went inside. Kathryn still had a key to our house, and countless times she'd come in when I wasn't there and borrowed this or that, or used my dryer, or just waited for me.

I was shocked at how unkempt the little house was . . . the bed unmade, clothes strewn about, dishes in the sink, wet clothes in the washer, and dirty floors. I hung out the laundry and did the dishes, then cleaned up the kitchen.

It was nearly noon when Kathryn drove into the yard. I could tell she was angry when she walked in.

"Really, you shouldn't have done my housework," she said defensively. "I would've gotten around to it."

"Just trying to help—" I began.

Kathryn brushed on by me and poured herself a glass of tea from the fridge.

"I took Jennifer to Lisa's and dropped by to see if

you might want to go into town for lunch," I explained. "We don't see much of you lately."

She swallowed hard and turned away. She was a pretty girl, so slim, the fine features of her face half little girl, half woman.

"I've been meaning to come over. I planned to today," she told me. "I went over to see Jason's mother at the mill. I might go to work there again, and we got to talking, you know how it is." She smiled, then picked up a pair of Jason's boots and a pair of her sneakers and put them in the bedroom. "I hate this house," she said. "I know I've been neglecting it lately. I'd hoped we'd have our own place by now."

"Things don't always go the way we plan," I told her.

"Don't I know it! Jason won't even talk to me about when we can build now," Kathryn said. "I've been looking for a job. That's why I decided to go back to work at the feed mill. Mary Ann needs somebody and it's okay as jobs go, even though the pay isn't the greatest."

"Maybe Jason will have a good crop this year," I began.

Kathryn's eyes flashed. "Maybe he won't spend it all on stock!" she snapped.

I put my arm around her and she leaned against me for a moment.

"Baby, do you feel sick, or are you and Jason having trouble?" I asked.

She sighed. "I'm okay, Mom. I'm just in a rotten mood. I guess I'm bored and I'm sick of this house. I'm sorry. I don't mean to take it out on you." She hugged me, and for a moment I just held her. There was too much tension, so I couldn't ask her what I'd come to talk to her about.

"Tell you what," she began suddenly. "I'll straighten up here a little and do a few things I need to, and then I'll come over and we'll go into town if you have time. Will it be too late for lunch?"

"Oh, no," I told her. "We can go have a snack."

"And I need to shop for groceries," she put in. "I'll just be a little while."

I went out to my car, hurt by her hostility, upset by our recent lack of closeness, and afraid to confront her with the talk Kathy had heard.

For some reason I drove on around the loop of country roads that would take me by Kathryn's in-laws' feed mill on my way home. *Well, Kathryn was just upset,* I told myself. *She was disappointed because they haven't been able to start building. And probably Jason's been working hard and maybe he's not in the best of moods either.*

Then another thought occurred to me . . . maybe Kathryn already heard the vicious gossip and didn't know if I'd heard it yet. Of course she'd be upset!

I neared the feed mill and decided to stop and see Mary Ann. I parked in front and went inside. Mary Ann was in the office on the phone. She raised a hand in greeting as I stepped inside, then motioned me to a chair. I sank down and waited for her to finish her call. I knew that she and Clint were the same age, but she looked older. She always dressed nicely, but it was the lines around her eyes and mouth that betrayed her, telling of the years of unhappiness.

"Oh, hello, Donna." She smiled as she put down the phone. "So glad to see you. How are you?"

"I'm fine," I lied. "I was just driving past from visiting Kathryn and I thought I'd stop. We haven't seen each other in awhile."

"I'm glad you did," she said. "How is Kathryn? I haven't seen her in weeks, I guess."

I struggled to regain my composure at the shock. Kathryn had lied to me, saying she'd just come from seeing Mary Ann. "Oh she's fine," I replied. What else could I say? "She mentioned something about seeing if you could use her back here in the office."

"I'd be glad to have her," Mary Ann said. "I need more time off. There are things I'd like to do at home that I never have time for, putting in these long hours."

We talked about housework and our gardens and trying to keep up with all of that and our jobs, too. She asked about Jennifer and Randy and told me their older son's wife was expecting again and that she was looking forward to having another grandchild. I said I had to be going, and she thanked me for coming and walked to the front door with me.

In the car, I drew a long, shaky breath as I turned the key. Why did Kathryn lie to me about where she'd been? I hadn't even asked her! Unless she's hiding something . . . or unless what Kathy overheard has some truth to it! The thought tore at my heart. I decided I had to come right out and ask Kathryn . . . give her a chance to explain. I prayed to God that the story was nothing but a vicious rumor.

At home, I made us bacon and tomato sandwiches. Kathryn was longer in coming than I'd expected, but finally she drove up.

"Oh, you made lunch." She smiled. "That's nice." She slid into a chair and sipped her tea. It made her look like my little girl again for a moment.

"Kathryn, there's something I have to ask you," I made myself say.

She looked up, wide-eyed, holding her sandwich.

"There's a terrible story going around," I went on, "that you're having an affair with Jason's father."

I saw the bright spots of color come to her cheeks. "I'm what?" she asked, laughing shakily. But her eyes didn't meet mine and she was flustered and shaken, the way Kathryn always was when she lied to me. I felt sick. This wasn't the reaction I'd wanted. She wasn't saying what I wanted her to say.

"Really, Mother." She sipped nervously at her tea. "Where did you ever hear a story like that?"

"Kathryn, tell me the truth," I demanded.

"How can you believe such a thing?" she began.

"Because I don't know what to believe," I snapped. "Because I don't know why you lied to me about going to see Mary Ann this morning, but when I stopped by to see her she said she hadn't talked to you in weeks."

Her eyes met mine, black as coals in her suddenly pale face. "What right have you to check on me?"

"I wasn't checking," I protested. "Mary Ann and I happen to be friends. I hadn't seen her in awhile, so I stopped by to say hello. I didn't ask her if you'd been there this morning. She asked how you were because she said she hadn't seen you in weeks."

Kathryn hesitated. She looked angry and a little frightened, too.

"Is it true, Kathryn?" I asked.

She drew a long, quivering breath and leaned her head on her arms so her silky hair hid her face. "It isn't the way you make it sound," she whispered.

I sank down in the chair opposite her. "Then how is it?" I asked softly.

"You . . . you don't understand," she began.

"You're right about that," I agreed. "I don't understand."

"We get together and talk sometimes."

"Talk, Kathryn? Just talk?" I cried. "You mean you meet your father-in-law in secret so the two of you can be alone together to talk?"

"Something like that," she mumbled.

"If it's innocent, why doesn't he come to your house or you go to his? Why are you sneaking off together into the woods between the fields? You must know his reputation with women . . . all those stories about his cheating on Mary Ann, that over the years it's been one woman after another."

"Those things aren't really true!" she cried. "He told me he's always been accused of all sorts of things with women just because he's so good looking . . . because he still looks young. He's a really nice person. Clint would never intentionally hurt anybody!"

Just tear up all our lives and ruin my daughter's, I wanted to scream.

"You believe that?" I demanded. "You mean you've listened to that line from him? That's about the oldest line in the world . . . that people don't understand him. I suppose Mary Ann doesn't understand him, either."

"She's always working," Kathryn cried defensively. "Running that precious feed mill that was her family's business. And Jason is wrapped up in his cows and his fields and his tractors, like a little kid playing farm!"

"He happens to be trying to earn a living," I interrupted. "Isn't he?"

"Sure, sure," she said bitterly.

"Kathryn, how far have you gone with Clint?" I asked softly. I wanted her to look up at me and honestly say they'd spent time just talking. Oh, how I wanted her to say that! Instead, she put her face in her hands and started to cry.

"You mean you're really having an affair with him?" I choked.

"We didn't mean for it to happen," she sobbed. "I've been so unhappy lately, so lonely, like there's nothing important going on in my life. He understood. It just happened, that's all."

I wanted to slap her! And I wanted to put my arms around her and make everything all right. I also wanted to kill Clint Henderson! I got up and walked to the back door and stood looking out at the marigolds blooming around the pond. Tears were streaming down my face.

"You slipped off and met him in the fields," I said dully. "And the two of you went to the woods. Is that true?"

"Mama, I'm sorry," she wept. "I know it was wrong. Like I said, I didn't mean for it to happen that way . . . neither of us did. Now we don't know what to do."

"It seems as if you've already done it all," I told her wearily. "You let Clint's hired hands see you. They've already been laughing about it in town. You know how gossip is. How long is it going to be before Jason hears it, or Mary Ann, or you father? It will kill your father, or maybe he'll kill Clint. What will

Jason do? Surely you don't expect him to understand. Or do you and his father just plan to deny the whole thing?"

"I don't know," she sobbed.

"If things were that bad, if you were that unhappy, you could have left Jason and come home, at least for awhile. You could have tried working at a job—"

"I hated that job at the real estate office," she cut in. "My boss was always on my back. I couldn't please her. Clint said I shouldn't have to work."

"Like Mary Ann's never had to work?" I asked.

"She works because she wants to."

"Have you asked her?" I demanded. "Maybe she has to work at a job somewhere to keep her mind off Clint's affairs. And maybe she has to run the mill to earn a living, like Jason and his brothers do most of the farming because their father is off in the bushes!"

I went back and stood across the table from her. She looked up at me then with tearful, troubled eyes. "Oh, Kathryn, don't you see?" I asked softly. "He's probably used this same line on who knows how many women over the years. Poor, misunderstood Clint. And now he's telling you there's nothing you can do about your affair. And I doubt very much there is anything you can do to stop the stories you've started, or keep your father, me, Jason, and Mary Ann from being hurt . . . or even to straighten out your own life!"

Kathryn sat staring into space, tears running down her face. I saw that she probably realized for the first time what she'd done to herself and the rest of us. I reached for her hands and held them in mine. I wished that she were a little girl again so that

I could protect her.

"I never really thought about it," she whispered. "I felt guilty and I guess I knew it was wrong, even though I believed him. But I never thought about people finding out."

"What do you think Jason will do if he hears about it?" I asked.

She was silent a long time. I knew what Randy would do . . . he'd be furious. I'd try to keep him away from Clint until he calmed down. It might be better if Kathryn wasn't around when he heard it, either. He was a good and gentle father, but a thing like this he'd never understand! But I didn't know Jason well enough to imagine what he'd do . . . whether he'd leave, throw Kathryn out, go after his father. I just couldn't guess.

"Jason would kill me," Kathryn said softly. "He said if I ever cheated on him it would be all over, that he'd divorce me. He blames his father for cheating on his mom. He was embarrassed by some of the gossip. They get along, on the surface, but I don't think he'll ever forgive his father for some of the things in the past."

"Knowing that he feels that way, you fell for Clint's line anyway?" I gasped.

"I didn't mean to. He was so nice, so understanding. Jason and I had quarreled and I was going to leave him, but Clint talked me out of it. He found me sitting in my car crying and we talked a long time. He said he'd see that we got the new house this fall, even if he had to sign for the loan himself.

"Nothing happened that time. He was just so kind and sympathetic. He told me to meet him the next day to talk again, and I did." She shook her head.

"Several times we just talked. Then things changed. We just. . . ." She shrugged and made an empty gesture with her hands. She couldn't stop shaking. "Oh, Mama, what am I going to do?" she sobbed. "Why didn't I just leave? What am I going to do?"

I put a sweater around her shoulders and she clutched it to her, still shaking. She couldn't be cold. It was ninety degrees outside.

"Mama, I'm sorry," she said. "What am I going to do?"

"Why don't you lie down for awhile?" I suggested. "Let me have time to think."

After Kathryn curled up on her old bed in what was now my sewing room, I paced around the house. We could deny the whole thing. We could say I'd heard what I had from Kathy and asked Kathryn about it. She could say it simply wasn't true and I could stand by her, insisting that it wasn't. I could even talk to Clint. Surely he'd go along with our story if I confronted him. We could tell Randy and Jason about the gossip, but insist that there was simply no truth to it.

But even as I planned it out I knew it wouldn't be that simple. Kathryn couldn't lie that well. She'd never been able to keep secrets or even tell convincing fibs. I'd always known when she was telling me anything but the truth. And even when I'd pretended to believe her, her conscience would torture her until she told me.

It'd been the same with her father. We'd laughed about it sometimes . . . little unimportant things she'd tried to put over on us and failed. So I was sure now that even if it was better for all concerned, Kathryn would never be able to tell that lie and stick to it.

THE DARK PATH IN THE WOODS

She could move back home, after I got Randy calmed down, but that would be an admission of guilt. I wasn't sure Randy would ever understand or really forgive her, and I was sure he would never forgive Clint. And what would Jason do?

Kathryn slept. She was still asleep when Randy came home from work. I told him she hadn't felt well and had fallen asleep. Jennifer had come home from Lisa's and was watching TV. Randy told me he'd promised to help Peter work on his lawn mower and went off across the road to his house. I woke Kathryn and told her what I'd thought about denying the whole thing. She didn't reply.

"Honey, you know I'll stand by you," I told her. "No matter what. You can always come home."

"No matter how stupid I am?" she asked sadly. "No, I don't think I can come home, not right now anyway. I know you're right about everything. Maybe by some miracle Dad and Jason won't hear about it. I'll make sure Clint and I are nowhere near each other again. I'll come over here a lot and I'll look for a job. Jason and I will just have to solve our problems the best we can. But I can't move out, not right now anyway." She got up and combed her hair.

"Honey, what if Jason does hear about it?" I asked. "I can probably handle your father if it comes to that, especially if Jason doesn't know. But if Jason—"

"Maybe it won't happen," she said, "Who would tell him? It would take a lot of nerve for someone just to walk up and tell him. The farmhands wouldn't. Maybe nobody will."

She left, and I somehow finished supper and pretended everything was normal the rest of the evening.

Kathryn came to the store and spent several hours with me the next day. The day after that she stopped by after she'd been job hunting and we had sodas together. She talked about going back to work at the feed mill with Mary Ann.

"I'd like to, in a way," she said. "But I'm afraid something would happen, like somebody would say something or Clint would come in and people who have heard gossip would be reminded. And I feel awful, like I've done something terrible to Mary Ann. Mom, how could I be so dumb?"

She hadn't heard from Clint. But she hadn't been home much during the day, and anyway, she'd been the one who'd gone to him. Maybe he'd lost interest when she hadn't come around . . . or maybe he'd realized the terrible risks they'd taken.

A couple more days passed uneventfully. I started to relax and so did Kathryn. Strangely enough, it was Jennifer who heard the gossip from the kids and blurted it out to Randy and me one evening when she came in from Lisa's.

"I want you to hear what that stupid Ryan Jorgenson was saying about Kathryn!" she cried, her eyes flashing. I stretched out my hand to stop her but it was too late. "He says Kathryn's having an affair with Clint Henderson, her father-in-law. Isn't that the most ridiculous thing you ever heard? He says his brother saw her meeting him in the fields and they parked in the woods. What would she want with an old man like that? I've a good notion to tell Kathryn and let Jason beat the daylights out of Ryan for saying such a thing!"

"Oh, Jennifer," I finally managed, "that's ridiculous. Just don't pay any attention to it. The more you listen to what people say when they tell things like that, the more they talk."

"They ought to be made to shut their mouths," she fussed, "before somebody does believe it."

"Like I said, honey. . . ." My voice was calmer than I expected. "Just don't listen. Now, if you're going to take a shower before supper, you'd better get with it."

Lisa's mom had taken them to the pool, and I knew Jennifer was anxious to wash the chlorine out of her hair. She turned and hurried off.

I glanced up at Randy and his face was a frozen mask as he stood in the kitchen doorway.

"You've already heard that garbage, haven't you?" he asked.

"Yes, I heard something about it," I admitted. "I guess it's something those farm hands started."

"Who did you hear it from?" he cut in.

"Kathy heard it in the supermarket a few days ago," I told him. "She told me about it."

"Why didn't you mention it to me?" he asked, his eyes dark with anger.

"Because it's just what you said, garbage," I replied. "It's best to do as I told Jennifer. Ignore it."

"They couldn't have picked a more likely target," he said, "after all the messing around Clint's done over the years. But why link him with Kathryn?"

"Because it sounds worse that way." I sighed. "More of a scandal, almost incest. But let it go and it will die down like all the other gossip about him over the years."

"But I happen to know a lot of that gossip had

some basis," he argued. "No woman is off limits to Clint! You don't suppose. . . ."

I busily set the table. "It's a ridiculous story. As Jennifer said, what would Kathryn see in an old man like that?" I tried to shrug it off, but when I glanced up Randy's eyes were blazing. He caught my arm.

"Did you talk to her about it?" he asked.

I hesitated. To simply brush it aside as gossip had been easy, but having to look into my husband's face and answer his question . . . that wasn't easy. Randy and I had something special, and it wasn't based on lies or half-truths.

"Yes, I talked to her about it the day after I heard it," I admitted. "She wasn't feeling well that day and it upset her. She went in and lay down and fell asleep."

He still held my arm. "Is there any truth to it?" he demanded.

I lied to him then. "Of course not. He's her father-in-law . . . older than we are, Randy. I guess she stopped by once when she saw him in the fields someplace and sat in his car talking to him."

"If I thought he'd so much as made a pass at her, I'd break his neck," Randy gritted, turning away. "Why in the world would she get in his car?"

"Out of the sun." I shrugged. "He's always been nice to her."

"I know how nice Clint is!" he snapped.

"You'd think nothing of it if it was Jason and me," I told him. "He's stopped by the house a few times because he happened to be going by and I was here alone. We had coffee—"

"Of course I thought nothing of it, Donna," Randy cut in. "Not with you and Jason. With Clint, it's a different story."

"I'm sure he thinks of Kathryn as a child," I began.

"Any woman between sixteen and sixty is fair game to him!" Randy lashed out. "Between his looks and his money, he's usually had his way."

"But Kathryn is his son's wife," I argued.

"I'm not sure that would make any difference to him," he growled.

"Well, let's put that garbage aside while we have supper," I told him, and he seemed to agree.

I went to get Jennifer. "Maybe the less said around your father about that rumor, the better," I murmured.

Her eyes met mine. "Sure, Mom," she said.

We ate without further discussion. I could see that Randy was brooding a little, but I was sure I'd convinced him the rumor was just that, an empty rumor, and he wouldn't go storming off to Clint or Kathryn.

After Jennifer had gone to bed, though, he did bring it up again.

"Did Kathryn mention that gossip to Jason?" he asked.

"I don't know," I lied. "We were both angry that people would say things like that. We didn't really talk about anything else. I mean, I don't know whether she discussed it with Jason or not."

Randy got up and walked over to the open door. "I feel like I should do something about it . . . talk to Clint maybe, tell him to shut his field hands' mouths."

"How can he do that?" I asked. "People will say what they're going to say. Even if he fires them, they'll only talk that much more. I think the less attention any of us pay it, the sooner it will die down."

Randy drew a deep breath. "I guess you're right. If I thought Clint had any ideas about Kathryn . . . but I guess Kathryn has better sense than that. Everything is alright with her and Jason, isn't it?"

"As far as I know." Another lie. But I had to put his mind at ease. What could he do to help the situation? Confronting Clint or Kathryn wouldn't help anyone.

I called Kathryn the next day from the store and told her what had happened. She came over a while later looking worn out.

"Sometimes I think Jason does know." She sighed. "It seems like the harder I try to get along with him, the more he tries to pick a fight with me. He's said things that might be hints . . . asked me where I've been every day lately, if I've seen either of his folks."

"Maybe he's just tired," I told her. "I'd seen the tractor lights at night. Everybody was working into the nights to get the cotton and soybeans planted before the next rain."

"I don't know." Kathryn sank down on one of the little vanity stools I had scattered about the shop. "I feel so empty, as if nothing in my life is important. I don't know whether I love Jason anymore or if he loves me. Nothing is turning out the way we thought it would."

"You're disappointed about not getting your new house," I told her. "But, Kathryn, would that make any real difference? If you can build this fall and be in it by winter, do you think that would really make that much of a difference?"

"I've been wondering that myself," she admitted. "I thought it would. I kept looking forward to it, our own house and being able to start a family. But then I figured, after we have the house and a baby, what then? We'd still have the same old routine . . . working, trying to juggle our money. What would we have to look forward to then? Jason and I don't have any fun anymore. He's always tired and worried and his mind is off somewhere. If I work, we spend all the money, if I don't, we spend it all. What's the point in anything?"

My heart ached for my disillusioned child. How could I tell her what each of us has to learn for ourselves . . . how to enjoy life. I remembered what Randy had said about that apartment in Jackson where Kathryn had been born. We'd both hated it but we'd worked hard and scraped by.

Maybe that was one of the benefits of growing up poor. My brothers and I didn't expect toys or entertainment. We'd had a ball and bat and I had a doll my mother had made me. My play dishes were acorn cups and the ends of tin cans. But we'd all been happy. Randy's family had it worse. I guess I'd been trying to make it up to him all our lives . . . for the doing without, for losing his mother and his father. Now he could buy a fishing rod and reel or a tool of some kind and we'd scarcely feel it. He bought a new set of dishes for me simply because I was tired of the old ones.

Our kids had more than we'd ever been able to imagine having, and now our pretty daughter sat before me telling me there was nothing important to her. Had we spoiled them that badly? We hadn't meant to. We'd only meant to make them happy.

But I couldn't crawl into her head or her heart.

For me, fun was going fishing with Randy, cooking hot dogs on the backyard grill, and talking until after the sun went down. It was watching TV with him in the evening, going for a ride in the twilight, or walking across the road to see Kathy and Peter. Happiness was the lovemaking with Randy that had become as familiar as the heat from our wood stove in the winter, but just as necessary and comforting. After all these years he could still nuzzle my neck and it was like it had been when we were first married.

"I wish I could tell you, Kathryn," I said. "Sometimes that's what life is, just hard work and getting by. But if you have the right person and love each other—"

"I'm not sure I do," Kathryn cut me off. "Mom, I want to move back home and think things over, try to decide what I want to do with my life."

I was torn between wanting to tell her she'd already made that decision and not being able to turn her away if she needed us. "This was what I was afraid would happen," I told her. "When you insisted on marrying so young, I was afraid one day you'd regret it."

"I wish you'd stopped me," she said.

"We couldn't." I sighed. "If we'd refused to give our consent, you'd have run away with him."

She nodded. "I know. Sometimes I can't remember how I felt then. We were so sure. But now everything has fallen apart."

I didn't know what to say. Maybe if she did move back home that she could finish growing up, find herself.

"Whatever you decide, honey," I told her. "I wish I could do it for you, but I can't. I guess you'll have to find your own way and make your own decisions."

"I know, Mom." She got up and hugged me.

"Whatever you decide, we'll stand by you," I reminded her, never doubting that Randy would feel the same as I did. She was still our precious daughter.

I didn't mention Kathryn's visit to Randy that evening. He came in tired, and his back was hurting the way it did sometimes. He didn't complain, but I could tell by the tired way he walked and the lines that deepened on either side of his mouth. I poured him a glass of tea, and he sprawled out on the sofa. Jennifer was going to a movie with Lisa and her mother, and I'd given her money to treat them to a hamburger. After she left, I fixed our plates and Randy and I ate in the living room.

"I guess I'm getting old, Donna." Randy grinned. "These long shifts kills me."

"I wish production would slack off," I told him, "so you could get a rest once in awhile."

When there were layoffs, we worried and prayed for production to pick up at the factory where he'd worked for over fifteen years. When he was tired and they were working twelve-hour shifts, I wished for a layoff.

"We're never satisfied, are we?" Randy asked, reading my mind.

I went over and sat on the floor and rested my head against him. He started to stroke my hair.

"I worry about you," I told him.

"You better," he said. "I'm the best you could get."

I laughed. "You're feeling better already. Now I don't feel sorry for you anymore." I started to get up, but he held me there by him.

"We're lucky, Donna."

"I know." I wondered if it was something special we did or just luck that kept us together and happy. "Maybe we just don't know any better," I said.

He chuckled, and I got up and put our dishes in the kitchen. The phone rang and I picked it up.

"Donna, this is Jason." His voice was so harsh I wouldn't have recognized it. "Kathryn wants to move back home. You better come get her before I kill her and my father, too!" The receiver slammed on the other end.

"Oh, no!" I cried.

Randy sprang up from the sofa. "Donna, what is it?" he asked.

"That was Jason," I told him. "He said to come get Kathryn before . . . before he killed her and Clint both!"

Randy was out the door before I could finish, and I ran after him. "Randy, wait!" I cried.

I managed to scramble into the pickup before he spun out of the driveway. "I'll kill him if he touches her," he swore. "He better not have laid a hand on her."

I wanted to calm him down so he wouldn't be so worked up when we got there, but my heart pounded in my chest and my tongue felt like cotton in my mouth. What if we were too late?

"Randy, please try to hold your temper," I pleaded when we rounded the curve by their house. I could see Jason sitting on the front steps.

Randy slammed on the brakes and was out of the

truck all in one motion, standing before Jason by the time I reached his side. Jason was crying.

"You better not have touched her," Randy threatened.

"I wanted to break her neck," Jason choked. "But I couldn't!" His fists were balled at his sides. "My brother told me a week ago what people were saying, and he told me then not to lose my cool . . . not to believe it. I didn't want to believe it. Lord knows I didn't! But tonight when I came in, she was packing and said she was leaving me and moving home. I asked her if it was true, and she admitted it!" He slammed one fist against his leg. "She admitted it! Why didn't she lie to me?"

Randy drew a long breath, and I brushed by him and ran into the house. Kathryn sat on the bed, frozen among the boxes and suitcases she'd been packing.

"I told him I wanted to move home for awhile and he went berserk," she said. "He started slamming things around and he asked me if what he'd heard about his father and me was true." She was sobbing so hard she couldn't finish.

"And you admitted it?" I asked.

She nodded. "I tried to explain . . . to say I was sorry. . . ."

"We ought to leave you here!" Randy spoke from behind me. "Trash! Clint Henderson's trash and that's what you are! I ought to kill him and save Jason the trouble—"

"Randy, please," I pleaded. "She was wrong, I know that. But she's our daughter. We have to stand by her. Clint will pay in his own way for everything he's done."

"He'll burn in hell!" Randy shouted.

"Probably," I agreed. "Where's Jason?"

"On the porch." He stepped by me and jerked Kathryn to her feet, then reached back to slap her.

"Randy, no!" I screamed. "That won't do any good! Please!"

Kathryn cringed, terrified, between us.

"It would sure make me feel better," he said hoarsely as he flung her on the bed and strode out.

"Then go hit Clint Henderson!" I called after him. "That's what he deserves!" I turned to Kathryn. "Get your things together. I'll drive your car."

I helped her carry her things out. Randy and Jason were standing out under a tree. I saw Randy reach out and touch Jason's arm in a gesture of comfort. My heart was breaking for us all.

Finally, we had what belongings of Kathryn's we were taking and I put her in the car. I went over to where Randy and Jason were.

"I'll take her home," I said. "Jason, I'm sorry."

He stared at his feet. "It's not your fault, Donna. I'm sorry I yelled at you on the phone."

"I know." I put my arm around him. "Do you want Randy to stay here with you for awhile?"

He nodded. "If you don't mind. He's making more sense than I am about this whole thing. I don't have anybody else right now—" His voice broke.

The rage was gone from Randy's face. He was still angry and sad and hurt. I put my hand on his shoulder and he patted mine. "Go along, Donna. Get her home and in bed or somewhere before I come in. I don't want to see her tonight," he said.

I took Kathryn home and gave her a sedative and put her to bed, leaving most of her things in the car.

Then I called Brenda and asked her to take my turn in the store the next day.

Randy came in later and sank down on the sofa. "I took Jason to his brother Jeremy's," he said wearily. "Jeremy talked to him a week ago, trying to keep this from happening. He'll stand by him till Jason gets himself under control. Then I stopped by Clint's."

"What happened?" I gasped.

"I told him what he was . . . that he didn't deserve decent sons like he has. He told me not to make a big thing out of it. Imagine that! He ruined his son's marriage, ruined my daughter, and he told me not to make a big thing out of it! I told him to never let me catch him around any of my family again and let it go at that."

I sank down in a chair.

"Is Kathryn asleep?" he asked.

"I don't know. She's in bed," I told him.

"Didn't we teach her right from wrong?" he asked. "Donna, didn't we do that? I told her when she started dating not to cheapen herself. I heard you tell her to value herself, to be sure the man she loves was worthy of her. Jason is a good boy, that's why we gave in and let them get married."

"Who knows why?" I sighed. "Randy, I've been over it and over it. She made a mistake. She was wrong and she listened to Clint say things she wanted to hear. She let herself believe what she wanted to instead of the truth. She made her decisions. She'll have to pay for them."

"But how it hurts!" Randy said, and suddenly he was crying. I went over to him "Our little girl," he choked.

"I know," I whispered, and I was crying, too.

"I wish Kathryn were back in diapers!" Randy said.

"That wouldn't change anything. She'll still have to grow up and make her own mistakes," I told him.

"Maybe we could have kept her from making this one. Maybe we shouldn't let Jennifer go off so much," he said.

"She only goes out with Lisa and her mother, people we know. It's the same as Kathryn did. We have to trust her. She'll make mistakes, but never, I hope, anything like this."

"I hope not." Randy rubbed his hands over his face.

Kathryn looked for a job, but there wasn't much in our little town in the way of office jobs. It was June and school had been out a couple of weeks. The new graduates had already made the rounds. And gossip made its rounds quickly in our town, too, so maybe that had something to do with it as well. Kathryn looked pale and withdrawn, and I knew she probably wasn't making much of an impression on the employers she did speak with. She went to Montgomery, a larger town about twenty-five miles away, and put in applications there. But nothing came of them, either.

"I'm going to start on the factories," she said finally one day when she returned.

I ached for her. A factory job wouldn't be so bad. It was the beaten look she had that hurt me. I'd taken her back to the house where she and Jason had lived to get the rest of her things. She only took her clothes and personal items, leaving her pretty dishes in the cupboards, bed linens on the bed, towels in the closet. Well, it wasn't as if anyone would be moving in there or doing anything with her things. Jason's clothes and personal things were gone, too, so apparently he wasn't staying there, either.

One day at the bank I ran into Clint. He looked away and hurried off, before everything had happened he'd have stopped and talked in his loud, friendly way.

Kathryn was out the day Mary Ann came over. She hadn't been to our house since before the wedding and I was shocked to see her at the door.

"Hello, Donna," she said. "Can I talk to you and Kathryn?"

"Of course, come in," I said stiffly, but still trying to be friendly. "Kathryn's out job hunting, but come in. Would you like a glass of tea?"

"Yes, I would." She followed me to the kitchen and sat down at the table. She looked tired, but Mary Ann had looked tired as far back as I could remember. "I wanted to come talk to you," she said as I poured our tea. "I wanted to say I'm sorry about everything that's happened."

"I am too, Mary Ann," I told her. "But none of it was your fault."

"No, nor yours," she said. "My daughter-in-law Janet first told me what she'd heard about Kathryn and Clint. I'd hoped that it wasn't true, but over the years . . . well, I'm sure you know. Everybody's heard about Clint's involvement with various women. He was good looking and had a way with women, and some thought we were rich, which we're not. They made it easy for him. I'm not excusing him, of course, but maybe you can understand a little bit. People have faults, big or small. Some men drink and some gamble, and with Clint it's women."

I couldn't understand her attitude, but I let her talk. She seemed to need that.

"I was going to leave him when I first learned he was cheating on me," she went on. "But I was expecting our oldest son and he promised it would never happen again." She sighed wearily. "But by the time it did, Jeremy was on the way.

"Then my father died and Clint and I took over running the feed mill, paying off my brothers and sisters who didn't want it anyway. He inherited land and we bought up more, and he was a good provider . . . and good to me and the children except for that one thing. If I'd left him, we'd have had to divide the property that he intended to go to the boys.

"He was proud of the boys and took them with him a lot . . . to the fields, fishing, hunting, into town. He taught them to use the farm equipment and had them farming as soon as they were big enough. They liked that, the same as he always has. I couldn't deprive them of the closeness they had with their father, and I couldn't part with them myself. And Clint would always say he was sorry." She closed her eyes, as if against the memories. "That his flings meant nothing, that he needed me."

She opened her eyes again. "I don't expect anyone to understand that, but I believe him in a way. He never wanted a divorce . . . never seemed to want anything lasting with any of those women. I didn't think, I mean, I never would've believed that he'd get involved that way with one of our daughters-in-law. When Janet told me, I refused to believe it. Clint is big on family, wanting his sons and their wives and children around a lot for holidays and family reunions. Now they've all turned against him."

"What else could he expect?" I asked. "Kathryn was wrong, of course, but if he hadn't—"

Mary Ann held up a hand. "You're absolutely right," she agreed. "Kathryn is hardly more than a child. I love her. That's why I'm here. You mentioned she might want to come back to work at the mill, and I'd like that. I want her to know that I don't blame her too much for what happened."

"She feels terrible about it." I sighed. "She's afraid she can't work with you after what's happened."

"Will you send her to see me . . . or bring her? I don't blame her. She's far from being the first fool. And in a way we're all fools, somehow or another. I wish she'd come back to work for me at the mill . . . if she wants to work."

"She needs to work," I said. "I'll talk to her."

"How is she?" Mary Ann asked.

"Sorry and hurt and ashamed," I told her. "Mixed up."

She nodded.

I asked about Jason. She looked bleak and said, "He works all the time, every day. He's staying with Jeremy and Janet. They've always been close. He won't talk to Clint at all . . . told him to stay away from wherever he's working. He hasn't talked to me about any plans of any sort. I don't think he talks much to anybody right now."

I promised I'd tell Kathryn how Mary Ann felt about wanting her back at the mill, then I thanked her for coming. I didn't know whether I could have come and bared my feelings like that if our positions had been reversed. I admired her for that.

When Kathryn came home, I told her about Mary Ann's visit and what had been said. She sat at the table with her head in her hands.

"I guess I'll go see her. I owe her that. I don't see how she can help but hate me, though," she whispered.

"As she said, you're not the first fool," I told her.

She lifted her head and blinked back tears. "One of many. I don't know whether that makes it better or worse."

"I don't know, either," I agreed.

She traced a pattern on the tabletop. "Mom, what would you have done if Dad had been like Clint?"

"I don't know," I told her honestly. "I really don't know whether I'd have stayed with him or divorced him. I'd probably have killed him." It was half an attempt at a joke, but neither of us smiled.

"You know, I've tried to think what I'd have done if it had been Jason," she said. "And I can't decide, either. I guess I'd do what he's done. I'd have moved home and never wanted to see him again."

The next day Kathryn went to see Mary Ann. When she came back I could tell she'd been crying. She said she was going back to work in the office there.

"Clint never goes there," she said. "Mary Ann really runs it herself. And Jason only used to come in to see me while I worked there before. If there's talk . . . well, I guess I'll have to live with that. It's a job and I feel like Mary Ann really wants me there."

The summer wore on. Kathryn worked steady. Weekends she worked around the house and yard, silently doing tasks she'd hated and complained about while growing up.

She seldom had much to say, and kept to herself a lot. Some girlfriends called or came by, but she seemed to cut them off. She'd spend time with Jennifer, helping her with sewing or cooking or something, but even then she was quiet. There was no more giggling or joking around.

At first, Jennifer resented Kathryn for moving back. "She did what they said she did, didn't she?" Jennifer asked. "I don't see how she could do something like that!"

"Jennifer, I'm going to discuss this with you once and only once," I told her. "Don't judge your sister. When you're her age, if you've made no mistakes of your own, if you've never hurt anybody and been sorry, never hurt the people who love you, then you can judge her, but not until then."

She stared down at her bare feet on the kitchen floor. "I guess I see what you mean," she said. "I'm sorry, Mama."

Kathryn went to her room early every evening and stayed out of Randy's way as much as possible. He acted as if she wasn't there, speaking to her only when he couldn't avoid it.

It hurt to see them so far apart. They'd been so close. We'd joked about Kathryn being his and Jennifer being mine. He was the one she'd gone to for help with her schoolwork, and often with her problems. I noticed that he was stricter now with Jennifer than he'd been before, wanting her home earlier, being sure of where she was and who she was with when she wasn't at home. Our house was too quiet. Even when Randy had been dog tired and his back ached, he'd never been too tired to joke around with the girls.

Is this where it ends for us? I wondered. *Where love and family stops being fun?* Oh, we still loved each other. Randy and I were still lovers and friends, but some of the spirit seemed to have gone out of our lives.

Kathryn offered to pay rent, and I discussed it with Randy.

"She eats so little," I told him. "I'd give anything to see her eat a decent meal. And she helps me so much around the house. I hate to take anything."

"Tell her to put it in the bank," he said abruptly. "We don't need her money. Maybe she'll want to go to college or something later on."

I told her.

"What I should do is get a place of my own," Kathryn said quietly. "I think my being here just reminds you and Dad of how much I hurt you."

I put my arms around her. "Oh, honey, not yet anyway. Stay with us for awhile. Sometimes things take time to heal. You're not yourself."

She hugged me back and tried to smile. Often when she didn't talk, I noticed that she'd have tears in her eyes. She'd get up and leave the room when sentimental songs came on the radio, and I'd hear her crying in her room at night.

For awhile people asked about Kathryn and Jason splitting up, wanting to know if they were going to get a divorce. I turned them off, telling them that was Kathryn's business, not mine. Nobody mentioned to me what had happened between Clint and Kathryn, but then I didn't give anyone much chance, changing any subject that might lead to a discussion about my daughter.

Fall came and Jennifer went back to school. At least the summer heat was over. Cotton trailers and trucks full of beans passed the store. The men in the fields worked every day and into the night . . . picking cotton, getting the beans, baling hay. It had been a good year.

On my days off and during the evenings, Kathryn and I put up tomatoes, green beans, and okra from my garden. I remembered how arrogantly she'd said she wasn't bothering with a garden, but now she helped willingly.

Once we met one of her girlfriends in a grocery store. The friend had a baby in her arms. Kathryn and I fussed over the baby, and as we walked away Kathryn sighed.

"Sometimes I wish I had a baby," she said.

A baby to suffer through this, too? I thought to myself.

"Oh, not really, I guess," she said quickly. "We couldn't have afforded one and I'd feel bad that it didn't have a home and parents together. And I know I wasn't ready to raise a child. I guess I was still too much of a kid myself."

Then I asked her if she'd seen or heard from Jason.

She shook her head. "No, it's strange. I know he's working the fields all around the feed mill, but we never see each other. I've thought about calling him to see if he wants me to get the divorce, but I just keep putting it off."

We heard things. Kathy saw Jason uptown and said that he'd lost weight. Clint had a heart attack. He was expected to recover, but Kathryn worked longer hours so that Mary Ann could stay at the hospital.

Finally, I saw Jason at the bank. Kathy was right. He'd lost a lot of weight and was lean and hard now, instead of stocky and a little chubby, the way he'd been.

"How are you, Donna?" he asked.

"Fine," I told him. "You doing alright?"

He nodded, then stopped beside me. "How's Kathryn?" he asked.

I hesitated. What could I say? That she cried a lot? "She's okay, I guess," I faltered. "She works at the mill, you know."

"Yeah, I know. I wonder, do you think she'd see me?" he asked.

"I really don't know how she feels about you or a lot of things," I said honestly. "She doesn't talk much. If you want to see her or talk to her, why don't you call her?"

He nodded again. "Maybe I will."

I didn't mention to Kathryn that I'd seen him. I really didn't know how she felt toward Jason . . . whether seeing him would hurt her more, or if things could ever be patched up between them. I just didn't know. If only he hadn't said maybe he'd call.

Days passed and he didn't call, so I was glad I hadn't mentioned it to Kathryn.

Then on Sunday he did call. Kathryn talked briefly on the phone and then came into the kitchen where I was.

"Jason called. He asked me if I'd go for a ride and talk over some things with him," she said.

"Are you going to?" I asked.

She nodded. "If only I could keep from crying,"

she wailed. "I don't even know what I'm crying about . . . for myself, for him, or for our plans that didn't turn out. I just don't know."

Tears welled up in her eyes, and I held her in my arms and stroked her hair.

When Jason came over, she walked out to the pickup. I remembered how she'd run to meet him, during those turbulent days when she was demanding we let them get married.

Randy and I were in bed before they came in, and the next morning Kathryn and I both had to go to work, so we had no chance to talk. That evening she helped me with the dishes.

"Jason asked me to come back to him," she said quietly.

"What are you going to do?" I asked.

"I don't know."

We were silent, doing the dishes and straightening the kitchen. When we were finished, I sat down at the table.

"I don't know what to do," she said. "He was the only boy I ever loved. I never even really had a crush on anybody before him. I'm so alone without him."

"But that's not enough," I told her.

"I know." Her eyes were dark and brooding. "He says nothing has any purpose without me. He's lonely, too. I told him that wasn't enough." She laughed emptily and touched my hand. "Like mother, like daughter?"

I held her hand. I'd never thought we were very much alike, Kathryn and I. She'd always been so bright and happy-go-lucky. Jennifer was my serious one, my worrier, and the one who worked hard at things and persevered.

"I wish I was like you," Kathryn said, as if reading my thoughts. "I wish I was strong and good. You've always held us all together and you love Daddy so much. I mean, you put your arms around him and you kiss him and rub his back, fix his meals, and put up with all his moods. I never saw all that until after I moved back."

"He does the same for me," I told her. "He's good to me."

"Sure," she agreed. "But I thought a man was supposed to be that way . . . make the living, solve the problems, all the things Daddy did. But I never really noticed what you did. You were just my mother, there when I called or needed you."

"I should have grabbed your hair and said, 'Now pay attention!'" I laughed.

"Maybe you should have," she said wistfully. "No, you can't see it until you're ready. You taught me to cook and keep house. But I think I played house until I got tired of it, and then I didn't know what else to do. I wanted Jason to give me a house, things. I never gave much myself though . . . never thought about how I could make our lives better at the time."

"Do you think you and Jason could make it work now?" I asked.

She studied her hands. "I wish we could. But I don't know whether he can really forgive me. If he can't, there would always be that between us. Every time we had a problem or a disagreement, it would crop up."

She was right, of course.

"I guess only time will tell about that. He said he'd pick me up after work tomorrow evening," Kathryn said.

THE DARK PATH IN THE WOODS

I talked to Randy and told him what Kathryn had said. "Honey, she needs you," I told him. "You were always so close. She's still your daughter. She still loves you and she needs for you to forgive her and talk to her. Maybe you could talk to Jason, too. He told her he wants her back, but if he can't forgive her it will never work."

Randy was silent.

"She didn't intentionally hurt us," I told him. "She hurt herself most of all."

He just nodded.

Later, Randy asked Kathryn to help him carry in wood for the heater, and they stayed out by the woodpile for a long time, talking. When they came inside, Randy had his arm around her and they both looked as if they'd been crying.

Soon, Clint was out of the hospital and Mary Ann gave Kathryn time off, Jason wasn't so pushed with fieldwork and they spent some afternoons together. She seemed happy, though I could tell she was still worried and uncertain. Randy and Jason went fishing together one Saturday, and they were all cooking fish when I got home from the store.

Kathryn pulled me aside. "Mom, I'm going home with Jason tonight," she said, looking as if she expected me to stop her.

"You're still married to him. I guess you can spend the night with him if you want," I told her.

"I wish I could be sure things would work out," she told me, worried.

"I wish I could be, too, honey," I said.

"He's so sure we can work everything out," she said.

"Then maybe you can." Oh, how I wanted to see

her happy again!

They left together that evening, and the next day they came back after her clothes.

It's been a year since then . . . a good year. Kathryn and Jason seem to have worked things out. They both seem happy. They decided to remodel the old house they'd been living in instead of building a new one. Kathryn still works at the feed mill with Mary Ann.

Nobody sees much of Clint. Kathryn says Jason has forbidden him to come to the house, and they never go to Mary Ann and Clint's place. When the families get together, it's at one of the boys' houses and Clint isn't asked. Mary Ann seems to understand.

Kathryn is still quieter than she used to be and only rarely do I hear her giggle with Jennifer. Jason doesn't smile as quickly as he used to, either. He's good to Kathryn, and he's become very close to Randy and me . . . he'll bring a pile of wood for us or come by and ask Randy to go fishing.

Last week Kathryn came to the store.

"Mama, tell me about having a baby," she said, smiling and crying at the same time. She'd been to the doctor and he'd confirmed her pregnancy.

"I'm so happy about it, and Jason wants it so much," she bubbled. "But, Mama, I'm going to need you!"

I held her close. "You'll do fine," I told her. "You'll give us a beautiful grandchild."

And as I held her, I hoped she'd never hurt for her child the way Randy and I had for her . . . that terrible helpless, can't-make-it-better ache! But I didn't mention it. The past was past, and I knew the baby would bring us all happiness.   THE END

LOVERS AGAIN AFTER 5 YEARS APART

The bell over the motel office door jingled noisily, and I turned from the window where I'd been staring out at the dirty springtime snow. For a moment I didn't recognize the man hunched in the doorway, wearing only half enough clothes for the bitter cold day.

"Kimberly?" he asked.

I recognized him as soon as he spoke my name. He was the only one who ever called me that. To everyone else I was Kim.

"Marcus!" I could barely whisper his name.

For five years I'd wondered what it would be like when we met again, if we met again, because in all that time I'd never heard one word from him except what he'd told his folks to tell me.

He came inside and let the door close behind him. He'd changed so much! The past five years he spent in the state penitentiary had aged him. He was very thin, and his eyes were like burned holes in his face.

I backed away, around the end of the counter, searching for words.

"I won't hurt you, Kimberly. I won't cause you any trouble," he said, but his expression was as threatening as the dark sky outside. "I just want to see my daughter."

"She's not here," I stammered. "She's in her day-care center."

"When can I see her?" he asked.

I glanced at my watch. It was a little past noon. "The children nap from twelve-thirty until two," I said, more to myself than to him. Madison loved being with other children. She'd complain if I picked her up before three o'clock.

"You do pick her up in the evening, don't you?" he asked.

"Of course!" I snapped. "I usually pick her up about three."

"I don't know what time it is," he said quietly.

"It's only a little after noon," I told him.

He turned toward the door. "I'll wait outside."

"It's too cold," I said. "Stay in here where it's warm. Would you like some coffee?"

He went over by the fireplace and glanced at the coffeepot on its stand behind the counter. "No, I don't need anything," he said.

I poured us each a cup of coffee anyway, trying to regain my composure and get control of my churning emotions. I'd loved Marcus so much, but that had been so long ago it seemed like something that had happened to someone else. And this man was a stranger.

I set his coffee on the corner of the counter where he could reach it. Then I sipped my own. I noticed his fingers trembled as he picked up the cup and set it back down.

"Marcus, I had no idea that you were coming," I began, trying to ease the terrible tension between us.

"No idea I was out?" He arched one eyebrow. "Seven years to life! I was a model prisoner." His tone was angry and bitter. "Time off for good behavior, and it helped that they're so crowded they're glad to turn some of us loose to get rid of us. I was paroled last week."

"I'm glad for you."

"Yeah, me, too." He picked up his coffee cup and sipped at it, then set it back down. "I served over five years for somebody else."

Marcus had maintained all through his trial that he was innocent of shooting Lou Amos in the holdup of his grocery store. But it was proven that his gun was the murder weapon.

"Are you married?" he asked.

I stared at him. "Of course not. You and I aren't even divorced."

He looked surprised. "I figured your father or Justin Williams would have gotten you a hush-hush annulment or divorce. Mom said she thought you had married again."

"I don't know why she'd think that," I said.

I looked out the window. It had started to snow again, little peppery snowflakes swirling in the cold wind. Ed and Maggie Smith, the motel owners, had driven down to Springville at the foot of the mountain to shop. I worried about them getting caught in a snowstorm halfway up the mountain on their way back to Mountain's Peak.

Marcus had his back to me, holding his hands out to the warmth of the fire. I saw that his shoes were worn, his trousers were threadbare, and he had only a light jacket on. Everything looked too big for him, and I guessed they were his brother Fredrick's clothes. I didn't know what to say to him.

"Mom said she didn't know where you were," Marcus said softly, "that you just came by once in awhile. But Fredrick's wife Lisa, said you lived in Mountain's Peak. I asked at a grocery store. They said you lived at this motel. Do you work here?"

"Oh, yes, I work here at the motel and at the restaurant over there," I told him. I motioned to the log structure a short distance away. I wanted to tell him that his mother did know where I was, where I'd been all this time. But I didn't want to argue with him.

"Kimberly, I want you to know I understand why you feel the way you do toward me," he said quietly. "I know it was too long to ask any woman to wait."

You could've asked! I wanted to scream at him. *You could've written. You could've let me come see you.*

Outside, the snow swirled thicker. "I'm afraid it's going to blizzard," I told Marcus, feeling the beginning of panic starting to grip me.

I didn't care if it snowed ten feet deep or if the wind blew a hundred miles an hour . . . if Madison and I were together. But the thought of our being separated in a storm was unbearable. I reached over and turned on the sputtering radio just in time to get a weather bulletin. Snow and high winds were expected for the mountain passes. That was it. I'd go get Madison whether she was ready to leave her friends in the nursery or not.

"The weather is going to get worse," I told Marcus. "I'm going to go get Madison."

He turned and his eyes searched my face. "What do you do about the office?" he asked.

"Leave it," I told him. There was no money in the office since it was the middle of the week. What we had to make change with was in a desk drawer in the Smiths' living room behind a locked door from the office. Another door from the office led into the two-room apartment I shared with Madison. I opened the door and pulled my heavy coat from a hook and started putting it on.

"I want to see her," Marcus said.

I stood looking at him. "All right, but—" I hesitated.

"But what?" he asked.

"I told her that her father was dead," I blurted. "I told everyone that when I first came up here. I had to tell her what everyone else believes."

"I guess you wished that," he said bitterly.

"I didn't," I told him angrily. "But I had to have a job. I had to make a life for Madison and myself."

"I guess it would be better for you both if people didn't know about me," he agreed.

"I don't know what to tell Madison. I guess I could tell her you're a friend," I said, worried.

Marcus frowned and didn't say anything.

"Do you want to go with me to pick her up?" I asked.

He nodded.

I had a heavy old jacket of Ed's that I wore to carry in wood and to empty ashes. I took it from its hook behind the door and held it out to Marcus.

"Wear this. You'll be warmer," I told him.

He hesitated and then took the coat.

"Whose is this?" he asked, noticing that it was a man's.

"Mine. It was Ed's. He and Maggie own the motel. They've been like family to Madison and me," I said.

"That's good," he mumbled. "You want me to drive you there? I borrowed Fredrick's truck to come up here."

"My car has snow tires," I told him.

Marcus followed me out to my old car and smiled for the first time.

"This is the car your folks gave you in high school!" he exclaimed.

"Yeah." I laughed. "Well, as long as it runs, I couldn't see any reason to change cars."

"I thought your dad would've gotten you a newer one," he said.

"I seldom see my parents," I told him.

My car started on the second try and I drove through the slushy streets and swirling snow.

"I can keep Madison with me most of the time I'm working, and the Smiths love to keep her, too, because they don't have any grandchildren," I told Marcus, making conversation to fill the awkward silence between us. "But she gets too lonesome and wants to play with children. I guess it's best for her. She's spoiled, I'm afraid. She's been the center of my life and then the Smiths just dote on her." I was tempted to add that I let them, since her own grandparents showed no interest.

"I've always wondered what she looked like," Marcus admitted.

I turned, surprised. "I gave your mom pictures to send to you," I said.

His eyes searched mine angrily, until I had to look back at the street in front of the car.

"I never got any pictures," he said coldly.

I wanted to pursue the subject, but we were at the nursery and I met another mother as I got out of my car.

"Hi!" she called. "Thought I'd better get Benny before it gets too bad to drive."

"Me, too," I agreed. "Even though Madison isn't going to like being picked up in the middle of the day."

Marcus had gotten out of the car and walked beside me. I couldn't help wanting him to see Madison. I wanted to tell him that she was beautiful, that she seemed to have gotten the best of both of us. Well, let him see for himself the daughter his mother had told me he didn't want to hear about!

Madison was carrying her plate to the kitchen when we stepped inside. She made a little puckered face. "Oh, Mom!" she said.

I glanced at Marcus. His eyes had followed mine and he was looking at Madison. I tried to imagine how it would be seeing her for the first time.

Madison put her dish away and came over to us. "It's not time. I could stay—" she began.

"No, honey," I told her as I got her coat from the rack. "It's snowing hard out. I'm getting you home while I still can."

She sighed, resigned, and slid her arms into her coat. She was looking curiously at Marcus.

"This is Marcus," I told her. "He's an old friend."

She nodded thoughtfully.

Marcus knelt beside her. "You're Madison," he said softly, his voice husky. "You're a pretty little girl."

She smiled at his compliment.

"Can I carry you to the car?" he asked.

She nodded, and Marcus scooped her up and turned toward the door. I waved at Dawn, who ran the nursery. She smiled and raised one hand.

Madison scrambled onto the seat between us and we rode most of the way home in silence. Marcus's eyes never left Madison's face.

"Do you live in Springville?" Madison asked him. Everybody we knew who didn't live in Mountain's Peak lived in Springville.

"Yes, yes, I do," he told her.

"How come you never visited us before?" she asked.

"We hadn't seen each other in a long time," I told her. "Marcus was up here and happened to stop by the motel and he wanted to see my pretty little girl."

She giggled at my flattery.

Ed and Maggie were getting out of the car at the motel when we got there.

"There's Papa and Gram!" Madison cried. "Where have they been?"

"Shopping in Springville," I said.

"They probably brought me something," she began excitedly. I caught the sleeve of her coat.

"Madison, listen to me! They probably did, but you don't ask. You wait until they give it to you and then say thank you. Remember? Don't ask," I stressed.

She looked a little defiant, but then she nodded. I parked the car and Marcus opened the door. Madison was off and running toward the Smiths' side of the motel.

"I'm sorry." I sighed. "They spoil her so badly, but I haven't the heart to stop them."

"Kimberly, she's beautiful," Marcus said in a strangled voice. He followed me from the car and stood uncertainly in front of the motel door.

"Come inside," I told him.

I opened the door to my living room and took off my coat. Ed came in from their side and I introduced Marcus as a friend from high school. Maggie and Madison came into the office. Madison clutched a new pink sweater, coloring books, and a puzzle.

"Spoiling her some more, aren't you?" I smiled.

"Well, you know, Kim. We can't help it." Maggie glanced curiously at Marcus.

I introduced him the same as I had to Ed.

"Do you live in Springville?" Maggie asked.

"Yes." Marcus nodded, obviously uncomfortable.

"I'm going to warm us some soup," I told Maggie.

"I ate already," Madison said. "Papa's going to help me with my puzzle."

"Could you make it later?" I asked him. "I'd like to have her with me for a little while."

"Sure. Go with your mama," Ed told Madison. "We'll get to that puzzle later."

She followed Marcus and I into our apartment and I closed the door.

"Have you had lunch?" I asked Marcus hanging up our coats. He didn't look like he'd had a square meal in a month.

"I'm fine," he mumbled.

"I'm starved," I told him.

Madison had gotten out crayons and was starting

in on the new coloring book sitting at the coffee table.

"You can talk to her while I fix something," I told him.

I went to the kitchenette and warmed soup and then scrambled eggs for sandwiches.

An eternity before, Marcus and I had dreamed of a home of our own where we could be together, I remembered. We'd never had one meal, or one night, in our own place. Suddenly tears swam in my eyes and I turned away to brush at them with a dish-towel, swallowing the lump in my throat and forcing myself not to think of any of that.

"Come eat with me," I told Marcus. "Madison, bring your things here."

"I'm busy, Mom," she objected.

Marcus came over and sat down. I set a bowl of soup before him and the plate of sandwiches.

"You shouldn't have bothered," he said.

"No bother," I told him, trying to sound bright and friendly, but my voice cracked. I sat down in my chair and tears spilled over and ran down my face.

"I'm sorry." Marcus reached out to touch my arm, but I knew if he did I'd crumble all to pieces.

"I'm okay." I swallowed hard and shook my head, wiping away the tears. "Just got sentimental there for a minute. Go ahead and eat."

I regained my composure and I saw Marcus struggle for his, but then he ate hungrily, even letting me refill his bowl for him.

Such polite strangers, I thought as I cleared away the dishes. Marcus had gone back to watch Madison.

I went over and sat on the sofa, listening to them

talk about the picture Madison was coloring. She finished and looked up at me.

"Mommy, Papa wants me to do the puzzle with him," she pleaded. "He's waiting for me in the office."

My eyes met Marcus's and he nodded.

"All right, honey," I told her. She hurried out the door that opened into the motel office.

"They seem like good people," Marcus said.

"They are," I told him. "I came up here to work the summer . . . after you left. Ed had had a heart attack and they kept me on, even though by then they knew I was going to have a baby. They were like family. After I had Madison, it was more so. Their only son drowned when he was fifteen. They adore Madison like a grandchild. They do spoil her terribly, but sometimes I think she's their entire life. They put up a swing set for Madison, made her a sandbox, bought her a wading pool. Each Christmas the tree is just for her. Every time they go to Springville they bring her gifts. But who else has Madison got?" I sighed. "My folks have no interest it her." I didn't mention his.

He nodded. "Well, I'm glad you have people like that."

I got up to put more wood in the heater. "Are you living with your folks?" I asked.

"Until I can get on my feet."

"How are they?" I asked.

His eyes searched mine as if surprised that I'd ask. "Old . . . not well. Dad's paralyzed from his last stroke."

"I'm sorry," I murmured.

"When did you see them last?" he asked.

I tried to think. "Oh, it's been a year or more. Let's see . . . it was the summer before last."

"The summer before last?" he cried, jumping to his feet. "A year and a half ago?"

"Yes," I told him, shocked at his outburst. "I never felt particularly welcome there. Oh, your mom wanted to see Madison, but just to see her. They didn't seem to want any ties."

"What about the money?" he demanded.

I didn't know what he was talking about and backed away from him. "What money?" I asked.

"The money I sent you, Kimberly," he said angrily. "I sent you every cent I could manage! Every single month! I had them sell my bike right after the trial so you could have the money."

"Now wait a minute!" I cried. "I never got any money from anybody. You told me to stay away from you and not let anybody know we were married until the trouble was over. I came up here and got a job, and I called your sister Nicole and told her where I was. She said she'd tell your mom. They knew we'd been seeing each other, but I didn't tell them we were married or about the baby. And I never got any money from anybody!"

"Didn't they give you the money from my bike, the money I sent?" His eyes flashed.

I shook my head. "I called them after you were convicted and asked for your address."

He swore and slammed a fist into his other hand. He walked over to a window and stood looking out with his back to me. After a minute he turned to face me. "Go on. Did they give you my address?"

"No." I sank down on the edge of the sofa. "At first your mother said that they didn't know where you were . . . that you'd said you'd let them know. I kept calling them, and after a couple times she said that you'd told them not to give me your address . . . that you wanted to break it off with me."

Marcus's face was pale. "Go on," he told me when I paused.

"Well, that's when I told her about the baby. Madison was due in a couple months then. Your mother said she was sorry that they couldn't help me and asked why my dad didn't help me. I told her I didn't need anything . . . that I wanted just to get in touch with you. She said you'd told them you wanted nothing more to do with me, but she asked me to let her know about the baby. After that, I sent her Madison's pictures, and I stopped by a few times. She said she sent you a picture of Madison," I whispered.

"Listen to me!" Marcus grabbed my arm. "I sent money for you. They said you wouldn't give them an address and that they didn't know where you were living, but they thought you were living with a man. They said you'd come by the house now and then and get the money and my letters."

I stared at him, shocked, trying to decide what to believe. Marcus was here, wanting to see Madison, even though his mother had said he didn't want to see or hear from me and had no interest in our baby.

"Why would they lie like that?" I gasped.

"I'll tell you why," he said. "For the money! That's why!" He let go of my arm, straightened up, and took a deep breath.

"You mean, you sent money that—" I began.

"That they kept!" he cut me off. "They kept the money I sent for my wife and child!"

I shook my head, unable to believe all I was hearing.

"Didn't you tell them that you didn't want to hear from me?" I asked.

"I wrote you," he told me. "I begged them to try to get your address so I could write you. They told me you said you didn't want anything from me except the money. I sent letter after letter. A month ago I wrote that I might be getting out."

I drew a long breath and shook my head. "Marcus, I never heard a word from you . . . no letters, no money. After awhile I stopped asking for your address. They said . . . well, I told you. I figured it was over with us. Madison and I made out all right."

He paced up and down the room, his hands balled into fists. "I'm afraid to go back there," he said tightly. "Afraid of what I'll do."

I got up and put the coffeepot on the burner.

"I have to get Fredrick's truck back to him before dark, though, and I have to go to work tomorrow. I'm on parole," he went on.

"Where are you working?" I asked.

"A sand and gravel company," he said. "Minimum wage. I was going to tell you I'd see you got child support as soon as I could, but all this time you never got what I sent. How did you manage?"

"I was lucky to find people like the Smiths," I admitted. "I lived with them when I first came here, then they divided their quarters and made this apartment for Madison and myself. They pay me pretty good, considering we live here, too, and they feed Madison half the time. I work at the restaurant. There's always something to do if you live here and know how busy it can get."

"Kimberly, I didn't mean for it to be that way," he said.

"I know." The coffee was ready and I poured us each a cup. "Marcus, don't do anything rash." I knew his temper. "Don't do anything that will get you in trouble. If your folks—"

"What do you mean if?" he demanded. "Don't you believe me? I have the money order receipts to prove I sent the money!"

"I don't care about the money," I told him. "Maybe they needed it worse than I did. They must have, to have done something like that."

"Is that all?" he asked. "You can just write it off like that? They needed it so that's fine with you?"

I walked to the heater and warmed my hands. "It's not worth your doing something crazy about it. No, it isn't fine with me, but I probably would have given it to them if they'd asked. And I wish they'd given me your letters." I turned and faced him.

"You must have felt very bitter toward me," he said.

"Yes," I admitted. "At first, when I thought you didn't care about me or our baby."

"How could you believe that, Kimberly?" he demanded. "You knew how I felt about you."

I closed my eyes, not wanting to remember. "People change, Marcus. We were awfully young and things change people."

"Things? Like going to jail?" he asked. "Did you think that changed the way I felt about you?"

"Well . . . yes. Marcus, your mom said you didn't want to hear from me. What else could I believe except that it had changed you and the way you felt?" I demanded.

He cursed under his breath. "I wrote to your folks. They sent the letter back. I wrote my lawyer and asked him to try to find you, but he never answered."

"I'm sorry, Marcus." I sat down on the sofa with my coffee cup in my hands.

"So you told my daughter I was dead," he murmured.

"I told you why," I said.

"Am I dead to you, too, Kimberly?" he asked.

I looked up at him, not knowing what to say.

"I guess I am," he concluded. "Well I knew it might be like that. Is there someone else?"

"No." I shook my head. "It's just that it's been a long time. I never expected to hear from you again. I've made a life for Madison and myself. Marcus, I think I'm in shock. It's hard to believe that you're here, much less all you've told me."

He sat down beside me on the sofa. "Do you think we could rebuild things between us?" he asked.

I tensed. "Give me some time before I answer that," I told him, unable to meet his eyes.

"Okay," he agreed. "Can I come back and see you and Madison?"

I nodded, not trusting my voice.

"There are some things I have to do," he said quietly. "I have to find out who should have been in prison instead of me."

I looked up at him then and he laughed bitterly. "You believe I did it, too. My family thinks I did it, of course. My family stole from me all this time! No, Kimberly, I didn't kill old man Amos or rob him. I know it was my gun, or they said it was. I couldn't prove where I was because I'd left your house and

Mom was asleep when I got home and I don't know where my father was. He came in after I did and didn't know whether I was home or not. But I didn't do it."

I started to say something, but he held up a hand to stop me.

"Somebody knows who did it," he went on. "The person who did it knows and he's probably still in Springville thinking he's off the hook because I put in his time for him. But only a few people knew where I kept the gun. I'll find the one who took it. Then I'll get a better job and have something to offer you and Madison."

"What are you going to do about your folks keeping your money?" I asked.

"What do you want me to do about it?" he said softly.

Suddenly there was a familiarity about our sitting side by side . . . about his question, too. So often during the year we'd gone together he'd said those very words. I reached for his hand and it closed around mine.

"Nothing, Marcus. Just let it go," I told him. "It's done and you can't undo it. There will just be trouble if you say anything."

He swallowed hard. "Alright," he agreed. "I'll let it go for now anyway."

I pulled my hand away and stood up, wanting to put some space between us.

"Kimberly, you look the same," he said in the soft tone that had always melted me. "Only prettier. I'll give you some time. Just let me come back and see you and Madison. Can I come up Saturday if I can find a way?"

I blinked back tears and nodded my head. I went to the little table I used for a desk and wrote the motel's phone number on a piece of paper.

"Call collect if you need to," I told him.

He took the paper and put it in his shirt pocket.

"I'll call Madison so you can tell her good-bye." I took the coat I'd loaned him from its hook. "And wear this in case you run into bad weather." I noticed with relief that the wind seemed to have died down.

I called Madison from the Smiths' living room, and she followed me back through the motel office to our apartment.

"Marcus is leaving now," I told her. "He wanted to tell you good-bye."

She went in and Marcus picked her up for a moment. I could see him savoring the way she felt in his arms.

"You're a pretty girl," he said huskily. "I'd like to come back and see you and your mommy again."

"Okay." She smiled. "Will you bring me something?"

"Madison!" I scolded.

"You don't have to bring me anything," she said quickly.

Marcus kissed her and set her back on her feet. "I have to go," he told me. His voice was ragged and he brushed my cheek with his lips before he hurried out. I didn't go to the window to see him leave.

After Madison was asleep that night, I went out into the office where Maggie was handing a guest a key. I poured myself coffee from the pot behind the counter and went and stood before the fireplace. Maggie looked up at me after the guest left.

"Kim, are you all right?" she asked.

"Sure." I forced a laugh. "Why shouldn't I be?"

"Your 'old friend' who came today," she said quietly. "He's Marcus Conner, isn't he? He went to jail a few years ago for a shooting that occurred during a holdup in Springville, right?"

I nodded.

"Is he Madison's father?" she asked gently.

"Is it that obvious?" I asked.

"Yes, it is." She smiled. "Did you know he was coming?"

"No." I sipped my coffee.

"I don't know how to ask this," she said worriedly. "You know Ed and I love you like a daughter and Madison . . . well, sometimes I've been afraid we're too attached to her. We wouldn't want anything to hurt either one of you. This man, is he causing any trouble for you, Kim?"

"Oh, no," I assured her, sounding more sure than I felt. "He just wanted to see Madison. He's just been paroled. I guess he's trying to make a new start. He wouldn't hurt us or anything like that."

Maggie looked relieved. "Ed and I were worried. Don't take this wrong, but we never really bought that story about your husband being killed in a motorcycle accident in Colorado. At first, we kept waiting for someone to show up, especially after Madison was born. But no one ever did and we were relieved because you seemed so content here with us."

"Maggie, don't worry," I told her. "I am content here. I wouldn't want to live anywhere else."

She laughed and came around the counter and hugged me. We sat down on the chairs in front of the fireplace.

"Ed and I talk about it sometimes . . . tell each other we can't be selfish with you or Madison. After all, you're young and have a right to lead your own life . . . get married and have your own home."

"I am married . . . to Marcus," I told her.

"We didn't know that. We worried when that young lawyer friend of yours, Justin Williams, was coming up here to see you so often for a period of time. He's such a fine young man, and he seemed to have so much to offer and thought so much of you. Sometimes we'd hope that things would work out for you two. Other times we'd wonder what we would do if you married him and you and Madison went to live on Springville."

I laughed at her. "I like Justin a lot but only as a friend," I said. "I just couldn't see myself as a lawyer's wife living in Springville or anywhere else. He said we could live up here, but I didn't believe our lives would ever fit together, or that I loved him that way."

"And this Marcus?" she asked. "How do you feel about him?"

I tried to figure that out myself. "I don't know," I said finally. "It's been a long time. We've both grown up."

"I . . . well, it's hard to believe you ever cared for someone like he must have been," she mused.

"I knew another side to him from what everyone else did," I told her. "Or thought I did. Now I'm not sure."

We talked for awhile longer, and then I helped her lock up the office and we said good night.

But Marcus did cause me trouble that night. I

tried to watch TV, but I found myself watching the screen with my mind somewhere else, not following the story at all. Finally, I turned it off and went to bed. But that was worse. I lay in the darkness, listening to Madison's even breathing from the bed next to mine, and my mind kept wandering back to other times and other places.

Finally, I got up and made hot chocolate. The apartment was chilly, so I built up the fire in the wood stove and cuddled into an afghan. But the memories kept flooding back. . . .

I'd grown up in Springville in what seemed like another lifetime. I had a brother, Brett, eight years older than me, but we never really knew each other at all. He left when I was ten to join the military, and we rarely heard from him. I didn't understand or even think much about it at the time.

My father owned the largest car dealership in town and some other business property he rented out. We had a big three-story house and my folks both drove new cars. We always had a maid living with us to take care of me, the house, and the cooking. We had just about everything anybody would want, and I thought we must've had quite a bit of money. I thought the reason we seldom had dinner together as a family was because my father was so busy and worked late. Mom went out with friends a lot, unless she had one of her frequent headaches, and then she stayed in her room. I knew my folks argued sometimes, but other kids said their parents did, too. My folks didn't set a curfew for me, or any rules at all. I pretty much did as I pleased.

I guess I was about thirteen the night the police brought my mother home drunk for the first time.

Though it was the middle of the night, my dad wasn't home. The maid and I had to take Mom upstairs and get her to bed. The next day she said she hadn't been drunk . . . that she'd had a migraine headache that paralyzed her so she couldn't walk or talk right. She and my father had a big fight about it the next night.

"For heaven's sake, Hillary, if you can't hold your liquor or control your drinking, stay off the street!" he yelled at her.

After that, it was easy enough for me to see when my mother had been drinking, which was most of the time. And that was only the first time the police brought her home like that. Many times after that friends, the police, or often people I didn't know would bring her home. Usually my father wasn't there and I'd go down and wake the maid and we'd get her into the house and up the stairs to her room. After awhile she didn't bother to make excuses anymore.

Sometimes people would drive her car home. If the police brought her, they'd usually tell me where her car was. I'd leave a note on my dad's dresser where to find her car and he'd have it taken care of . . . they didn't share the same room anymore. The nights she drank at home she just passed out in her room, and all we had to worry about was seeing that she didn't pass out with candles burning on her nightstand. She set it on fire once and her bed twice, but the maid learned to help me keep tabs on that.

I don't remember how old I was when one of my girlfriends told me that my father was having an affair with Laura, his secretary, and that he stayed at her apartment several times a week. My girlfriend's family lived in the same apartment complex, and I guess by then it was pretty common knowledge.

One night I went out riding around with some friends and we drove by Laura's apartment. There was my dad's car. Later I found out Laura wasn't the only woman in my father's life.

So that was how it was. My mother had her liquor and my dad had his women. I guess I was lucky that I didn't get into trouble of any kind or take up with a rough crowd. I even made fairly good grades in school.

The summer I turned seventeen I got a job at a drive-in restaurant. My dad laughed at me because he gave me a liberal allowance and he'd given me a new car the year before. But I was bored because all my friends had jobs, were going to summer school, or were going away on vacation with their families. It was fun earning my own money, having my own job.

That was how I met Marcus. Oh, I'd seen, him around for a long time. Springville wasn't that big of a town, and with only one high school, most of us kids knew each other by sight at least. Marcus had dropped out of school and ran with a tough crowd of bikers. He was a year older than me, and I might not have known who he was if it hadn't been for his sister, Nicole, who was in my class. We weren't close friends, but we'd been in the same classes even back in grade school. I knew Nicole and Marcus came from a large family and that their father was sick and couldn't work. Fredrick, the oldest brother, went off to join the Army, and then there was Marcus, Nicole, and several younger kids. I felt sorry for Nicole. She studied hard and made good grades. She'd worked a part-time job at a fast-food place for a couple of years, and as far as I knew she didn't date at all.

Marcus and his friends came into the place I was working pretty often, roaring in on their bikes, acting loud and tough. Marcus wasn't the biggest or oldest in that gang, and he certainly wasn't the loudest. In fact he was kind of quiet. One evening they came in and his friends started making a mess of the booth where they were sitting. They dumped the salt and pepper out onto the table, wadded up napkins and threw them around, and poured sugar on the floor.

"Don't let them get away with that," I protested to my boss.

"Ignore them and they'll go away," she said.

"Ignore them and they'll trash the whole place," I told her.

The three boys with Marcus were the ones making the mess. Marcus was watching me as I filled sugar jars and napkin holders. I tried to ignore what those three were doing and the way Marcus's eyes roved over me. I could feel my face getting flushed and that made me even angrier.

When they started on the catsup, I walked across the little dining area and stared back into Marcus's eyes.

"Are these your friends?" I asked.

He smiled cockily. "I guess you could say that."

I reached out and snatched the catsup from one fellow's hand before he could spill any more on the table.

"Real pigs!" I told Marcus. "You have real pigs for friends!"

I turned and marched off. It was nearly closing time and I went back to help my boss clean the grill.

"Now you did it." She sighed. "They'll make a worse mess and we'll be forever getting out of here."

I could feel Marcus's eyes still on me, and I turned and gave him a cool stare. He said something under his breath, and one of the guys laughed.

"I said, clean it up!" Marcus said, so low I could barely hear him.

The others looked kind of funny and then started picking up napkins and wiping up the mess, scooping the salt and pepper into an ashtray. When they'd done about all they could, I grabbed a cloth and went over to wash the table.

"Oh, just get out of my way," I told them.

"You're cute when you're mad, honey," one said, and I noticed the way Marcus glared at him.

They eased out of the booth and filed out, walking like each of them thought he was God's gift to women. I cleaned up the mess while my boss locked the door and watched them leave on their motorcycles.

"Thank goodness they all left," my boss said. "Kim, I'm afraid of that tough gang. The guy who kept looking at you looks hard as nails. Maybe you should call somebody to see you get home."

"I'll be okay," I told her. There was no one to call. By that time of the evening Mom would be drunk or passed out, and my dad wouldn't appreciate my calling him at Laura's just because a boy had looked at me.

My boss had parked on one side of the building and I was on the other. I guess she was really nervous because she was in her car and gone before I even got to mine. I'd just gotten in my car when Marcus rolled his bike out of the shadows and over to the driver's window.

"Hello, Chickie." He grinned.

I'd rolled the window down and his closeness startled me, but I didn't let on.

"My name isn't Chickie," I told him coolly.

"What is it?" he asked.

I looked at his face in the dim light and a strange excitement seemed to race through my veins . . . half fear, half daring.

"Kimberly Matthews," I told him.

"Kimberly Matthews. Pretty name, Kimberly. Why are you working in a place like that? Why are you working at all? Your old man has bucks."

I pulled out my ponytail and shook my hair loose, aware that he was watching.

"I work because I want to," I told him.

He laughed. "Because you want to?"

"You do what you want to, don't you?" I challenged. "Run with those creeps."

He winced and I could tell he didn't like what I'd said about his friends.

"Don't you?" I repeated.

"Yeah, I guess I do what I want." He shrugged.

"Well, my, my." I smiled. "That gives us something in common."

"What else do you suppose we have in common?" he asked.

"Not much," I told him.

"We could have a drink and talk about it," he suggested.

I'd put the keys in the ignition. All I had to do was

start the car and back out and leave him, but I hesitated for some reason I couldn't understand.

"No, I don't think so," I told him.

"Why not?" he asked. "You too good to be seen with me?"

I laughed and saw the surprise on his face.

"I don't want a drink," I told him. "I might have a soda with you someplace."

His eyes searched mine. "All right," he agreed. "You name it."

"The Sunrise Diner," I told him. It was a big drive-in that stayed open all night.

"Okay." He nodded. "Leave your car and get on behind me."

"Uh-uh." I shook my head. "I'll take my car home. You can follow me."

He nodded.

As I drove home with Marcus following me, I thought to myself: *This is crazy! I'm usually careful whom I date.* I'd never met a boy I wanted to get serious with, and I found wrestling sessions in the backseat of a car to be anything but pleasing. I also didn't care enough about dates or being popular to give in just for one of those reasons.

I parked in the driveway and got out, pulling off the vest I had to wear at work. Marcus cut his motorcycle motor and rolled up beside me.

"Look, I don't really want my hair torn out of my head," I said, "so how about not going ninety miles an hour?"

He smiled. "I wouldn't think of mussing your hair."

"And I've never been on one of these things before," I confessed.

"Okay, I'll take it easy," he agreed.

I leaned against my car a moment, trying to figure out why I was doing such a thing.

"Aren't you afraid to take off with me?" he asked. "You don't even know my name."

"Oh, yes I do. You're Marcus Conner. I've known your sister Nicole a long time. Should I be afraid to go with you?" I was serious.

He grew serious, too. "No, Kimberly, you shouldn't be afraid. I won't do anything to hurt you." His mouth got a soft, different look. "I've seen you around a long time and wanted to talk to you, but rich girls like you don't go out with guys like me."

"At least I wouldn't call you names," I objected.

"What do you mean?" he asked.

"You said 'rich girls like me' and said what I wouldn't do before you even know me. I wouldn't jump to conclusions about you like that," I told him.

His eyes widened. "Wow!" he said softly. "You can lay it on, can't you?"

"It's the truth, isn't it?" I asked.

"Yeah." He nodded thoughtfully. "Well, we'd better go before I say something else wrong."

Marcus told me how to get on the bike behind him and helped me. "Just hang onto my waist," he instructed.

The bike lurched when he started it, and I clung to him. There was something about being that close to him with my arms around his lean, muscular body that was a lot more exciting than anything else I'd ever done!

When we walked into the drive-in together, there were some of his friends and some of mine . . . but definitely not having anything to do with each other. His friends spoke to him and stared at me. My friends spoke to me and stared at Marcus. We got some soda and sat in a booth by ourselves. We were sitting side by side, and Marcus leaned his head close to mine.

"Did you see the looks you got?" he asked. "Your friends are shocked."

I straightened up and looked at him. "What difference does that make to me?" I asked.

He was thoughtful for a few moments. "You're a lot different than I thought you'd be, Kimberly," he said finally.

The jukebox started a new tune and I told Marcus what songs I liked, mostly sweet, sentimental ones. We talked about things we liked and things we couldn't stand and laughed a lot.

Finally, I asked him to take me home. Most of my friends had left, but his were still hanging around, and I felt Marcus's arm go around my waist as we stood up to leave.

When we got to my house, he caught my hands when I got off his bike.

"Will I see you again, Kimberly?" he asked.

"I suppose so; unless one of us leaves Springville." I laughed.

"I mean, will you go out with me?" he persisted.

I pulled one hand free and traced the line of his cheek with one finger and kissed his lips the way I'd been wanting to all evening.

"Probably so, Marcus," I told him. Then I said good night and ran up the steps to the house.

He was waiting for me when I got off work the next evening.

"Oh, no!" my boss gasped. "He's waiting for you! I told you not to cross him and his friends. Shall I call the police?"

"Marcus?" I laughed. "He's not at all like people think. He's not trouble."

"You're crazy," she said, shocked.

Marcus walked me to my car. "Want to go have a soda?" he asked.

"Not particularly," I told him. "Let's go someplace we can dance."

"I can't dance," he said.

"Don't you want to dance with me?" I traced one finger along his chin and saw him sort of melt.

"Well, I guess," he agreed.

We went to a little place where I'd been a few times before. It was a crummy bar but there was a nice patio on one side and there was a three-piece band. Marcus and I danced like we'd been dancing together all our lives until they closed the place.

I'd driven my car, and we'd left Marcus's bike at my house. He kept his arm around me as I drove home. After I'd parked in the driveway, he pulled me into his arms before I could open the car door.

"Kimberly, I never knew anybody like you before," he breathed into my hair.

My breath caught in my throat. I was too wound up over him, too.

"Oh, Marcus, I never felt this way about anybody before, either." I clung to him.

"This is for real, isn't it?" he asked.

"I don't know," I told him shakily. "I feel a little like it's a bubble that will burst any minute."

He kissed me and it was like fire, melting what little resistance I had left.

"I love you," he said, his lips against mine.

"I love you, too." I buried my face in his shirt a

minute and tried to catch my breath. Then I pushed his arms away and reached for the door handle. "Marcus, I have to go in," I told him.

"Don't go," he pleaded.

"I have to," I said. "I'm scared to death!"

I jumped out of the car, ran in the house, and left him sitting in my car. After awhile I heard his bike motor start and fade off into the night.

I didn't work the next day, so I fixed us a picnic lunch and drove to Marcus's house, a run-down old place that had been built onto until there was hardly any yard left. He came running out when I honked the horn. I drove out into the desert along a track of a road that followed a dry riverbed.

"Kimberly," Marcus began, "you'll get us stuck out here and it's a long walk back to civilization."

I found the spot I was looking for and cut the motor. "I've been here before." I laughed.

His expression darkened. "With who?"

"Nobody," I told him. "I come out here to sketch."

I got my drawing things out of the car and a blanket that we spread on the smooth, round pebbles of the riverbed. A constant breeze stirred the branches of the low mesquites that shaded us from the hundred-degree desert sun.

"This is beautiful," Marcus said. "I didn't even know this was here."

The desert lay flat and empty and seemed to stretch out forever in all directions except north. In that direction, a range of mountains rose abruptly out of the desert flatness, their tops covered with feathery green forest.

"Have you been up there?" I asked.

"A couple of times," he said. "On bikes with the

guys. We should go up there."

We agreed that we'd drive up into the mountains when we could spend the whole day. It was as if life was new. We wanted to do and experience everything together.

I got out my drawing things and Marcus carried the ice chest to the shade of the mesquites and opened sodas for us. But soon we were in each other's arms and there was no denying our passion. The dual excitement of fear and daring the first time I had gone out with Marcus raced through me, only this time it was combined with desire. He lowered me onto the picnic blanket, and in the hot desert air we showered each other with kisses. He was such a mystery to me and I needed to know every inch of him, someone who made me feel safe, wanted, and yearning for more.

Later, while we lay next to one another savoring the feel of the other's skin on our own, Marcus whispered, "We could get married, Kimberly."

"We could," I agreed. "As soon as you get a job."

He drew a long breath. "There aren't many jobs for me."

"You could go back and finish school," I told him.

He sat up and stared out into the distance. "I can't. I'm so far behind, and I should have graduated this spring. I can't go back and sit in school. It would take me years, and I just can't."

"You could go to vocational school then," I suggested.

"I don't know anything about that," he admitted.

"We could find out." I ran the palms of my hands over the smooth, tan skin of his shoulders. "I'd go with you to find out about it."

"I started to take carpentry in shop before I quit school," he said. "I liked that."

We spent the whole day together . . . talking, laughing, loving, dreaming. After that, I spent nearly all my free time with Marcus. He worked now and then at a junkyard, taking parts off wrecked cars. He still hung around with that wild, tough crowd but not when he could be with me.

One evening the phone was ringing when we walked in the door at my house. It was someone calling from a bar, wanting us to come get my mom.

"Come with me," I told Marcus. "You can drive her car."

We went to the bar, and Marcus drove Mom's car home while she rode with me. He helped me get her into the house and up the stairs. By then she'd passed out completely, and I took her shoes off and left her on the bed in her clothes.

"I see what you mean about your mom," Marcus said when we were back in the kitchen fixing a snack. "I didn't believe it was that bad."

"You thought money cured everything, didn't you?" I asked.

"I guess I did," he admitted. "I worry because I know I'll never make as much money as your father."

"And I know I'll never drink as much as my mother," I told him.

"Silly," he said, pulling me into his arms. "That's not logical."

"It isn't the money, it's the people and what they do," I said.

In the fall we both went back to school. It was my senior year. Marcus took carpentry at the vocational school and I coached him so he could get his high school equivalency. My friends couldn't believe I was going with Marcus.

"Kim, he's a biker!" my best friend Annie protested. She'd been away all summer. "He's not your type at all. I can't believe you're actually serious about him."

I refused to discuss it, and after awhile everyone stopped trying to talk to me about him. Marcus told me his mom said I was "slumming" and that I'd drop him for somebody with money after the novelty wore off. His sister, Nicole, and I seldom saw each other at school that year, but she was none too friendly, either.

One day Dad was home when I came in from school.

"Kim, what's this I hear about you going out with Marcus Conner?" he asked. I noticed he'd had his hair styled and tinted to cover the gray.

"I've been going with him for a couple of months, Daddy," I told him.

He frowned. "For heaven's sake, can't you find somebody better? Do you have to pick a hoodlum like that?"

I put my books down and faced him.

"You laughed at me when I got a job last summer and you offered me more allowance," I told him. "But I wanted my own job. I want to pick my own friends, have my own relationships."

"Okay, okay," he said. "I just don't want you getting in over your head with a bunch like that."

"I'm not the one who has to be carried home from bars," I told him. "And I know all about Marcus. I'm not in over my head."

"Okay," he said again. "Just so you know what you're doing. I've got to run."

Things went fairly peacefully during the fall and winter. After the weather got cold, Marcus and I spent a lot of evenings at my house. I'd fix our supper out of whatever happened to be in the refrigerator, or I'd stop at the supermarket on my way home from school. Mom was gone most of the time and didn't even attempt to shop or cook or anything like that anymore. In the evenings, Marcus and I would study in my room and sometimes he'd stay until after midnight. We were in love and going to be married as soon as I graduated and he finished his courses at the vocational school and got a job. We had everything all planned.

After Christmas, Mom got in a fight at a club and hit another woman. They made her leave, and on the way home she got stopped for drunk driving. My dad managed to keep her from going to jail, but it cost him a lot and he was furious. He took her car away and threatened her with divorce.

"Kim will graduate from high school in less than six months," I heard him tell her. "I can rent an apartment and sell this place. And just remember there's no alimony in this state. So you stay home and behave yourself . . . or else!"

"You mean Kim can have her car and come and go as she pleases, entertain that gigolo of hers?" Mom screamed at him. "While I'm stranded here like a prisoner?"

"Unless you want to be stranded without a roof over your head," Dad told her. "Kim isn't costing me money to keep her out of jail, smearing my name."

"Oh, aren't you the pious one?" Mom cried bitterly. "How many women are you keeping at the moment?"

He told her to shut up, and then left.

After that, things got worse. Mom still drank, but cooped up at home she turned mean and ugly and took it out on anybody who was around, which was mostly me. We couldn't keep a maid anymore because Mom was so mean they were afraid of her. I couldn't take Marcus there anymore, either.

"You're just like your father, Kim!" she screamed at me. "Sex is all you think about. It would take a harem of women to keep him happy. Is that how you are, Kim? How many besides Marcus have been in your bed?"

I covered my ears against my mother's accusations. I stayed away from home as much as I could. Marcus and I would drive out to the riverbed and stay until it grew too cold and dark. Other times we'd just drive over to the city park and eat hamburgers and do our studying.

"We'll be married soon with a place of our own, Kimberly," Marcus promised me. "Honey, I hate it being this way for you."

"It will be over soon," I told him, huddled in his arms.

Once I had returned home to find that Mom had all the locks changed so I couldn't get in. Marcus boosted me onto the porch roof so I could crawl in my window. After that I kept clothes and even blankets and pillows in my car, even though Dad had keys made for me the next day. Another time I came home to find she'd shredded all my drawings and paintings. I wept bitterly against Marcus's chest.

"I guess that next to you, those were what I loved

264

the most," I sobbed.

Marcus offered to drop out of school and look for full-time work, but I insisted he stay on and finish. "It's the only way we're going to have a decent future," I told him. "Otherwise you'll be stuck in part-time junkyard jobs forever."

"I'm so worried about you." He sighed, smoothing my hair.

"I'll be okay for a couple more months," I tried to reassure him.

I didn't tell him about the time I came home and found most of my clothes thrown out the window onto the porch roof. After that, I packed most of my belongings that I cared about into the car and left them there.

Usually I tried to wait until Mom would be asleep or passed out before I came home, but one night as I started upstairs she dropped a heavy flowerpot on my head, cutting my scalp.

I ran back to my car and drove to the hospital, blood streaming down my face. They put stitches in and called my dad.

Mom insisted she'd thought I was a burglar, and Dad threatened to send her to a hospital where they treated alcoholics.

"That does it!" Marcus swore when he heard about it. "We're getting married and you're getting out of there if we have to live in that riverbed."

We had less than a month of school left, and we had some money saved from my allowance and Marcus's part-time jobs. We drove across the state line and got married, but agreed to keep it secret until we had a place of our own. He wouldn't let me borrow money from my dad.

"I'm not taking handouts from him," he said angrily. "I know what he thinks of me, and he doesn't care enough about you to keep you safe from that madwoman."

We looked at cheap apartments, but at a lot of places, the owner or manager said they had no vacancies once they found out we were still in school and didn't have steady jobs.

"I'm afraid for you to stay at home," Marcus worried. "I'm afraid she'll put a butcher knife in you while you're asleep."

"I'm okay," I tried to tell him. "I lock my door from the inside and pull the bureau across it."

Marcus had a good chance for a job with a contractor friend of his shop instructor so we pinned our hopes on that. I suspected that I was pregnant, and even though it wasn't the best timing in the world, we were both happy and excited about it.

The weather was warm by then, and one evening we drove out to the riverbed and stayed until nearly midnight. We were both excited that having to keep our marriage a secret would soon be over and we could live the rest of our lives as a happy family. He kissed me gently and told me how happy he was that he'd found me, I showed rather than told him how much he meant to me. We had made love many times before, but this time it was different. We knew that our future was right around the corner and we came together as husband and wife.

I dropped Marcus off at his house then drove home and went to bed.

Annie met me at my locker the next morning. "I'm surprised you're here!" she gasped. "Have you heard about Marcus?"

"What do you mean? I was with him until midnight last night," I told her.

"They've arrested him for killing Lou Amos last night," she said. "Kim, I'm sorry. I thought you'd heard."

I walked out of the school, ran to my car, and drove to Marcus's house. His mother let me in. She'd been crying and explained that the police had come for Marcus in the night. Lou Amos, who ran a little grocery store in their neighborhood, had been shot sometime after midnight when he'd surprised a burglar in his store.

"They found Marcus's jacket in the store," she wept. "I told them he could have left it there some other time. Then they found his gun in the garage where he kept it."

Marcus hadn't had his jacket on when I was with him the night before, and I couldn't remember when he had last worn it. The weather had been warm. His mother said that the police weren't allowing anyone but his lawyer to see him that day. I went home and called the jail, but they wouldn't let me talk to him.

I sat around in a daze until it was time for the afternoon edition of the paper, and then I went out and bought it. The account in the paper matched almost perfectly what Marcus's mother had said.

Marcus called me that afternoon. "Kimberly, listen to me," he said. "My lawyer got permission for me to make this call and I don't have much time to talk, so just listen. Don't talk to anybody about all this—"

"Marcus, I can't believe you did it!" I cried.

"Will you listen?" he demanded. "I didn't do it, but

267

I'm worried about you. There were only a few people who knew where I kept my gun. If they think you're going to be my alibi, you might be in danger. Anyway, I don't trust them with me in here. It would be better if they think we've split up. If they think that, they're less apt to bother you to get at me. Do you understand?"

"I guess so," I agreed reluctantly. "But we were together until after midnight—"

"That's when it happened. Anyway, we don't have any witnesses, even to that. Just do what I'm asking you. Stay out of sight, act like we've split up, and don't say anything to anybody until this gets straightened out."

"I love you, Marcus." I sobbed.

"Oh, baby!" His voice broke. "I love you, too, and I'm so helpless in here. Please do as I say and be careful."

I promised I would, and he hung up the phone.

Somehow I got through the rest of my exams at school that week. I went and talked to Norton Williams, who I read was appointed as Marcus's lawyer. I told him about being with Marcus the night of the murder.

He shook his head. "Kim, Marcus is right. Even if somehow we could prove that it happened while you two were together who is going to believe you? Of course you'd try to protect him. Marcus thinks one of his 'friends' who knew where he kept his gun did it. If that's true, that person will try to shut you up if he thinks you can prove you and Marcus were together during the time of the burglary. And Marcus is afraid of what those guys will do with him in jail. He did run with a pretty tough bunch, you know.

Probably the best thing for you to do is what he says
. . . stay out of sight as much as possible, at least
until we can get him out on bail."

But that hope was soon shattered when Marcus
was denied bail.

Somehow I got through graduation and tried my
best to pull myself together even though all of my
dreams for the future had been taken from me in
one fell swoop.

"Kim, it's better that you found out about Marcus
before things went any further," my dad told me.

He let the subject drop, but at home with Mom it
was a nightmare.

"Where's your boyfriend now, Miss Smartie?"
she'd jeer drunkenly. "In jail for murder, that's
where. I hope they send him to the electric chair."

I couldn't stay there anymore. One of the coun-
selors in school had told Annie about summer jobs
available at a resort near Mountain's Peak, and she
begged me to go with her to apply.

"You need a change, and I've heard it's a really
neat job," she said. "I know it sounds like a drag,
cleaning rooms, but I heard that after we're off work
we can use the resort facilities . . . swimming, tennis, young guys with money."

I rode up in her car with two other girls. We
stopped for hamburgers at a rustic restaurant in
Mountain's Peak.

The others lingered after we finished eating, but I
was feeling queasy so I went outside for some air.
There was a motel a short distance from the restaurant with a help-wanted sign in the window. I was
afraid too many girls would be applying for jobs out
at the resort and I needed anything I could get.

LOVERS AGAIN AFTER 5 YEARS APART

I walked over to the motel, stepped into the office, and met Maggie Smith. She explained that she wanted someone who could stay at the motel twenty-four hours a day if necessary because her husband had had a heart attack and was in the hospital in Springville.

"I really need the job," I told her. "I'll stay whatever hours you need me."

"I thought maybe someone older." She hesitated. "But if you can stay, we'll give it a try."

I explained about my friends going out to the resort area. "I can stay today until they go back," I told her. "You can show me what to do and then I'll come right back up here in my own car. Most of my things are already packed."

She said that would be fine, and I went back to tell Annie and the others.

"Are you crazy?" Annie cried. "That sure doesn't sound like fun, and we'll never get to see each other. At least come with us to put in an application at the resort."

"I need a job more than you do," I told her. "And I already promised Mrs. Smith."

When I got back to the motel, Mrs. Smith was crying. The hospital had called and asked her to come down as soon as she could.

"Show me what to do and I'll stay until you get back . . . tomorrow or whenever," I offered.

She hurriedly showed me forms to have guests fill out, and there was a list of charges. She took me into her quarters behind the motel office and showed me a spare room.

"You can sleep here," she said. "And fix whatever you can find to eat, or there's the restaurant next door. Do you need money for meals?"

I told her I had enough in my purse. She handed me a gown and a robe of hers to use. I watched her drive off.

Annie came over from the restaurant, I told her what had happened and to go on without me.

"Well, I guess they really need you," she said. "I still don't understand you, Kim."

I called Marcus's lawyer and told him where I was and how to reach me, and then I called Marcus's mother and my dad.

Mrs. Smith called me several times that evening. An older woman had come by in the morning and cleaned the rooms that had been used. In the afternoon Mrs. Smith finally came back looking exhausted, but said her husband was doing better.

The next morning, Mrs. Smith had the lady who'd cleaned the rooms watch the office while she drove down to visit her husband and dropped me off at my house.

I hurriedly tossed the rest of my belongings into the car and drove back up to Mountain's Peak.

Mrs. Smith and I soon became friends, and she told me to call her Maggie. I stayed on in the spare room of their apartment because she didn't want to be alone. After her husband came home from the hospital he need constant supervision.

Annie and the others had found the jobs at the resort were already filled, so I didn't hear much from them. I bought the Springville newspapers to keep up with any information about Marcus. When there was no mention of his case in the paper for over a week, I called Mr. Williams. He said there was nothing anyone could do until Marcus's case came to trial. It was late summer by then, and the trail lasted one day. It seemed over almost as soon as it began, and Marcus was found guilty . . . seven years to life!

I couldn't believe that could happen. None of it seemed real, especially when his mother said Marcus didn't want to hear from me. But by then my baby was showing, and I faced the fact that I was alone. . . .

I woke stiff and cold on the sofa with only the afghan around me, and I pulled it closer to me. I tried to tell myself that it had only been a dream . . . that Marcus hadn't really come back, that everything was as it had been for over five years, and that there would be no changes in the little niche I'd made for myself and Madison. But I knew that wasn't so. Marcus had come back.

I got up and filled the wood stove to warm up the coffee I'd made the night before. No use going back to bed; the sky was already turning gray with another cold dawn. I stood staring out the window. The first snow had fallen before Thanksgiving, it was now March and I was tired of it, even though it was Mountain's Peak's winter livelihood. Skiers came to the slopes, filling every available motel room, pouring into the restaurant until the owners, Betty and Dana, begged me to work the rush hours.

Madison woke up, so I fed her breakfast and drove her to the day-care center. Then I returned home and took a shower, put on a pair of jeans and a flannel shirt, and told myself I felt better. Ed was in the office when I went in.

"We're almost filled up for the weekend," he said. "The phone's been ringing since daylight for reservations."

"They're forecasting more snow, aren't they?" I asked.

"Yes, four to six inches," he replied.

"Have you got anything for me to do?" I asked.

"Maggie wants to show you the dress she's making Madison for her birthday," he said and laughed. "That's probably the most important thing. I can't believe she's going to be five in a week."

"She'll go to kindergarten at the elementary school next year," I told him.

"Maybe we should put a brick on her head to keep her from growing so fast." He chuckled.

I went over and admired the dress Maggie was making for Madison, and we discussed the party we'd be having. You'd have thought it was a national holiday from the preparations Maggie was making for it!

Then I headed to the restaurant for coffee, toast, and local gossip.

"Hi, Kim," Betty greeted me. "I'm glad you're here. Would you stand by in case Dana needs help? I want to run down to Springville for supplies."

I told her I would, and I sat down at the counter with some other locals. But that morning I couldn't seem to concentrate on any tidbits of local news.

Finally, I made some excuse and went back to the motel, going through the routine of making beds and straightening up.

After awhile Ed called me, handing the phone through the door of my apartment.

"Hello?" I said into the receiver.

"Hi, Kim. It's Justin Williams. How are you?"

"Fine," I told him. "They're predicting snow and the slopes should be great. Come on up."

He was silent a moment. "That wasn't what I was calling about. I just found out Marcus was paroled."

Justin and I had gone to high school together. He'd gone on to law school and then had taken over his Uncle Norton's practice when the older man was forced to retire because of bad health.

"I know," I told Justin.

"You've seen him?" He sounded worried.

"He was here yesterday," I replied.

"I see. Well, how is he?"

I tried to think how to describe Marcus. "I don't know, Justin," I said finally. "He's nervous, uptight."

"Do you think he'll make any trouble for you?" he asked.

"No, I don't think anything like that," I said.

Two years before, Justin had come up here for a weekend of skiing and we'd reunited. We'd had fun . . . playing with Madison in the snow, drinking coffee, dancing at the lodge, and talking in front of the fireplace until all hours.

"I'll get you a divorce," Justin had offered. "Kim, marry me."

But it hadn't been that kind of feeling for me . . . no fire in my veins, no hunger for his lips on mine. I loved him . . . but as a friend. He had been understanding enough about it. We were still friends. I'd painted desert and mountain scenes to hang on the walls of his new office, and when Marcus's sister, Nicole, had asked me to help her get a job as a receptionist, I'd mentioned to him what a good worker she'd always been.

"Is there anything I can do?" Justin asked, pulling me back to the present.

"I don't think so," I replied.

"I have a special on divorces this month," he said, trying to sound lighthearted.

I laughed. "Not right now, Justin. Let's just let everything—"

"Rock on?" he finished for me.

"Yeah, for the time being. Justin, I don't know what to think of this, but Marcus says he wrote me and sent money to me through his folks. He says they told him they didn't know where I was and that I wouldn't give them my address. He says they told him I'd come by and pick up the mail."

"And they told you that he didn't want to hear from you, didn't they?" he guessed. "Sounds like somebody is lying."

"Who?" I asked.

He sighed. "Honey, I wouldn't put money on it either way."

"He says he didn't do it . . . the burglary I mean," I told him.

"Kim, did you think he'd tell you if he did?" he asked.

"Well, I don't know. I just don't know what to think. Oh, and another thing, he said he wrote to your uncle, asking him to find me or get my address, but that he never got an answer."

"Kim, don't set yourself up to get hurt," Justin warned.

"I'm not," I told him. "I was just telling you what he said."

"Sure. Well, call me anytime and if there's anything I can do, you know I'll come running."

I knew he meant it, and I said I'd keep in touch.

After Marcus's conviction, I'd made myself face the facts. Lou Amos had been shot with Marcus's gun. The crime had apparently happened shortly after I'd left Marcus at his house, less than two blocks from Amos's store. And Marcus was what he was, one of a wild crowd of young toughs who'd been questioned about other burglaries and thefts. His brother Fredrick had been accused of car theft but had been released for lack of evidence before he'd left for the Army.

The worst part was that I knew Marcus was desperate for money to get us a place of our own. If he'd done it, and a jury thought there was evidence enough to convict him, he'd done it for me. Or had he? I wondered. He'd told me not to try to get in touch with him before the trial, and afterward his mother said he'd written that he didn't want to hear from me. Maybe I'd always been wrong about Marcus. Maybe he always had been what other people had tried to tell me, instead of what I thought he was.

But now he was back, saying that he cared about Madison and me, that he'd sent money and letters I'd never received, that he hadn't committed the crime he'd been convicted of.

Too many memories still lurked in my heart in spite of my doubts about him. I was torn between wanting to see him again and being afraid of what would happen if I did.

By Friday evening the motel was full, we hung out the no-vacancy sign and closed the office. There was nothing I cared for on TV and Madison was asleep, so I sat down by the stove in the main room of our apartment to work on an afghan I was knitting.

There was a knock at the door, but before I could

reach it I heard Marcus's voice calling, "Kimberly, it's me."

I opened the door, and he stepped in from the cold, his hair ruffled from the wind. Despite of all the changes, he was as familiar as he'd ever been. It was as if the years had never passed, as if we'd never been apart.

"I couldn't stay away from you," he whispered, and we were in each other's arms, clinging as if no force on earth could ever separate us again. We went to my room and he kissed me. All of the feelings I had for him came back and a desire stirred inside of me that I hadn't in so many years. I kissed him back more passionately than ever before, and we found ourselves entwined, rediscovering our love after being separated for so long. It started rushed and frantic, like we couldn't get enough of each other, but then slowed down to a tender and loving pace.

Later, we lay close together on the sleeper that the sofa turned into. "I can't believe this," he murmured into my hair. "Oh, honey, I wanted you so much. I was so sure I'd lost you."

I clung to him, close to tears.

We talked for hours, the way we had under the mesquites in the riverbed, and in my room at my folks' house. Marcus said he was unable to stay with his folks after he knew that they'd lied to keep us apart and had moved in with a co-worker. He'd hitched a ride up the mountain as soon as he'd gotten off work that evening. We got up and made pancakes in the middle of the night, and talked until the sun started to rise.

Skiers' car motors woke me only a few hours after

I'd fallen asleep. I dressed and slipped out of the apartment to go help with the breakfast rush at the restaurant. When I returned, I found Marcus and Madison eating cereal, watching cartoons, and talking as if they'd known each other always.

I could only spend a few minutes with them, and then I went to help Maggie clean the rooms people had checked out of already.

After the noon rush at the restaurant, I carried our lunch back to the apartment. Madison finished hers and begged to go outside with Ed, who was scraping ice off the walks. I let her go and sank down on the sofa into Marcus's arms.

"How long before you're off and running again?" Marcus asked. "Isn't it rough working two jobs like this?"

"It's usually only on weekends," I told him. "And then only when there's snow and good skiing. During the week it's slow and we catch our breaths. Summers are busy but it's different, not so hectic and we have more help cleaning rooms. I'm off now until the supper rush. Dawn, the day worker, said she'd come in to do the rest of the rooms."

He reached over and took an envelope from his jacket pocket and laid it in my lap, then took out his billfold and pulled out some bills.

"I told you that I'd start helping you and Madison. It isn't much," he began.

I snatched his billfold and put the money back into it. "Marcus, you need heavy clothes, a car, and decent meals. It's been a long winter and I have money saved. Madison and I don't need anything," I told him.

I opened the envelope. It contained money order

stubs that he'd told me he'd sent. I put them back and laid it aside. "Marcus, I believed you," I told him. "Did you ask your parents about it?"

He shook his head. "I was too mad. If my mom admitted it, we'd have gotten into a fight. And if she denied it—" He made a helpless gesture. "—that would have made me just as mad."

"Let it go," I told him. "What's done is done."

Again we lay awake far into the night . . . savoring our love, talking about things we were going to do with Madison in the summer and deciding how we would tell her that Marcus was her father.

I wanted to tell Marcus to stay with us, not to go back down to Springville, but I was afraid to bring up the subject.

"Oh, honey, I hate to leave," he said suddenly, as if reading my mind.

"Then don't," I told him. "Stay here with us. Ed would sign for you, saying you work for him. He'd do it for Madison and me. You can find work cutting wood, and as soon as the weather lets up people will be wanting cabins built or repaired."

Marcus propped himself up on one elbow. "Someday, sweetheart. Just as soon as I get things taken care of in Springville," he said.

"What things?"

"Only three people besides myself knew where I kept my gun," he said. "The Cooper brothers and Randy Reynolds—"

"Oh, Marcus!" I cried. "There's nothing you can do about it now. You won't be able to find enough proof to reopen the whole thing."

His eyes narrowed, and his mouth became a tight, angry line.

"I can lean on them until somebody cracks. Maybe I can't ever prove anything in court, but I can make somebody pay," he said.

"And then what?" I flared. "Go back to prison for that? Marcus, use your head. That would only be making matters worse."

He made a fist and punched the pillow. "What do you expect me to do? Say, 'Oh well, it's only five years out of my life' and let them go on laughing because they put one over on me? I promised myself every day I spent there that somebody would pay."

"Oh, honey, I'm so sorry." I pulled him into my arms. Right then I had no doubts. One of the others must have done it. Marcus wouldn't be that bitter, threatening to risk everything we had, if he wasn't innocent. "But don't throw away our chance to be together now. I couldn't stand to lose you again," I said.

He softened then and held me in his arms. But I couldn't be sure of what was in his mind.

I helped with breakfast at the restaurant the next morning. Ed and Maggie said they'd stay in the office and Dawn was coming in to clean rooms. I found a sweatshirt and long underwear and jogging pants of mine that were big enough for Marcus, and we drove out to watch the skiers and let Madison go sledding on a smaller slope with some other children.

"Madison asked me if I was going to stay," Marcus said thoughtfully as we sat in the car watching her play with the others.

"What did you tell her?" I asked.

"I have a job in Springville that I have to go back

to, but that someday I'll come up here to stay."

I decided to issue the ultimatum that I hoped would change his mind. He wanted Madison to know that he was her father, and we'd talked about how to explain it to her.

"Marcus, if you go back down there, just for revenge, I don't want Madison to know that you're her father," I said firmly.

There was anger in his dark eyes as he turned to look at me. "But you agreed we'd tell her today," he said.

"I don't want her hurt, and she will be if she knows you're her father and then you go back to jail for trying to get revenge for something you can't even prove!"

He watched Madison come flying down the hill. She spilled at the bottom and laughed.

"Let me work this out, Kimberly. Give me a little time," he begged.

"Marcus, give it up!" I demanded.

He turned, eyes flashing. "I can't! Can't you understand that? I can't just give it up!"

I let the subject drop. He'd mentioned hitchhiking back down to Springville, but I'd said I'd drive him that evening.

Back at the motel he put his arms around me.

"I guess we'd better be leaving pretty soon," he murmured. "I don't want you driving back up here too late at night. Honey, you know I hate to go." There was anguish in his voice.

I touched his face. "The roads are clear and we're not supposed to get any more snow. I could drive you down early in the morning," I suggested.

"You make it easy," he said, grinning. Then he

took my chin in his hand and kissed me. I held onto him as tight as I could, fearing it might be the last time I would get the chance to show him how much I loved him. Being with him at that moment reminded me of the last night we'd spent together five years ago making love in the riverbed. There was the same anticipation of our entire future being at our fingertips, only this time I knew that stories don't always have a happy ending. I think he felt the same because we made love with a ferocity we never had before.

I carried Madison, who was half asleep, to Maggie and Ed's apartment before dawn the next day. They'd agreed to take her to the day-care center. Marcus and I ate a hurried breakfast and carried our coffee to the car. He drove through the sleepy little mountain village and started down the long, winding road to Springville.

"You know, people do commute," I told him, looking out at the other cars behind and ahead of us. "If we got another car you could stay with us."

"And work for minimum wage in Springville?" He laughed bitterly. "I took some woodworking courses. I'll get something like that after I get things taken care of."

I leaned my head against his shoulder wishing he'd just give up on it, but afraid to say any more.

I left Marcus at his job and watched him walk through the gate with the lunch I'd made him.

One supermarket opened early, I drove there but had to wait half an hour for them to open. I shopped for groceries. One thing about Mountain's Peak: Prices on everything were higher so we tried to do all our shopping in Springville.

LOVERS AGAIN AFTER 5 YEARS APART

I got to Justin Williams's office just as he was unlocking the door. Nicole was beside him.

"Come in, Kim." He grinned broadly. "You're looking great. Must be all the cold mountain air." He chuckled.

I laughed, too, and said hello to Nicole. She returned my greeting, but her eyes were worried and she didn't seem happy to see me. I followed Justin inside.

"There's something I want to show you," he said, leading the way to his office. He took a piece of paper from his desk drawer and handed it to me. It was the letter from Marcus to Justin's uncle asking him to find me or send my address.

Justin closed the door. "You know, you asked me to review his case a couple of years ago and I did. If that letter had been there then, with no notation that it had been answered, no copy of a reply, I would have answered it myself. My uncle was careful about things like that," Justin said.

"What do you mean?" I asked.

"I had Nicole pull Marcus's file for me back when you first spoke about it awhile back, then I gave it back to her to put away," he said.

"You think she took the letter out and then put it back?" I asked.

"The family didn't want him getting in touch with you," he reminded me.

I sat down in one of the leather armchairs. "I just can't get over it . . . that they'd deceive him that way just for a little bit of money," I said. "I guess it seemed like more to them than it would have to me if I'd needed it."

"Have you heard any more from Marcus?" he asked.

I studied my hands. "He spent the weekend with Madison and me."

He drew a long breath and I looked up at him.

"Justin, you know I didn't want a divorce when you offered to marry me. Marcus came back, and it was the same as it had been before," I finished in a low voice.

He got up and stood at the window, looking out onto a little courtyard. "You're throwing your life away on him, Kim!" he warned.

"What if he really didn't do it?" I asked. "Justin, he's so bent on finding who did even though I've begged him not to try to do anything about it! He wouldn't do that if he was guilty!"

"It makes a great act!" He swung around to face me. "It gets all your sympathy. I imagine he's most convincing, but he's still what he's always been."

I stared at him angrily, searching for words.

"I'm sorry," he said. "You know how I feel about you. But, Kim, if I thought there was a chance that he's not guilty, I'd reopen the case and try to clear him."

"But there were three others who knew where he kept the gun," I began.

"I know. And they all had good alibis. They really did, Kim. Randy Reynolds has straightened up and works as a plumber . . . he's married with a family. The Cooper brothers have an auto body shop. If Marcus tries to make trouble for any of them, well he's the one who will suffer for it. I really am sorry, Kim."

I stood up and gathered my things. "Well, thanks for letting me know about the letter."

"He's telling the truth on that score," Justin admitted. "Real great family, huh?"

I nodded, and he came over and took my arm. "Kim, you know if there's anything I can do, all you have to do is tell me."

I turned to him. "Let Nicole go somewhere for coffee with me?" I asked.

"Well, sure," he agreed.

But she wasn't eager to go. "I can't get away right now," she began after I asked her.

"Oh, go ahead, Nicole," Justin told her. "Have a gab session."

Reluctantly, she got up from her desk and followed me outside.

"Where's a good place?" I asked.

"There's a coffee shop in the mall." She motioned across the street.

We walked over and I chattered on about how good the warm desert sun felt. "Usually we're grateful for all the snow we can get," I rambled on. "But this year we've had it so long I'm tired of it."

We sat in a booth and ordered coffee.

"Have you seen Marcus since he's been back?" I asked.

"Once, at my folks' house," she said. "I understand he's moved out."

I nodded. "Nicole, did you know about that letter in Marcus's file?"

Her eyes avoided mine. "Justin showed it to me," she said. "It must have been written just before he took over his uncle's practice, before I came there. I'd never seen it before. It's too bad . . . I mean, about you and Marcus. Just a misunderstanding all around."

I knew she lied.

"I have to ask you something," I told her. "While Marcus was in prison, he sent money orders for me and Madison to your folks. Your mom told him she didn't know where I was. You had my address and so did she."

"Oh, no, Kim. He sent that money to Mom," she interrupted. "He just told you that. He sent it to help out. You know, with Dad being sick and all."

I searched her face.

"Really," she insisted. "I don't know what he told you, but that was the way it was. He's probably just trying to make himself look good in your eyes."

I nodded. "What about the burglary?" I asked quietly. "Do you believe he did it?"

"Well, who else could have?" She shrugged. "I'm sorry. I suppose he's given you that line about being framed, but look at the evidence . . . his gun, his jacket, and he was out at that time. He always needed money, and I guess he wanted it for you and him. Kim, I never could understand what you saw in him. You could have had anybody, even Justin!"

"I loved Marcus," I told her quietly.

"I'm sure you probably did," she said. "I just, well, I've already said too much about what's none of my business."

Later, I drove to my father's office and sat in the parking lot for a few minutes thinking about Nicole. I was sure she'd lied about the letter. And why should she be so against Marcus? Had he really sent his parents that money? I couldn't believe that. He hadn't been close to his folks and hadn't gotten along very well with his father. Would he suddenly have become a devoted son and turned his back on me?

I went in to see my father. He and my mother had divorced and sold the house. She lived in a small apartment complex he owned and he gave her a living allowance.

"Hi, Kim," Dad greeted me. He had his hair styled

a new way and wore clothes that would have looked better on a twenty-year-old man.

"You look fantastic!" he gushed. "Hey, let me buy you some new outfits—"

"Daddy, I don't need anything," I cut him off.

"Always the independent one! I guess you got that from me. What have you been doing with yourself?"

"Working," I told him. "The snow is still on and we're swamped every weekend." I sat down in one of his plush chairs. "Marcus has been paroled."

"So I heard," he said. "Is he giving you trouble? You should've gotten a divorce long ago."

"No, he isn't giving me trouble," I said.

"You're not going to take him back, are you?" he demanded. "Kim, surely you have better sense than that."

"Daddy, I don't think he did that burglary and shooting—"

"Oh, Kim, come off it," he interrupted. "I know you couldn't see him for what he was then, a cheap hoodlum after your money . . . my money. But you're older now. You should be able to see through him."

"He never asked for anything," I flared. "Nothing!"

"He drove your car, didn't he?"

"When we went somewhere together or I told him to," I agreed. "But he was trying to make it on his own. He wouldn't even let me borrow a month's rent from you."

"Better he had than to rob a two-bit grocery store," my father snapped.

I knew there was nothing to be gained by talking to him.

"Well, I just came by to see how you were," I told him. "How's Mom?"

"She was in the hospital for a couple weeks," he said, knowing there was no need to say why. "She's better now. How's Madison?"

"Fine," I told him. "I've got to be going. Just wanted to say hello."

"Sorry I got heavy on you about Marcus. It's just that you could do better," Dad said.

"I know." I kissed him good-bye and left.

What now? I thought. When I was back in the car I tried to think of who else I might know something. It was probably crazy, or at least useless, but I decided to go see Marcus's folks.

The house looked even more run down than I remembered. Marcus's father sat in a rocker on the porch with a blanket over his knees.

"How are you, Mr. Conner?" I asked him.

He looked up at me and I couldn't be sure he remembered me.

"Not well," he said. "Not well at all."

"Do you remember me?" I asked.

"Kim . . . Marcus's wife?"

"We never hear from him," the old man mumbled. "Never hear from him at all."

"Wasn't he just here last week?" I asked. "Wasn't he staying with you?"

"Yeah. While he was in prison, we didn't hear anything . . . no letters, nothing. He came back, but now he left again. The boy doesn't care about us. I'm old and sick. He doesn't care."

"Didn't he send you money?" I coaxed.

"No, no money . . . nothing." He shook his head.

I knocked on the screen door and Marcus's

mother came to answer it.

"Oh, Kim." She smiled. "Marcus isn't here. He hasn't been here in days." She didn't invite me inside.

"Then you don't know where he is?" I asked.

"No." She shook her head. "Working . . . maybe with friends. Kim, you're better off without him. He's nothing but trouble. Find yourself another man." Her eyes reminded me of the way Nicole's had looked.

"Mrs. Conner, did you send him the pictures I gave you of Madison?" I asked.

"Yeah, I sent them, but he never said anything about them. I told him in letters about your pretty baby, but he didn't seem to care." She smiled. "How is Madison?"

"She's fine," I told her. "Well, I guess I'll be going."

They were lying. They were all lying! I sat in the car and tried to decide how much Marcus's father understood . . . whether he didn't understand anything or whether he lied, too. Each one seemed to be telling a different story. I wondered what Fredrick would tell me.

I found Fredrick's address in a phone book at a gas station pay phone and scribbled it down. The attendant said it was in a new subdivision and gave me instructions for getting there. I found the address easily and knocked on the door of a little house. Fredrick's wife, Lisa, came to the door with a baby in her arms. She was obviously pregnant again.

"Lisa?" I asked. "I don't know whether you remember me. I'm Kim Marcus's wife. We met at their folks' house once."

"Oh, yes. Come in, Kim." She smiled.

I stepped into the tiny cluttered living room.

"If you're looking for Marcus, none of us have seen him in days," she offered.

"Well, I was," I told her.

"Did he come to see you?" she asked. "Fredrick loaned him our truck a few days ago. He said he was going to see you."

"Yes, he did."

A little boy came into the room. He and the baby had the same big eyes as Madison's. We made conversation about the kids for a few minutes and then Lisa asked me to sit down. She sank down on the sofa.

"I was just wondering about a few things," I told her. "Marcus said he wrote to me at his folks' house, but his mother always insisted that he didn't want to hear from me and I took her word for it."

Lisa looked sad. "I know they did that. Listen, don't tell Fredrick or anyone that I talked to you."

"I won't," I promised. "You mean you knew that he wrote me there?"

She nodded.

"Did you know his mother told him I picked up his letters there?" I asked.

She nodded again. "Kim, I knew about all that . . . what they were doing . . . but Fredrick said Marcus owed it to them and I didn't really know much about what had gone on before. We weren't here when Marcus got in trouble. Fredrick was still in the Army, and we didn't get back here until Marcus had been gone a year or so. I thought it wasn't right, but it wasn't any of my business, and I didn't want trouble with Fredrick or his folks."

"You knew about them keeping the money?" I asked.

She nodded.

"Do you know whether it was sent to me or to them?"

"I think it was sent for you, but don't tell anybody I told you all this."

I promised I wouldn't tell and told her I had to be leaving. Her story seemed to back up other things I'd learned. But no matter what, that didn't prove anything about Marcus's guilt or innocence, I reminded myself.

I started back to Justin's office, not really knowing why. I certainly didn't have any new evidence of any kind. If I wanted to find out who Marcus had sent the money to, all I had to do was ask that a tracer be put on one of the money orders to see who it had been made out to. I could ask Justin to do that, and if they'd forged my signature . . . suddenly I felt as if a very big threat had fallen into my hands. If they had forged my signature, it would be a federal offense!

I passed the Cooper brothers' body shop, and on an impulse I pulled in. Matt, the younger one, came out of the big shop door.

"Hey, Kim!" He grinned. "It's been years. You're looking good."

I got out of my car and stood leaning against it. "Hello, Matt. You look pretty good yourself," I told him.

"Except for the grease under my fingernails?" he asked.

I laughed. "Nice shop. Is business good?"

"Making a living," he said. "What can I do for you?"

"I wondered if you'd seen Marcus," I said.

"Yeah, he came by here over a week ago. He's got a real chip on his shoulder. I hope it doesn't get him back into trouble."

"What do you mean?" I asked.

"Well, he said he was going to find who framed him and take matters into his own hands. Haven't you seen him?"

"Yeah." I nodded. "That's what he tells me and I'm worried about it."

"It's a shame." Matt shook his head. "I'd like to help him. We offered him a job and he turned it down. I guess I'd feel just about as bitter if I were him."

"What do you mean?" I asked.

"If I'd taken a bum rap." He offered me a soda and then opened one for himself when I refused.

"Do you think he took a bum rap?" I used his words.

He took a sip of his drink. "Sure, he did, Kim. We were wild and acted tough, but it was Marcus who kept us all out of serious trouble most of the time. He wouldn't have done something like robbing old Amos. It wasn't his style. He might have punched him out, but he wouldn't have used a gun or robbed him."

"Not even if he needed money?" I asked.

Matt shook his head. "He was talking about selling his bike. He'd have done that first. He never even carried that gun. We all had guns. We thought it was a big deal right then, but it just wasn't something Marcus would have done. Heck, Kim, you had him so tamed down he hardly even rode with us anymore!"

"Then who do you think did it?" I asked.

He shrugged. "I've wondered about that. My brother and I knew he had the gun, and so did Randy Reynolds. I think we were the only ones, except for his family."

"Did his family know about it?" I asked. I hadn't thought of that.

"Well, it was right there in the shed. His old man was always prowling around, and so were the younger kids."

"They were mostly girls. . . ." I said.

"One of them could have had a boyfriend. Now, this is just a theory, something I thought of because I've wondered about it a lot," Matt went on. "Maybe one of the kids told somebody about the gun."

"But it was put back," I reminded him. "If somebody stole it and used it, he'd be more likely just to throw it away or keep it."

"There you go," Matt agreed. "I thought of that, too. I always wondered why it was put back. One thing is for sure, if Marcus had used it he'd have been smart enough not to put it back, and he wouldn't have left his jacket lying around, either."

We were silent a moment, both of us busy with our own thoughts.

"You and Marcus back together?" Matt finally asked.

I nodded.

"You always were good for him." He grinned. "Broke up our gang, but you were good for him. Probably just as well you broke up our gang, too. You know, Marcus was so straight after you two got together he should have been the last one to wind up in trouble. It just doesn't make any sense."

I thanked him for talking to me and got back into my car. He was the only one who'd had anything good to say about Marcus. I drove back to Justin's office.

"You're back," Nicole said, surprised. "Justin is in court."

I sat down in the empty waiting room. She went on with what she was doing for a few minutes and then looked up.

"I don't know how long he'll be gone. Are you going to wait?" she asked.

"I've been thinking," I told her. "About Marcus handing me that line about sending me money. He gave me the stubs of the money orders and, of course, they don't prove anything except that he bought money orders. I'm going to put a tracer on some of them and see who they were made out to."

She stared at me a moment in shock. "Why-why would you do that?" she managed finally.

"To know the truth," I told her. "Your mother says one thing, your father another, you another, and Marcus still another."

"My parents are old. They don't understand anything," she said, and I noticed her hands were shaking.

"They'd understand if they forged my signature," I told her.

She sort of crumpled and leaned her head in her hand.

"They needed the money," she choked. "I wasn't working yet. All the kids and Dad not working . . . and your folks had money. They'd have given you anything you needed."

"Did you help your folks forge my signature or

cash the checks?" I asked.

She was trembling. "Kim, I didn't actually realize how serious it was what we were doing. Look, if it's the money, I'll pay you back."

"It's not the money I care about," I told her. "I'd probably have given it to them if they'd asked. But was it fair to Marcus?"

"Kim, you don't realize how it was for us," Nicole cried. "We were always so poor and then that happened. I didn't know what was going on. The police came and arrested Marcus. . . ."

"I don't believe Marcus did it," I told her. "Your whole family knew about his gun." I was going to ask her if she'd told someone else or if one of the younger kids had, but she didn't give me a chance.

"Marcus is out now!" she told me. "You two can get back together or do whatever you want. My father is old. He would have died in prison! Mama would have grieved herself to death, and there were the three younger kids. You always had everything easy. What would you know about trying to scrimp along from one welfare check to the next? Old Amos always treated us like dirt and my dad couldn't take any more. But we didn't know what he'd done until after Marcus was arrested."

"So you just let Marcus take the blame?" I gasped. "Instead of your father?"

She was crying. "Kim, I'll pay you back that money a little at a time. Fredrick might help if I tell him you were going to check on the money orders."

I stood up. "I don't want the money!" I protested.

I went out into the warm sunlight and sat in my car. I'd let myself believe Marcus was guilty all that time. It had been easier than trying to find out the truth. I'd let myself believe his mother instead of contacting him on my own. I could have gotten his address from his lawyer . . . from the authorities . . . somehow. If I'd talked to Matt Cooper then, he would have told me about Marcus's family knowing about the gun. So many ifs! But mostly, if I'd believed in my husband, the man my heart had told me to believe in, things might have been different.

Justin pulled up after awhile and came over to my car. I told him what Nicole had told me and we went back inside. She broke down and told him the whole story.

"You know, the sad part is that your father would probably have been judged too incompetent to stand trial," he told her. "At least, he is now. And it would have been a whole different kind of case if Lou Amos had aggravated your father. That's not grounds for shooting somebody, but it would have been taken into consideration with someone like your father."

"I didn't know all that then." She sobbed. "I only knew he was old and Mama was carrying on, saying he'd die in prison, and that they'd take part of the money we got to live on away from us. Then when Marcus sent money for Kim, it seemed like we needed it worse than she did, and I never thought about how serious it was or getting caught or anything like that."

"I just want Marcus cleared," I told him.

He said to have Marcus come talk to him.

I picked Marcus up after work. "You still here?" he asked, sliding tiredly into the car beside me. He kissed me and leaned back against the seat. "What have you been doing all day?"

"Shopping for groceries and some decent clothes for you. I was also trying to straighten out your life," I said.

"What do you mean?" he asked, a little suspiciously.

"I know now that I should have gotten in touch with you a long time ago," I told him, "instead of listening to what your mother or anyone else said. I should've believed you. I went to see your folks and Fredrick's wife and Nicole today. When I threatened to have those money orders checked to see who they were made out to and whether my signature had been forged, Nicole broke down and told the whole story."

"I didn't think you cared about the money," he said.

"I don't. I care about having you cleared of a crime you didn't commit," I told him.

His eyes searched mine. "Kimberly, what do you mean?"

"Promise you won't do anything rash when I tell you who did shoot Lou Amos?" I asked.

He nodded.

"Nicole admitted that your father killed Lou after they'd argued and he thought Lou had treated him badly. Oh, honey, I'm sorry! They let you take the blame because your father was old and not well, and I guess they were afraid he'd go to prison and die there."

Shock and anger and finally acceptance crossed Marcus's face.

"Justin Williams is going to reopen the case and have you cleared," I said.

"You really dug it all up didn't you?" he asked.

"Are you sure about all this?"

I nodded. "Justin wants you to sign some papers, and then he'll go to the district attorney with it. He thinks he can protect Nicole and Fredrick and your mom, even though they were wrong in covering up for your father. And no court would find him competent to stand trial the way he is now. They probably wouldn't have even then." Tears filled my eyes and ran down my face. Marcus pulled me into his arms and he was crying, too.

After awhile we went to see Justin, and then we went home to Mountain's Peak. I told Ed and Maggie what had happened, and Ed went to Marcus's parole officer with him the next day and told him he was giving Marcus a job.

It took a few weeks to have Marcus entirely cleared, and even longer for a lot of the scars to heal. His father was declared incompetent, and no charges were even filed against his mother or siblings. I guess everyone thought there had been enough suffering.

We still live in Mountain's Peak. Ed and Maggie offered to give us an acre of land to build a house on, just to keep their "family" all there with them.

Marcus does carpentry work for a contractor and works on our house when he has time. It will probably be ready to move into next summer. I hope so, because our two rooms get crowded enough with the three of us and by then we'll have a new member in the family.

Time and love and trust have healed most of the scars, but I think Marcus and I will always be a little closer, a little more careful of our love, because of the lies that kept us apart for five years.　　THE END

THE NURSES
CALL HER HOLLY

Ed lay on the bed with his eyes open. "I wish you didn't have to go to work," he said.

"Well, I've got to. And I've got to hurry, too." I stepped quickly into my white panty hose and drew them up. I glanced at the clock and frowned when I saw the time. I was going to be late for work—again. I shouldn't have let Ed make love to me.

"You ought to quit, Jane. We don't need the money, you know." And Ed was off on the same old nagging complaint. "After all, we're getting older now, and we should be thinking about starting a family."

I felt a little twinge of anger rise in me. I wished he would stop pestering me about having a baby. Right now I just didn't feel responsible enough to have a child. And besides, I didn't want to give up my job at the hospital or the money that came with it.

"Come on now, honey. Help me get ready, huh? Find my shoes for me," I urged him, hoping that he would change the subject.

"Oh, sure, honey." He slipped off the side of the bed and searched the floor for my missing shoes. "I've got them!" he yelled. I was in the bathroom fixing my hair and putting on a couple of touches of makeup. When I worked the night shift at the hospital, I didn't worry too much about how I looked. It was dark, and the patients would be asleep.

As I was bending over, tying my shoes, I felt Ed's hand running up my back. "Stay home tonight, huh? I've still got a lot of loving left for you. It seems a shame to let it all go to waste."

I jerked away from him and grabbed my purse. "Can't. Gotta go," I mumbled and gave him a quick peck on the cheek. As I shut the door, I saw him standing by the bed with a hangdog look on his face. Ed didn't like it when I had to work the night shift, and I really couldn't blame him. But it was part of my job at Memorial Hospital.

I drove quickly through the light traffic to the hospital.

It wasn't very far from my home. It was almost within walking distance, but I hated to be out on the streets at night. As I drove, I thought sadly about my husband. Right now he would probably be crawling back into bed or curling up on the couch to watch television. Certainly he would be lonely, and I felt responsible for that.

I'd promised him and myself that I would quit nursing when it was financially possible for me to do so. We had made plans about starting a family and settling down like every other couple we knew; but when the time came, almost two years ago, I just couldn't do it.

While Ed had been going to school, my job had

carried us through the rough spots—and there had been plenty of those. I had secretly been proud of the fact that I had earned enough to make it possible for him to continue his education, and he had appreciated my efforts.

Now, though, I knew he resented my job. At first I had stalled, saying that we needed furniture and clothes. But finally, after several months, Ed forced me to face the fact that I just didn't want to quit. He assumed that it was the money I made. And certainly that was part of it. But that wasn't the only reason—or even the main one.

The real reason that I refused to quit my job was that I didn't want to have a baby. I hadn't told Ed that. Somehow I knew I could never word it so he'd understand. It would just end up in another fight. The plain fact was that I was afraid to have a baby. I was afraid of the physical reality of it and the responsibility of raising a child.

"Going to be a rough night tonight, Jane. Full moon." Frank, one of the interns, greeted me as I entered the hospital. He rolled his eyes and made a scary face. He was what I suppose you could call the hospital clown, although he was very good at his job.

"You don't believe that stuff, do you?" I asked while I checked my roster of patients. I was relieved that I would have no hard cases tonight. Nothing of an emergency nature should happen while I was on duty, full moon or no full moon.

"Sure. It's a medical fact, didn't you know that? More rapes and murders and people going buggy happen on full-moon nights. Proven, and that's a fact. All that gravity drives people nuts." He shrugged his shoulders.

"How is Mr. Sorenson doing?" I asked, hoping he would get down to business. Mr. Sorenson had been brought in the other night suffering from a severe heart attack. He was a handsome, youthful-looking man and had been close to death. I hoped he had improved.

"Up and at 'em this morning, I guess," Frank joked. "Shouldn't be any problem, Jane," he added seriously.

I worked through the night doing mostly routine chores and checking on my various patients. I'd been right—this was going to be an uneventful night.

Then, around four in the morning, I heard the wail of an ambulance siren. Frank and an emergency nurse burst through the door and ran for the emergency room. Curious, and having nothing else to do, I followed, hoping I'd be able to help in some way.

I got there as they were wheeling in the victim on a stretcher. She was just a baby, not older than six months I estimated, and she looked horrible. Her face was very puffy, and her skin was pale and sweaty looking. She appeared to be in a delirium of some kind and kept rolling her head about crazily. Two other nurses and one intern were taking care of her. I noticed Frank talking to the ambulance driver, and I went over to them to see what the story was going on.

"That's right. A couple of high school kids out parking found her. She was locked up in an old sedan. They called right in, but it looks bad." The driver shook his head slowly and walked away.

"What's up, Frank?" I asked, wanting to hear the complete story.

"Desertion case, it looks like. A couple of lovers went out into the hills to find a nice quiet place. The guy must be a regular, because he recognized the car and realized it hadn't moved since the night before. Curious, he checked it out and found the baby inside. That's about it," Frank said, and then he followed the stretcher out of the emergency room.

The doctors worked on the baby for over an hour, getting her set up properly. I took a peek at her after they were through. They had put her in my section. As I walked into the dark room, I noticed they were feeding her intravenously, and they had probably given her a sedative because she was quiet now.

When I got close to her, I could tell that she had probably been a cute little girl before this had happened to her. I also noticed that her face had a few telltale black-and-blue marks on it. She had obviously been beaten as well as deserted. As gently as I could, I pulled her covers back and lifted the hospital gown to take a look at her body. It was a horrid mass of bruises and even some open wounds. There were ulcerated sores where the ammonia from her urine in the unchanged diaper had eaten into her tender skin. There were also a series of small circular scars. Somehow I knew they were old burns.

"Pretty grim, huh?" I heard Frank say softly behind me. I swallowed the lump in my throat and turned to face him. "How old is she, Frank?" I asked.

"Well, we figure she's about eight months old, but she's so undernourished she looks a lot younger. They haven't found her parents yet. The police are still checking on the car," he said.

"I hope they throw them in jail!" I said bitterly. "People who could do this to an innocent, helpless child are sick. They should be locked away with the criminally insane!" I turned from him and gazed again at the small, still form in the crib. "Is she going to make it, Frank?" I asked.

"Hard to say. She's in awfully bad shape, Jane. Well, give me a call if you need anything." Frank left, shutting the door quietly behind him.

I sat on a chair by the edge of the crib. This had been part of my training, and I had seen cases of child abuse several times during the course of my work at the hospital, but I had never seen a child abuse case as brutal or pathetic as this one.

By the time I got home, Ed was out of bed and getting ready for his own day at work. There were times when I wished I were a teacher, and this was one of them. I was pretty depressed and disgusted when I got home, and I guess it was pretty visible to my husband.

"Another bad night, huh?" I nodded my head. "Want a cup of coffee?" He poured us both a cup and sat down at the kitchen table with me. "You ought to quit, Jane. This job is getting you down, and you don't need it," he began to say. After the night I had put in, I didn't feel like talking to him at all, especially about my work. "We can start a family," he persisted. "You can have a baby like you've always wanted."

"Who said I wanted a baby?" I asked sharply. The

vision of the child lying in the hospital bed jumped into my mind.

"Well, you've always said you wanted—" Ed began, more than a little bit shocked.

"I don't now! I don't!" I shouted angrily. How did I know that I wouldn't resent having a baby to take care of all the time and begin to mistreat it? Tonight I'd seen the horrible results of what happened to some unwanted babies. I wasn't at all sure I wanted one myself, and if I didn't want one, wouldn't my feelings turn to hate if I actually had one? I wished I knew.

"What's got into you lately, Jane?" my husband asked, his anger matching mine. "You've always said you wanted a baby. Boy, you're getting to be something else! I'm telling you, you'd better start thinking about what you want to do more, work or be my wife. It's obvious that you can't manage to do both!"

"What do you know about it?" I shot back at him. Inside, though, I knew he was right. For a long time I'd been stalling, delaying making a decision. I was just too uncertain about starting a family. "Maybe I don't want one. Maybe I'd hate it and beat it up. Maybe I'd kill it."

"Oh, come on! What makes you say that? That's stupid," Ed said, stunned.

"Well, I don't know, Ed. I don't know if I really want children or not. I mean, I thought I did, at one time. But now I'm afraid." At last I had been truthful with my husband. It was a huge relief to get it off my mind.

"Afraid? Of what?"

I ran my fingers nervously through my hair.

"Tonight they brought in a child who had been horribly abused, Ed. She might die, and she's only eight months old. It's a lot of responsibility having a baby, and I don't know if I want that kind of responsibility."

"I've got to go to work," Ed said in a depressed voice. "I wish I could stay here and talk to you about this. I think I could make you see that there's no reason for your fears. But just think about it, huh? Think about all the love a child of ours would have, and what a good home we'd provide for it. Okay, honey?" Ed bent down and kissed me on the cheek.

I crawled into bed, exhausted, not wanting to think about anything. I didn't know what to do. A part of me wanted a baby and a part of me didn't. I didn't know which part to trust. And it was obvious that I was going to have to make some kind of a decision soon.

When I got back to the hospital that night, the little girl's condition hadn't changed. She was still on the critical list. I wanted to sit the night with her, and I got one of the other nurses to cover for me out on the floor.

"The day nurses named her Holly," she told me. "Kind of a Christmas name they thought up. They say maybe it'll bring her good luck."

Holly. I sat throughout the night with her, just listening to her uneven breathing. With every breath she took, she might have gone into convulsions again. Her condition was that unstable.

I was sitting by her, thinking of my own situation with Ed and what I should do about it, when suddenly her eyelids quivered and her head slumped down on the mattress. Then she began to arch and twist, and I realized that she was going into another convulsion.

"Don't die, Holly!" I cried, and I frantically began to try to keep her from injuring herself or strangling on the foamy saliva that was filling her mouth.

Frank was at my side a moment after I rang, and together we worked, trying to bring the seizure under control.

Finally, after what seemed like hours of tiring effort, Holly's breathing began to improve and her heart rate was near normal.

"I think she'll be all right now, Jane," Frank said wearily. "Thanks to your alertness. You must have been right on top of it when it happened. Otherwise, she could be gone by now. You've done a tremendous job."

I felt myself flushing at Frank's compliment. "It's only my duty. And don't get so dramatic about it. Holly is only another patient to me."

"Oh, sure," Frank said. He looked down at the baby lying quietly in her bed. "This kid isn't going to have much of a Christmas this year, is she?"

"No," I admitted sadly. "And it's her first one, too. It ought to be something special."

"Yeah, well—hopefully next year will be different for her." Frank turned to leave, but I stopped him.

"What are they going to do with her, Frank? I mean, after she is well enough to leave the hospital. Have they found her parents yet?"

"No, and I hope they never do. And if they do catch up with them, I hope they lock them up for about fifty years!" he snapped.

"But what's going to happen to Holly?" I questioned him again.

"I would imagine she'll go to a foster care home temporarily. If there's brain damage, which we won't be able to tell for a while, she probably will be placed in a custodial institution. Not many people want to adopt problem children."

After Frank left, I sat and watched Holly sleep. A long time passed that way, but to me it seemed like only a few short minutes. She was such a beautiful, sweet baby I couldn't understand how anyone could have beaten her and left her to die. It wasn't right. It wasn't fair. And I was glad I had been able to save her life. I was beginning to think that Holly was someone very special.

"They're going to put her up for adoption," I said to Ed when I got home.

"Who's going to put who up for adoption?" Ed was scuffling around the kitchen in his pajamas, fixing himself toast and coffee for his breakfast.

"The baby. Holly." A confused look came over Ed's face. "The baby who was beaten and deserted," I explained.

"Oh. Well, I hope she makes it," he said blankly.

"Don't you care?"

Ed stood and looked at me, his eyes searching mine. "Isn't that the kid who turned you against having a baby of your own? If so, then—no, I don't care very much."

"That's the cruelest thing I've ever heard, Ed! I don't understand how you can have such a cold heart. If only you could see Holly, then you would feel differently." I felt as though I was going to start crying.

"Hey! What's the matter with you?" he asked, noticing my emotional state. "Weren't you the one who didn't want to have anything to do with babies?"

"I saved Holly's life last night, Ed. I was praying she wouldn't die while I was trying to save her. She's so beautiful, and do you know what kind of life she might have if the right people don't adopt her?"

"What is this? I don't understand you, Jane. The other night you said you didn't want a baby under any circumstances—"

"But Holly is just special!" I insisted. "She's a special baby. She's had such a hard time, Ed, yet she balls up her fists and fights for her life. I didn't know babies could be so—"

"So real?"

"I watched her all night—after her attack. And this may sound ridiculous, Ed, but I want to adopt Holly."

"Jane, are you serious?" He came to me and took me in his arms. All I could do was murmur, "Yes." Inside, I felt panic. I wasn't over my fears yet, but I knew I had to have Holly for my own. "Can I go see her tomorrow?" Ed asked. "I know I'll love her, too, but I want to see her. I want Holly to know both of us before we bring her home!" he said excitedly.

We've been lucky. We've watched Holly's eyes light up at the sight of a Christmas tree and seen her delight in the gaily wrapped packages we'd bought for. Her first Christmas was something special—for all of us.

Ed and I have had Holly for two months now. Most of her scars and bruises have disappeared, and her cruel emaciation has turned to a healthy rosy glow. But Ed and I know that what she needs most is not food but generous amounts of love. If we're permitted to adopt her—and our lawyer is sure we will—we're ready to give her all the love any little girl could want.

I'm still afraid of the responsibilities I've taken on. Being a mother isn't as easy as being a nurse. But with my husband's help and with Holly's bright smiles, I know I can handle the job.   THE END

FORBIDDEN AFFAIR

The sun beat down on my back in long, hot, golden waves. I was lying on my stomach, face buried in folded arms, above the roughness of the beach towel and the grainy heat of the sand. *This is the way young girls stretch out,* I thought. *Old lady, you should be in a rocking chair on the cottage porch, rocking and watching the waves come in. Remember, you're no young girl. You're fifty—half a century has gone by since the day you were born.*

Sad thoughts, those, like autumn rain beating against my brain, but they didn't bother me. I felt as if I'd lost the capacity to feel. My husband, Al, had been dead seven months now, and they may as well have been seven centuries. Somehow I'd have to find a way to pass the time until I, too, finally died. So much of me seemed already dead.

"Go to the beach, Mother," my children had said. "Get a good rest. When you come back, we'll think about selling the house. Then you can get a little apartment close to us—that's what you need."

Yes, sell the house as we'd sold the shop after Al had died. How Al and I had worked, making a success of that shop. It was called The Display—we sold supplies to make displays for store windows, for wedding decorations, church bazaars—things like that. When Al had opened it twenty years ago, people had said it would never succeed, but it had. It had made a good living for us. After our kids, Amy and Edmund, had grown up, I'd worked full-time in the shop along with Al.

But then his sickness had come—the cancer—and it had been long and brutal. I'd turned the shop over to Barry Newton, our assistant, and gone with Al from one hospital to another, and, finally, nursed him at home until he entered the hospital for the last time.

After Al died, Barry had wanted to buy the shop and my kids had said that I should let him. "You've worked hard enough," they said. "You've got Dad's insurance, and with the money from the sale of the shop, you'll get along well without having to work again. At your age, you shouldn't have to."

Al and I had often rented one of the cottages at Sun Grove. It wasn't a fashionable place, but the rent was cheap and we liked it. Now, in early September, it was deserted. It would stay hot until the second week of October, probably. That was usually when the autumn storms started.

I'd been here a month already, just vegetating in the sun and sea air. Physically, I felt great, but the heavy weight on my spirit made me drag around slowly—to feel as if there was no purpose to my life. Nothing to stay for—but nothing to go home for, either.

Sighing, I rolled over on my back, and then I blinked behind my oversized sunglasses. A man was coming toward me. Since nobody had been in the other cottages for a week or so, I'd thought I had the beach all to myself.

He was a tall man, and very thin. His shoulders were somewhat stooped, his thick hair blowing in the breeze. You could tell he hadn't been out in the sun much. He looked as if he was getting over some sickness—a slow, exhausting sickness that had worn him out. At a distance, I thought he was my age or older from the listless way he carried himself, but when he came closer I saw that his skin was firm and unlined. In his late twenties, probably—a young man who walked like an old man with an old man's hopeless expression. Suddenly, I knew I had been lonely, because I was glad to see this stranger. I sat up and smiled. "Hi," I said.

He looked as surprised to see me as I'd been to see him. "Hi." His voice was rusty, as if he wasn't used to using it. He tried for a smile, but it wasn't much.

"I didn't know anyone was here. I thought all the cottages were empty. Maybe you just came down for the day?" He sounded hopeful, as if he wanted me to be here only briefly, as if he wanted the sand and the sea to himself.

"No—I live up there." I waved my hand at my little cottage that stood just beyond the nearest dunes. "I've been here for—oh, five weeks or so. And you?"

"I live in the blue cottage—the one at the other end of the beach. I—I just came a few days ago. A couple of days ago to be exact. This is the first time I've been this far down the beach." He sounded as if he felt he should explain his every move to me. As if I had the right to approve or disapprove.

I patted the sand with my palm. "Sit down." He

hunkered down, sitting on his heels, scooping up handfuls of sand and letting them trickle through his fingers. "My name is Nina Grogan," I said.

"I'm Ben Tuckwill." We were like a couple of shy children introducing each other on a playground. After a moment of awkward silence, he said, "Your tan—it's nice. You've got a really good tan. You're—toast brown. It looks nice with your hair."

"And you don't have any tan at all, so if you stay out much longer you'll get a bad burn." I pressed my thumb against the flushed skin of his upper arm, leaving a white mark when I removed it. "Yes, you're already burning. You ought to get out of the sun."

"I burn easily," he said as if he didn't care. He dropped down to sit on the sand, his pink legs out before him. Then he looked at me—a shy, sideways glance out of sad eyes. "Do you mind me sitting here?"

He was so unsure of himself he made me feel assured. I laughed. "Lord, no! It's your beach as much as mine." I reached into my beach robe pocket and offered him a stick of gum, which he chewed in silence except for his very brief answers to my questions. Yes, he was here alone. He planned to stay some time—he wasn't sure how long. "I've been sick," he finally admitted, adding quickly "—but they discharged me from the hospital a week ago. I'm not sick now."

After awhile it got uncomfortable between us because it was so awkward. "I'm going for a swim," I said and left him. When I came out of the water, he was gone. Later I passed him, lying some distance down the beach, sound asleep. I knew I should wake him, because he was going to be sick from that burn if he wasn't careful, but now it was my turn to be shy. Who was I? Some sort of nursemaid? I'd warned him about burning, and he was an adult.

After a little while I went into my cottage, showered and changed into my nightgown, watched my tiny portable TV for a while, then went to bed. A couple of sleeping pills knocked me out at last. Once I'd scorned all pills. Now I weakly depended on them.

But the next morning I had breakfast, three cups of coffee and some toast, eaten without appetite, and I thought of Ben Tuckwill. Finally, I got into my bathing suit and wandered down on the beach. He wasn't in sight, and I started worrying about him. At last, I walked down to the blue cottage and tapped on the door. I had to knock quite hard before he came to the door, a white terry cloth robe flashing bright against the angry red of his sunburn.

"Oh Lord, I warned you!" Sighing, I walked into the room and motioned him to lie down on the day bed, which was evidently where he slept. I dug into my beach bag and brought out a bottle of lotion. "I got this in Mexico a couple of years ago when my husband and I went to Veracruz on vacation," I told him. "It's powerful stuff—very good. Lower that bathrobe there, I'll oil you good. Then I'll give you a couple aspirin for the pain and fever. Maybe you should even see a doctor."

"No doctor." He glared out of his bloodshot, sore-looking eyes.

"Okay, calm down." I rubbed the oil on him in long, gentle swipes. It seemed strange to touch a masculine, muscular back again. I oiled him all over like a baby. Then I made him take the aspirin. "I'll bring over an ice bag and some chilled juice," I told him as I left.

"You need lots of liquids. I won't be gone long."

And that's how I got to know Ben Tuckwill. I nursed him through his sunburn and we talked. I told him about my life with Al and the children, to keep his mind off the pain, and as he got better he talked about himself, as if that was a part of his healing, too.

He'd had a good job as an account executive with an ad agency, making good money, and if he'd played his cards right there would have been more money as he fought his way up the corporate ladder. He and his wife, Lily, had a split-level house in a nice suburb.

Lily was intelligent and pretty. She was an interior decorator and good at her job. They had no children. Lily said only an insecure woman needed children for fulfillment. She was so sure of herself that Ben thought she was probably right. Too bad, because he liked kids. In college he'd been an English major, and he'd wanted to teach kids—teach them the beauty and order of a language perfectly used. But teachers didn't make much money and account executives did. But as he worked, his nerves had become tighter, knotting inside him day after day, and shadows had appeared and voices had whispered strange things in his head—voices that weren't real but only echoes. One day his supervisor found him crouched in the corner of his office, crying and whimpering and begging the echo-voices to be still.

It was a bad breakdown. He'd been in a private hospital for a while and then later, when it became evident he wasn't going to pop back just like that, he'd been taken to the state hospital. He'd been there two years until the gray, nightmare world had slowly cleared and, at last, painfully frightened, he had been able to face reality again. By that time, his home was gone, his job was gone, and Lily was gone. He didn't blame his agency for firing him, or Lily for divorcing him.

The next week Ben and I saw each other often. We'd spend the long, hot days together, playing like kids in the breakers, tossing a beach ball back and forth, making sand castles even—a lost young man and a woman who was growing old, we pushed time back for a little while. We refused to think of our past, just as we refused to think of the years ahead.

But something was happening to me, something that frightened me. My body was becoming alive again. Maybe I couldn't think so clearly yet, but I could feel, and what I felt was a growing desire for this young man. And it was such a strong desire— stronger and more demanding than any physical want I'd ever known.

This blazing, tormenting desire was something strange, and it terrified me and I called myself a fool. My God, I was twenty years older than Ben! He was just five years older than my son. This desire was unnatural. I was nothing but a dirty old woman to even think of it!

I tried to keep it light between us—fun—with me always shoving my age in his face like a barrier. But the situation was becoming explosive, and we both knew it.

Then there was the night we decided to grill hot dogs on the beach over a driftwood fire. It had been a very hot day, and the sand was warm under our bare feet, although the wind from the sea was chill—a reminder that summer was here on borrowed time. But Ben and I built a high, blazing fire against the chill. And, in the warmth of that fire, we could pretend it was August again.

After we'd eaten, we sat on the sand and watched the fire slowly burn down. I sat well away from him, but he pulled me over. As if I had no will at all, I leaned against him, resting my head against his shoulder. "If we had a radio, we could hear music," I murmured to break the silence.

"We don't need music, Nina," he told me, and then his arms were around me, swinging me back so that I lay across his knees. My lips parted with my panting breath. My eyes took in the beauty of his strong young face coming closer to mine, and then my lashes drifted down against my cheek. I was too limp, too shaken with desire to hold my eyes open. And he kissed me and kissed me. Then his hands were pulling my robe from me, peeling off my suit as if it were an extra skin that I didn't need.

I'll pull away in a moment, I told myself, but the moment passed and then it was too late to pull away. I could only cling to him as my voice murmured a cowardly—"No, Ben—no!"

Love with Ben was a frenzy—an intoxication. It was white-hot flames and rich red wine. Sometimes, with Al, I'd had trouble reaching a climax. There was none of that with Ben. My body rose to the heights, shivered with unbearable delirium, and then relaxed only to become deliriously aflame again.

When at long last it was over, we stretched out beside the slowly dying embers of our driftwood fire. By now even the sand had cooled, but our bodies were still warm and damp with love. "I love you, Nina," he murmured.

At this moment I couldn't argue or reason with him. I could only whisper, "Oh, Ben, I love you, too!"

FORBIDDEN AFFAIR

The next few days were like a honeymoon. Ben and I couldn't bear to be parted, even for a moment. He moved into my cottage, and we lived in a maze of love. For a while each day was enough by itself, but then Ben began to think of the future. Actually, the thing that brought his thoughts on was a letter from my daughter.

"You've been gone long enough, Mom," she wrote. "The weather's going to get bad and Edmund and I don't like to think of you out there alone at the beach. You've already stayed longer than we expected you to. I've found a very nice apartment just three blocks away from my apartment and seven blocks from Edmund's home. You'll be close enough so we can keep an eye on you.

"Edmund is in a hurry to put your house on the market, and I also have a buyer for your car. I can't see why you'd need one. The new apartment is near a shopping mall. I'm sure you'll like it very much. There are several widows living there, and you'll soon make friends with them."

Her letter went on and on, planning my life as if I were a tottering seventy instead of a vibrant fifty. I was still middle-aged, not old! And Ben's love had made me feel so very young!

Ben found me reading that letter and crying. He took the pages out of my hands and read them himself, and his face flushed with anger. "Well, you can tell your son and daughter they can stop worrying about you," he said. "Your future belongs to me now."

I stared at him. "What do you mean?"

"We're going to get married, of course," he said, putting one arm around me and hugging me tightly. "Oh, I'll have to think of some kind of a future for me.

319

I don't have much money. A lot of it went when I was ill, and the rest Lily got."

I pretended I hadn't heard him speak of marriage. I knew how impossible that was, but I didn't want to argue with him—not yet. I pounced on his own plans, trying to make him think about himself and what he would do when he left here.

"You wanted to be a teacher," I reminded him. "Why not go back to college and get your teacher's certificate?"

"I don't have that kind of money," he said, shaking his head, but his voice was wistful.

"So you could get some kind of job—any job. Work part-time and go to school full-time. Or, if it would take more money than that—work full-time and go to school part-time."

"If I only went to school part-time, it would take at least two years to get a teacher's certificate." He frowned. "I'll be thirty next month. I don't have time to waste."

Thirty! I wanted to laugh and I wanted to cry! He'd said thirty as if he was hovering on the brink of middle-age! Oh, our time values were all loused up!

"It's never too late to do what you want to do," I told him.

For a few moments his eyes were sparkling with dreams, and then he shook his head again. "I only want one thing, Nina—that's to marry you and take care of you."

So, I wasn't going to be allowed to put it off. I sighed deeply. "Ben, we are not going to get married. This time at the beach—it's been a magic, wonderful, perfect time—but it's all we'll have. There are too many years between us. Ben, you're not quite thirty.

FORBIDDEN AFFAIR

I'm fifty! Old enough to be your mother."

"Hush," he said in a kind of panic. "You're not old—and I don't care how many years you've lived. You're beautiful and young. You'll always be young."

I laughed sadly. "Now you're talking like a child. In just ten years I'll be sixty. Sixty, Ben—think of it. I'll be old!"

He flinched. Although he was a mature man, he was thinking that sixty was old. And, to him, it seemed so. I could remember how I'd felt when I was his age.

I still felt that way, although it was hard to realize how much of my life had gone by. I didn't even feel fifty! But there it was.

The argument went on, senseless and hurting to us both. Finally, I couldn't bear it. "We'll resolve this later, Ben," I told him. "You're right about one thing. At this time, your future is too uncertain for me to share. Go back to college and get your teacher's certificate. Then we can talk about it."

"Will you wait two years?" he asked anxiously.

"Real love can stand the test of time," I told him.

But I knew two years were too many at my age. No matter. In two years, Ben would have his feet under him again. He'd have the excitement of a new career, and he might, in that time, find a new love—a woman more his age.

But at least what I'd said sent him into a frenzy of planning. He wrote off for college catalogues and wrote letters to friends who might know where he could get a part-time job. "It's too late for the autumn semester," he told me. "But if I can be settled in some job soon, I'll be able to enter college in January."

In the meantime, the days were passing all too swiftly. I knew we couldn't stay here much longer.

Already the nights were chilly. It was only really warm in the middle of the day. Before long, the storm season would set in and then it could be actually dangerous. *I should go back home and try to set my own life in some sort of order,* I thought. Ben ought to decide where he wants to go to school and go there and job hunt in person. But, oh, it was so difficult for us to leave each other. We kept putting it off day after day. Next week would be time enough—and the next week

The storm started somewhere far out at sea as a slight disturbance. By the time it reached the coast, it was a lashing fury. We heard warnings on the radio, but it was still miles away. There was the chance it would blow itself out before it got to us. And it was hard to believe in danger, for the day was crisp and golden, the sky cloudless and polished blue. The sea was placid—and unless you looked closely, you wouldn't even notice the ripple of white-tipped waves that came in faster and faster.

"Maybe we should go into the village," I told Ben. "I've never been here this late in the year, but I've heard the storms can be very bad."

He shrugged and grinned. "So what's a little wind? The cottage is way up, on fairly high ground. I wouldn't mind a bit of a wind. It might even be exciting."

I laughed, thinking how much like a little boy he could be at times. And then, half an hour later, it suddenly wasn't a laughing matter. The sky became inky black and a cold wind blew in off the water—a great, terrifying wind that banged at the windows and shook the cottage walls. I tried to turn on the lights, but the electricity had gone out, and with it the radio. I lit some candles, but they kept blowing out in the draft that swept in around the windowpanes and below the door.

FORBIDDEN AFFAIR

"Nina, we'd better get out of here," Ben told me. I nodded and yanked on my raincoat and tied a scarf over my head. He had to struggle with the door to get it open. We ran out, but we only got a few feet. The wind actually swept our feet out from under us. The rain was coming down in blinding sheets, whipping and lashing us one way and then another.

"We'll never make it," he shouted against the roar. I knew he was probably thinking what I was thinking. Even if we could get to my car or his, it was doubtful we could drive them out of here. By now, they were probably mired down in the wet sand.

Leaning against each other, stumbling and lurching, we managed to get back inside the cottage.

"We should have left while we had a chance," I said slowly. "We should have gone days ago. Only—"

"Only we couldn't bear to leave each other." He put his arms around me, and I buried my face against his chest.

I wouldn't mind dying here in Ben's arms, I thought. In a way it would be an answer to the whole thing. Death would keep us together, while life would part us.

Even as I thought it I knew I was being selfish. Maybe it would be all right for me to die. Most of my living was behind me. But Ben still had his life ahead of me. *God, no matter what happens to me—bring Ben through safely,* I prayed—and at that very moment I heard the roof going. There was a terrible ripping sound. Everything seemed to be tipping, tilting, and things were falling around us. Then something struck a violent blow across my shoulders and that's the last I remember.

I opened my eyes in a swaying ambulance. Later I

learned that the shore patrol had found us pinned under the wreckage of the cottage. I was unconscious, but Ben had been conscious, although trapped in the debris and suffering agonies from a broken arm.

When I came to the second time, we were in the hospital's emergency room, me lying on one table and Ben sitting on another. A nurse was sponging my face off and a doctor or intern was questioning Ben. He asked Ben's name, and then patted him on the knee.

"Don't look so worried, man," he said in a crisp, jolly way. "Your mother got a bad bump on the head and quite a few cuts and bruises, but she'll be all right. You were both very lucky."

"She's not my mother!" Ben exclaimed. "She's—" His voice faltered. He swallowed, then went on, "She's just a friend."

I gave a shuddering sigh and closed my eyes against the pain. Ben hadn't meant to disown our relationship. Of course, he couldn't tell the doctor I was his lover. He might have said, "She's the woman I love. The woman I plan to marry." But I knew it was more than discretion that had kept him from saying that. I could see myself as he must be seeing me. Gray-faced, white-haired, looking old and shattered and ugly. We had left our Shangri-la, and the princess had abruptly turned into an old woman. It wasn't his fault—or mine. It was just the way things were.

The next day I felt much better. The doctor said I had a mild concussion and a bad cut on the cheek, which had needed a few stitches. I gave him my daughter's name and telephone number and told him to call and ask her to come and get me and take me home.

Ben came in after the doctor had left. His eyes were anxious, and he was a little shamefaced. "Thank God, you're all right, darling," he told me.

I smiled at him. Ben—so very dear. "We tried to prolong the summer, didn't we?" I asked. "And that's a dangerous thing to do. You can't hang on to summer after autumn comes." I was telling him two things and he knew it. I'd tried to hang on to the summer of my life when it was already autumn for me.

"I've had them call Amy," I told him. "She's coming for me. We'd better say good-bye now."

"But not like this!" he protested. "We haven't made any real plans. Nina, you're my lover!"

Slowly I shook my head. "No, Ben. I'm exactly what you said I was in the emergency room. I'm your friend—your very good friend—a friend you'll always remember. That's the way I want it—you cherishing beautiful memories. Far better that than hanging on to what would soon become an ugly reality."

I patted his uninjured arm gently. "You've got a wonderful time ahead of you. You'll go back to college and you'll teach and do with your life just what you wanted to do, and I'll know it, and feel good because in my little way I helped you make up your mind."

"But what will you do?" he exclaimed.

My lips curved in the shadow of an impish grin. "Why, when I thought I was going to die, I guess I realized I have a life to live, too. Maybe I have twenty or thirty years of life left yet. And I'm going to find something I want to fill those years with. I'm not young enough for you, Ben, but I'm not old enough to lie down and give up. There are a lot of wonderful things ahead for me, dear—and you can just bet I'm going to find them. And knowing that—well, you can feel good about giving me back my life like I gave yours back to you. That's what our love has done for each other. That makes it very special, doesn't it? It was a love worth having—for both of us."

He protested a little, but the storm must have shaken him into facing reality, also. What we'd had couldn't possibly last. But, oh, it had been good! It had been worth having. It had been so special that neither of us would ever forget our days of sun and sand, moonlight and love.

Well, Amy came to get me, and I sold the house as she and Edmund thought I should. But I didn't move into the apartment near them. I used the money to buy a small gift shop and I have living quarters in the back of the shop. I'm very busy building up the business and making it pay—and it is paying. I do volunteer work at a nearby hospital a couple evenings a week also, and I've made a lot of new friends, including a couple of very interesting men about my age. No, I'm not romantic about any of them yet, but they provide companionship and interest.

Maybe I'll never fall in love again, but maybe I will. If I do—and it's right—I'll accept it. If I don't—well, I won't regret it. I have my memories of the long years with Al—and the short weeks with Ben. They're enough to remind me that I'm a desirable woman. But I don't live in the past, for the present is very full, and the future is no longer something to dread.

THE END

A TEST
OF FAITH

My neighbor, Bea Stewart, laid her plump hand on my arm. "Honey, that man of yours isn't coming back, and you know it."

"He will come back," I protested. "Or he'll send for us. He's only been gone a month."

"A month!" Her hand tightened and her nails dug into my arm. "If he's coming back, why hasn't he called you?"

"You know why!" I gestured helplessly and pulled away from her. "Nobody has a phone down here."

"Then why hasn't he written? He can write, can't he?"

"Of course he can!" I fumed. Stan had been a good student. He'd have graduated at the top of his class if he could have finished. My Stan was very smart.

"Then why hasn't he written you?"

I closed my eyes and looked away from Bea's probing gaze. It was the one question I could not answer. But I knew Stan hadn't deserted me and our three kids. "Please, Bea." I was begging her to shut up. She was a dear, good woman, but she was overbearing and outspoken and didn't know when to mind her own business.

"You're a fool, Janie, if you don't sign those papers and get food for those poor kids."

I shook my head. "We have food." I glanced furtively at the old refrigerator. Inside, its shelves were almost bare.

Bea snorted. "What kind of food? Good food that keeps a kid healthy, or the kind that only fills their bellies?"

"We have food," I repeated.

"All right. All right." Bea threw up her hand. "You're a stubborn woman, Janie Kessler."

I nodded. I'd been told that before, and I suppose it was true enough. But some things are right and some are wrong, and it would be wrong for me to sign that paper the social worker had given me.

Bea gazed at me from under a head full of salt and pepper hair. I could see her aching for me, and I looked away quickly, hating the pity. Then she said good-bye and left, shaking her head and waddling a little, like a fat, friendly duck. On the table were the oranges she'd brought over. "I guess I bought too many last week," she'd told me. "They were on sale and I got carried away. I thought maybe the kids might eat them up before they go bad."

It was a flimsy story to save my pride. She'd bought them this morning. She'd do without something she should have bought for herself or Walt. All they had was his little Social Security check every month. Bea wasn't sixty-two yet, so she didn't get a share of Social Security. She couldn't work because of Walt's heart trouble. She was chained to Walt and hid her constant fear of dying alone. But she never complained.

In the kitchen drawer was the paper the social worker, Miss Tate, had left. It was the application for Aid to Dependent Children. If I signed it I'd be swearing Stan had deserted us, that we had no form of support.

Miss Tate had come to me. When I answered the door I drew back slightly at the sight of the pretty, well-dressed young woman. "I don't want anything," I said.

"I'm not a saleswoman. But I understand you may need help. I'm from the county welfare department."

"Who told you I needed help?" I asked, staring suspiciously at her through the patched screen.

"A friend," she said. "May I come in?"

I picked up Rosie, who'd toddled in, and put her on my hip, then opened the screen door. "You and your children live here alone?" Miss Tate asked me, taking a seat on the sofa. It was the best piece of furniture we owned and I was proud of it. Stan had bought it for me right after we moved here to Warren.

I shifted Rosie around and sat down with her in my lap. She leaned back up against me and eyed the strange woman quietly. My arms tightened around her warm little body. "Yes, we're alone right now," I said slowly. "But Stan, that's my husband, he's gone to northern Chicago to look for work."

"I see." She asked a lot of questions then. About how long he'd been gone and if I'd heard from him.

I ducked my head then, and I had to admit that I

hadn't heard from Stan except for two postcards he'd sent while he was traveling.

I glanced back up. Miss Tate flashed me a smile and I suddenly felt ashamed. Maybe even a little envious. Her hair obviously had been cut and styled in a beauty shop and her clothes looked new. I ran one hand over my faded black slacks. She looked about my age—twenty-four. "Times haven't been easy lately," I explained. "Stan has been out of work."

She asked more questions about the kids, and nodded in satisfaction when I told her Mark and Doug were both getting free lunches at school. Then she showed me the papers. All I had to do was sign them, and I could get help for me and my children. She laid a pen down next to the papers.

I licked my lips. It would mean immediate cash and food stamps. I could get the kids some meat and some vegetables and even ice cream. Lord, how Rosie begged for ice cream!

My fingers hovered over the pen. Rosie bumped against me, rocking back and forth a little. I touched the pen, and then jerked back like it was hot. "I'm sorry," I choked. "I can't sign. I just can't do it. It would be a lie; Stan will take care of us. He hasn't deserted us."

"Mrs. Kessler," Miss Tate said softly, "sometimes even the best of men break and run. Sometimes they can't go on any longer. It gets to be too much for them."

"Not Stan." I shook my head and blinked hard against the threat of tears. I hadn't cried once since Stan left, and I wouldn't cry now.

She sighed softly and her eyes drifted slowly over

me and around the room. I knew what she was seeing. A shabby little house. But it's filled with love, I
wanted to tell her. When Stan is here there is love
and laughter. So much you can feel and see it and
almost touch it.

She got up to leave and I walked her to the door,
still holding Rosie up tight against me. "Thank you,"
I told her. "Thank you for caring."

She glanced back at me, and then smiled, and
our eyes held for a moment. There was admiration
in her eyes now, not pity.

But after she'd gone I noticed she'd left the
paper. Like maybe she thought I'd sign it if I had to.
But I wouldn't have to. Stan would be back.

"Oh, God," I moaned aloud. "Dear God in heaven.
We are Your children. Give us strength." But sometimes it seemed like my strength was wavering.

Stan and I were dating the year Mama got sick.
Mama had worked in a dress shop for fifteen years.
We had a small house and she made enough for us
to live on. She was keeping Daddy's insurance
money in the bank. "It's to help you get started in
college or for a wedding, whichever comes first,"
she used to tell me.

I think we were closer than a lot of mothers and
daughters. We had to be. There were times when
she was my friend as well as my mother. She drew
me into the decisions that had to be made concerning our lives. We shared the cooking and housework, too.

I knew Mama had been losing a little weight.
She'd joked that soon she'd have to wear my
clothes instead of hers. It shocked me the day I discovered Mama actually could wear my clothes. I

was a skinny junior in high school! Yet Mama pulled on my jeans and one of my sweaters one day.

"Mama!" I stared at her. She was suddenly so thin it frightened me. "You haven't been dieting. There must be something wrong."

"Not a thing," she swore, but I started noticing things. Like how she was gobbling aspirins every time she turned around. And she was having trouble with her periods. They'd come and go with no regularity and sometimes she'd come home from work and lie down on the sofa. She'd refuse to eat and wouldn't move until it was time to go to bed.

I told Stan that I was worried about Mama. "Can't you get her to see a doctor?" he asked.

I shook my head. "I mentioned that once. She nearly bit my head off." My arms tightened around Stan's slender body. He was nearly six feet tall and he was still outgrowing his clothes. "I'm scared, Stan."

"Hush, baby," he murmured. "It'll be all right."

"I hope so," I whispered and raised my lips to his. We were young and in love. I adored him and he was so good. Mama liked Stan, too. She never minded when we hung around the house and watched TV with her, and her meals always contained a little extra when she knew Stan would be there for dinner.

Mama finally went to see Dr. Forrester.

I didn't know it until he called me at home after school one day. "Janie, I've put your mother in the hospital," he said. "She's furious with me, but she must have immediate surgery. I want you to pack a suitcase for her and take it to her."

I was so stunned I didn't ask any questions. I

called Stan at work. He had a part-time job working as a busboy for a pancake house. I explained and he promised he'd see me after work.

With trembling fingers I folded up Mama's best nightgowns and packed everything I could think of that she might need. Then I gathered up what money I could find in the house and called a taxi to take me to the hospital because I couldn't bear to wait for the bus.

I found Mama in a room she had to share with another woman. My heart almost stopped beating at the sight of her between those cold white sheets, wearing a coarse hospital gown. She was lying with her head turned toward the wall.

I crept across the room. "Mama," I said, leaning over her. Her eyes jerked open and when she turned her head, there were traces of tears on her cheeks. "Mama." I hesitated, frightened.

"Why, baby." She smiled brightly and sat up in bed. She hugged me and patted my shoulder. "Isn't this the silliest thing you ever heard of? Putting me in the hospital like this." Her hands worked restlessly over the sheet.

"What's wrong, Mama?"

"Oh, you know, female trouble. Dr. Forrester always gets into a panic. You know him. He lives on the safe side of the street. They're going to do some little tests on me and—"

"Dr. Forrester told me surgery," I interrupted. "Well, it takes surgery to do the test, honey."

"You mean like a biopsy?" I asked, remembering some things I'd learned at school.

Mama nodded, her lips pressed tight together. "Yes, a biopsy, Janie. But it's nothing to worry about—"

"Oh, Mama." I flung myself into her arms and we held on tight to each other. We both cried a little and neither of us spoke the dreaded word.

Dr. Forrester didn't pull any punches with me an hour later when I went into his office. "Janie, I know you're young, but you're all the family your mother has. I suspect that she has cancer. Frankly, her prospects are poor. So, little lady, you have a lot of things to face up to. And first things first. Do you have a place to stay?"

"Oh—sure." I gestured helplessly. There was the Barton family who lived next door. And there was Marsha Klein, my best friend. "What am I going to do?" I asked him.

"Pray," he told me. "You go home and pray long and hard. And I'm going to do the same. Then we'll do everything we can to save your mother. There is some hope, Janie. There's always hope. And faith."

He buzzed for Mrs. Zane, one of his nurses. "You take the rest of the afternoon off and look after Janie," he told her. "Take her home. Help her pack. Make sure she gets moved in with someone."

Mrs. Zane was a warm, motherly woman with gray hair and quick ways. She talked a mile a minute on the drive home while I sat frozen next to the car door. Once we were in the house, I didn't think I could bear to leave it. The house was part of Mama.

I thought of Marsha. I knew her mom and dad would take me in, but the Bartons next door would keep me close to home and I needed to be close to home. Mrs. Zane went next door and explained everything to them for me.

Mrs. Barton came over in no time, holding me, touching me, giving me directions. I gratefully obeyed. I closed and locked windows and doors. She picked out some clothes for me to take and moved me into their married son's old bedroom.

Mrs. Barton went with me to visit Mama that night at the hospital. We arrived with an armload of flowers from Mrs. Barton's garden. The two of them chatted and exchanged some looks I couldn't miss. I could feel them putting a protective circle around me.

When we got back home Stan's car was parked in front of my house. "May I?" I asked.

"Of course, dear," she said kindly.

I got out of her car and ran to Stan. He opened the car door and drew me inside. I went straight into his arms, and for the first time that day I cried. He didn't try to stop me. He held me close and stroked my hair and finally he tipped my face up and wiped away the tears. He kissed me gently. "I love you, Janie," he murmured.

"Oh, Stan. Stan." I began to sob again. He'd never said those words aloud before. I'd felt his love, but I hadn't been sure until now.

Stan and I both skipped school the next morning and went to the hospital to wait out Mama's surgery. Mrs. Barton was there, too. Stan's mother dropped by briefly, and she patted my hand and hugged me.

When Dr. Forrester came, the results were imprinted upon his tired face. Cancer. He did a complete hysterectomy, he told us while my nails dug into Stan's hand. "But it wasn't enough. The cancer is widespread. I don't know why she waited so long . . ." he said angrily, and then abruptly his voice softened. "But there's still a lot we can do.

There are new drugs all the time. And treatments. We have a fine hospital here. We'll do all we can."

He wouldn't let me see Mama until the next morning, and when I did, it was as if she'd aged twenty years overnight. "Why did you wait so long, Mama?" I asked her, remembering Dr. Forrester's words.

She moistened her dry, cracked lips. "Because I was weak, Janie. I guess I knew. Something inside me knew and I was frightened. I kept telling myself it was nothing, but another part of me said it was cancer, and I was afraid to find out."

"Oh, Mama." I took her hands in mine. "I love you so."

"I know, baby."

"What can I do?" I asked her.

"Do what you must. Do what you can." She paused. "When a person does what she can, then God does what He can."

"I know, Mama." It was one of her favorite sayings.

But through it all I was so helpless. I prayed. I visited Mama. I kept up my schoolwork. Dr. Forrester had done all he could, and more, it seemed. But it wasn't enough.

Mama died six weeks later without ever having left the hospital. I cried against Stan's chest. "It's not fair!" I sobbed. "We did everything. God didn't do anything. Nothing."

"But He did, honey. He took away her suffering. He took her home."

"Home." I spat out the word. "Home. You mean heaven. But is there a heaven?" I raised my eyes to his.

"For people like your mama there is."

But there wasn't anything left in me. I couldn't go on believing. I couldn't pray at the funeral. I only wanted to block the funeral out of my mind forever.

It was Mr. Barton who had to explain to me that there wasn't any money left. Everything from Daddy's insurance had gone for the hospital bills. Mama's small policy would barely pay for the funeral. There was only the house left.

Then he spoke the real horror. "You're still a minor, Janie. You'll have to go to court so the judge can decide about what to do with you."

When I told Stan he only nodded. "I'd been expecting something like that," he said. "There's only one thing to do, Janie. We'll get married now."

"Now?" I closed my eyes and for the first time since Mama got sick I dared to seek happiness. "Are you sure?" I asked him.

"Yes. I've never been more sure of anything in my life."

The Bartons protested. "Honey, you could live with us. Why, I'm sure we could qualify as your foster parents."

They were nice people, of course. But they weren't Mama or Stan. Everything had to be investigated. Stan's parents talked to a social worker and so did Stan and I. Then we had to go to court and talk to the judge. "You're so young," he kept saying, and I didn't think he was going to let us get married.

But finally he agreed because Stan's parents had agreed. We were to live with them because we couldn't afford to live in Mama's house. I was stunned to find out Mama had taken out a mortgage on the house. It was the first time she'd ever done anything like that without telling me.

The house went to the bank and Stan and I were married. We had two days in a motel room for a honeymoon. Then we moved in with Stan's parents and went back to school.

Almost immediately I realized Stan's parents were poorer than I'd thought. But they were good people. They took me in like I was a daughter and made room for me at their table along with their other four kids. I thought everything was going to be all right. Stan had his part-time job. We were both going to finish school. It wouldn't be long before Stan graduated, only two months.

What we hadn't planned on was Stan's father breaking his leg. There was insurance to pay for the hospital bill, but there wasn't any unemployment. Dad Kessler was his boss's only employee and his boss never made any unemployment payments to the state.

Mom Kessler went out and got a job in the kitchen of a small café, but the wages were terribly small. They tried every way they could to stretch the money she and Stan made, but it wasn't enough.

So Stan had to drop out of school. I cried and argued with him, and he got mad at me. "A man does what he has to do," he told me.

"It's wrong," I told him.

"I have to. You can see that. I'll go back to school, Janie. Next year. Maybe you and I can graduate together. Wouldn't that be fun?"

"Is that the truth, Stan?" I asked.

"The truth," he promised.

Stan got on at the local lumberyard. And it would have been as he said, but I got pregnant that summer. I looked around the small, crowded house and

A TEST OF FAITH

I knew how it was going to be. Stan and I would have to move out. He'd never go back to school. It was hard to accept. I hated myself for getting pregnant. I blamed God for letting it happen, but only inwardly. I never said one word to Stan or his family about how I felt now toward God and the church and Jesus.

Sometimes, when we were all sitting in church, I'd get a bitter taste in my mouth. I wanted to spit it out and cleanse myself, but I didn't know how. So I kept that part of myself secret.

Stan and I rented a little house not far from where I used to live. We had a lot of junk furniture, but it was so marvelous being alone. Like the honeymoon we never had. I felt like we were finally beginning our marriage.

I was happy through my pregnancy for the most part. When Mark was laid in my arms it was like a small miracle. I knew babies were small, but eight pounds seemed incredibly tiny to me. And perfect. I never knew babies were so perfect.

After Mark was born Dr. Forrester inserted an IUD. Only it didn't work for me. I lost it and got pregnant again. Mark was only a year old when Doug was born.

Stan got a raise that year and another one two years later. I was safely on the Pill this time, though Dr. Forrester didn't totally approve. He was one of those doctors who didn't quite trust the Pill, so he kept his patients on it for four years, and then off a full year before he'd let them return to it. Needless to say, that one year off the Pill got me pregnant with Rosie.

Now I looked around the bare, gray-looking

kitchen of the shack of a house here in Warren. I was twenty-four. I had three kids, and I didn't know where my husband was.

I shivered. We'd never meant to leave our hometown, but times got bad. Stan's boss at home closed up the lumberyard the day he turned sixty-five. He went out of business and no one else wanted to buy the lumberyard. Then Stan found out what it was like to go job hunting without a high school diploma. No one wanted to hire him. It didn't matter that he was a hard worker and had experience.

Stan's old boss was a friend of the man who ran the lumberyard here in Warren. He helped Stan get a new job there.

We came to Warren and to our disappointment the pay was lower than Stan was used to. "But we're here," Stan told me. "And I might find myself something better later on. It's a growing town."

Money was tight but we managed. That winter Stan fixed up the old house as best he could with scrap lumber and old paint that his boss gave him.

Stan fixed the backyard up for the kids with a swing in the big tree and a tractor tire filled with sand for Rosie.

More than once that winter I remembered Mama's words: "A person does what she can, then God does what He can."

Well, I was doing and Stan was doing, but God didn't seem to be doing much. Stan was laid off just before Christmas because of bad weather. Nobody buys lumber and paint in the winter if they can't use it. We managed through the holidays. I'd already bought most of the kids' gifts on layaway, and Stan was getting unemployment checks.

Then Stan got back on in February, worked two months, and then was laid off again because of the heavy rains.

He came home that day as down as I'd ever seen him.

Yet he had hope. "There's work in Chicago," he told me. "In the lumber mills." A salesman Stan knew had told him that his company was desperate for laborers.

"I'm going to go, Janie. I'm going to go out there and get a job with union protection and we're going to have a real home."

"You're going alone?" I asked, my heart crimping up tight.

"It's the only way. With the kids along we'd have to spend nights in motels. We'd have to buy restaurant food. You know me, I'll get by on nothing. No, you and the kids stay here. I'll send money and soon you can join me. I'll get us that house and . . ."

I pressed against him. "I'm frightened, Stan. We've never been apart. Not since we got married. Not once."

"I know, baby. But it'll be all right. Don't be frightened. God will provide." He held me back and looked into my face. "We've made it this far, haven't we? We've had our bad times and we came through. We had our good times and we'll have better. Right?"

"Right." I nodded, fighting to keep my chin from quivering and tears from spilling down my cheeks. I would not cry, I vowed. I'd keep faith in Stan and I would not cry. Stan might think God was going to do things for us, but I knew better. It was Stan I had put my faith in.

A TEST OF FAITH

The morning Stan left we were all up early. The boys were as excited as could be. They kept hopping around and trying to help, but they mostly got in the way.

"Write me a letter," Mark told his daddy. "Write me one I can read."

"I will, son," he promised and swept Mark up into his arms and hugged him. Then he hugged Doug, who was tugging at his pants leg, and finally he folded Rosie and me into his arms. I pressed my face against his chest, as if to steal some of his strength and warmth to last through the lonely days ahead.

The four of us stood on the front porch and waved as Stan drove away. I ached with unshed tears. He was taking part of me, too. I didn't dare cry, though. One tear and I'd have all three kids crying. Right now the boys looked upon their daddy's trip as an adventure. I had to let it stay that way.

Four days later there was a postcard from Stan. Bless his heart, he remembered to print it so Mark could read it. Even five-year-old Doug could read some of it. They nearly wore out that card reading it over and over.

Two days later there was another card from Chicago. Every afternoon at three o'clock I waited for the postman at the mailbox, but after that last card, not a word came from Stan. At first, I was only faintly annoyed, and then I began to get scared.

As the days and weeks and finally a full month passed, I was terrified. I'd wake up in the middle of the night, alone in bed with my thoughts. Stan down in some canyon where the car had rolled off. My Stan in a hospital someplace, unconscious or a victim of amnesia. Stan killed by a hitchhiker.

Getting through the days became harder and harder. But I knew that Stan would write or come back when he was able. It wasn't like Bea and that Miss Tate thought. Stan had not deserted me.

Rosie's cries jerked me out of my thoughts and I hurried back to her. She was standing up in the crib she'd now outgrown, but I couldn't afford to buy her a bed and there wasn't any point in buying anything here, once we moved. I snapped off the thought and picked up Rosie, who was holding her arms up to me. She cuddled against me and rubbed her eyes and I smoothed her blonde curls. "Hungry, Mama."

"I know," I whispered. I was hungry all the time. Bea was right, of course. I'd had food to keep stomachs full, but not the kind of good healthy food that satisfies a body.

I carried her to the bathroom, then to the kitchen. Her eyes lit up at the sight of the oranges. I peeled one for her and sat her down and gave her one section at a time.

She giggled as the juice dripped down her chin. My mouth watered. I swallowed, taking one section and just letting it lay on my tongue to savor the fresh crisp taste and smell. Just one bite for myself and I'd save the rest for the kids.

The boys hit the house after school, wanting to eat. Mark was in the first grade and Doug went to afternoon kindergarten classes. But I was able to send him early in time for lunch. Without those two free lunches every school day I don't know what I'd have done.

I'd had too much pride to apply for the free lunches, but not Stan. When he was out of work and on unemployment, he went to the school and arranged for the boys' lunches. "We're not going to deny our kids what's available," he told me.

I gave them each an orange and put the others in the refrigerator to save and dole out one at a time. And I still had to fix supper. There wasn't much left. There was a dab of brown beans I had to cook without even a bit of bacon to flavor them and I made gravy out of canned milk and fat and flour. It filled us.

The next afternoon the postman brought mail. But none from Stan. There was a second warning about the overdue electric bill. The gas had already been turned off. Which meant we didn't have hot water and the stove didn't work. But I had an old electric hotplate that I could cook and heat water on.

Sighing, I pushed the warning from the electric company down in the trash. I couldn't worry about it until it happened. Besides, I'd hear from Stan anytime now. Probably tomorrow.

I divided two oranges among the three kids after school the next day. "Mama," Mark said. "I need money for school."

"For what?" I asked.

"For the bus for the trip to the zoo."

"I want to go, too," Doug cried.

"You can't go. It's not for kindergarten kids," Mark said disdainfully. "Can I have some money, Mama?"

I closed my eyes. I would not cry. I would not cry. I slipped out of my chair and went out to stand on the front porch where I'd waved good-bye to Stan. I'd found myself out there a lot lately, looking, thinking Stan might come back and surprise us. Maybe he hadn't been able to find work. Maybe he was ashamed to come back and bring us bad news. Maybe . . . I cut off the wandering thoughts. I couldn't know, and "maybe" did me no good.

The screen door opened and closed. It was little Mark. I sat down on the steps and he stood beside me and put his hand on my shoulder. "It's okay, Mama, I don't have to go to the zoo. I've been before. And Daddy will take us again. I'll bet they have neater zoos in Chicago than they have here."

"Oh, Mark," I whispered and hugged him. "You are a good boy."

But surely there must be some way I could find him some money. I opened my purse and counted the money that was left from Stan's last unemployment check. If I had three more quarters I could give him the change and I'd still have some left over.

The next day was Friday. I'd always gone shopping on Friday, but not with the amount of money I had left. I was sitting at the table at noon, trying to figure out what I could buy with the money when Bea popped up at the back door. She let herself in, a paper sack in her hand. "The egg man came yesterday," she said, meaning a local farmer who made door-to-door deliveries. "I guess he got my order mixed up. He left me about two dozen eggs too many. You know Walt doesn't care for eggs. He's not supposed to eat them anyway with his heart like it is and . . ." She started to sit the sack down.

I squeezed her hand against the top of the bag. "Bea, you have got to stop this. You can't go on buying stuff for us."

She jerked her hand back and for a second I

thought she was going to slap mine, as if I were a small child. "A person has got to help out another if he can. And I can," she blustered. "So there!" She turned and stomped out of the house, letting the screen slam behind her.

I felt weak. I sank down to the table. Eggs. We hadn't had eggs in three weeks. I couldn't help it. I cooked two for Rosie and me and we ate them without butter or bread.

Then I sat there, looking at the yellow-stained plate and something hit me hard. I couldn't go on like this. I couldn't let Bea feed us. For the first time I faced the fact that Stan might not come back. I faced it full on. No, I didn't believe Stan had run out on me, but something could have happened. Something he couldn't help.

I had to do something, and I had to do it right now. My children's lives depended on it.

I swept up Rosie into my arms and took her over to Bea's. "Would you watch her?" I asked. "And keep an eye out for the boys when they get home from school?"

"Of course. Probably do Walt good to have some young ones around. He's really sour today. Won't hardly get out of his chair."

I have to do what I can, I thought as I started out a few minutes later. There was just me. No one else.

I went to the better section of town and started knocking on doors. I'd carefully rehearsed my speech on my way over. "Hello, I'm Janie Kessler and I'm looking for work. I'm a good housekeeper and I'll do anything you want."

It wasn't easy going door-to-door. I had more than one slammed in my face. Some thought I was trying to sell something. One woman thought I was begging. But, finally, one woman let me in. "I've been ill," she told me. "If you could just get this place straightened up, I'll pay you fifty dollars."

Grateful, I took the job. I vacuumed and dusted and polished furniture under her direction. Then I tore in on the kitchen. It was so filthy it turned my stomach just to touch parts of it, but I did what I had to do.

It was dark when I was able to leave with the money tucked into my wallet. I walked to a grocery store and got milk and bread and more beans. I passed wishfully by a row of steaks that were on sale, but they were so still expensive. I couldn't buy anything like that. But I did get one pound of hamburger. My kids would have meat tonight. And tomorrow I'd go looking for more work, and the next day, and the next.

I walked home, exhausted, yet filled with fresh hope. I walked into the house and found all three kids there alone. "Where's Bea?" I cried.

"Walt got sick," Mark told me. "She said I was a big boy and to look after Doug and Rosie. She said Walt had to go to the hospital. An ambulance came, Mama. They took old Walt away."

"Oh, God." I sank down to my knees and drew my three babies into my arms. They were so little, yet so brave.

I forced myself to my feet and fixed supper for them. They gulped down the milk and meat and bread. I was clearing off the table when Bea came back. She came to my door and I let her in. "I'm sorry about the kids," she said.

"It's all right," I said. "There was nothing else you

could do."

She looked so bleak and tired, I didn't have the heart to say what was on the tip of my tongue. Dear God, the things that could have happened to my babies! I didn't even dare think about it.

Bea shifted her bulk around and sank down in one of my chairs. "I don't know what I'm going to do," she said, her voice low and harsh. "The hospital wants some money. They want it right away. Walt's on Medicare, of course, but I'm supposed to pay the first two hundred dollars. Now where am I going to get two hundred dollars?"

"If only I had it," I whispered.

"I know. Poor Walt. He's in such pain. He—he might not make it this time."

"He will. He will," I told her and hugged her. I remembered what Bea had told me. You help a person when you can. Maybe I could.

"Bea, you stay here with the kids," I said. "I have to do something. I think I can solve your problem."

I went straight to the church and Reverend Crone. His wife let me in and I explained Bea's situation. "Is there any way the church can help? Is there an emergency fund or something?"

"Yes," he said simply. "Of course we'll help."

I felt stunned, taken aback. I hadn't thought it would be this easy. I'd reached out and there was help.

Reverend Crone promised to take the money down to the hospital first thing in the morning, and I went home with my heart lighter than it had been since Stan had left. Bea cried when I told her. "So many, so many good people in this world."

"So many," I echoed and I held her until she

stopped crying.

Bea went home and I put my little ones to bed and listened to their prayers. A part of me listened with a new heart as they blessed their daddy.

With them in bed, I walked through the house and picked up things. Tomorrow I'd look for work again, and I'd be able to give Bea a little money for looking after the kids for me.

I walked out on the front porch for a breath of fresh air and to gaze down the street as I did so often, looking off in the direction Stan had gone. I looked up into the star-filled night and the beauty of it overwhelmed me. There was no room for self-pity on a night like this. I sighed and turned around to go back into the house. Then it occurred to me. The mailbox! I hadn't checked the mail today, and there was something in there. My hands started to shake even as I reached inside—because I knew. I don't know how, but I knew.

I drew out two letters and both had Stan's handwriting. Trembling, I pressed them to my breast and slipped inside the house. Sitting on the edge of a chair, I held them out under the lamp. One was old and soiled. I looked at the postmark—three weeks old. Somewhere along the way the letter had gotten wet. It had my name and my address and the town name on it, but the state and zip code had been washed away by the water. And the markings. I didn't know there were so many towns named Warren in the country. There was a Warren, Arkansas. One in Missouri, Michigan, Nebraska. And finally here. The letter had finally come here.

It was so precious, so dear, it almost hurt to open it. But I did. With trembling fingers, I tore at the envelope and my breath caught as two twenty dollar bills fell into my hand. Slowly, carefully, I opened the letter from Stan. He'd gotten a job in a lumber mill. He'd also gotten an advance in pay. This was for me and the kids and soon he'd be able to send for us! I gulped back a happy cry. The other letter was only a week old and there was more money.

But it was Stan's letter, his words of love that filled me with real happiness. I'd been right. Stan hadn't deserted us. He'd kept his faith and love.

"A miracle," I whispered, and so it was. I slipped down to my knees and I could hear Mama. "A person does what she can, and then God does what He can." Today I'd done what I could. And God had done His part.

I'd been through a test of faith in my man and my Lord, and today I'd found my Lord again. My heart was overflowing with such joy I couldn't find words to express them in prayer. But I knew God understood. He'd heard my joy, my thanksgiving, my return to His fold.

A single tear slipped down my cheek. I could cry now. Everything was going to be all right. THE END